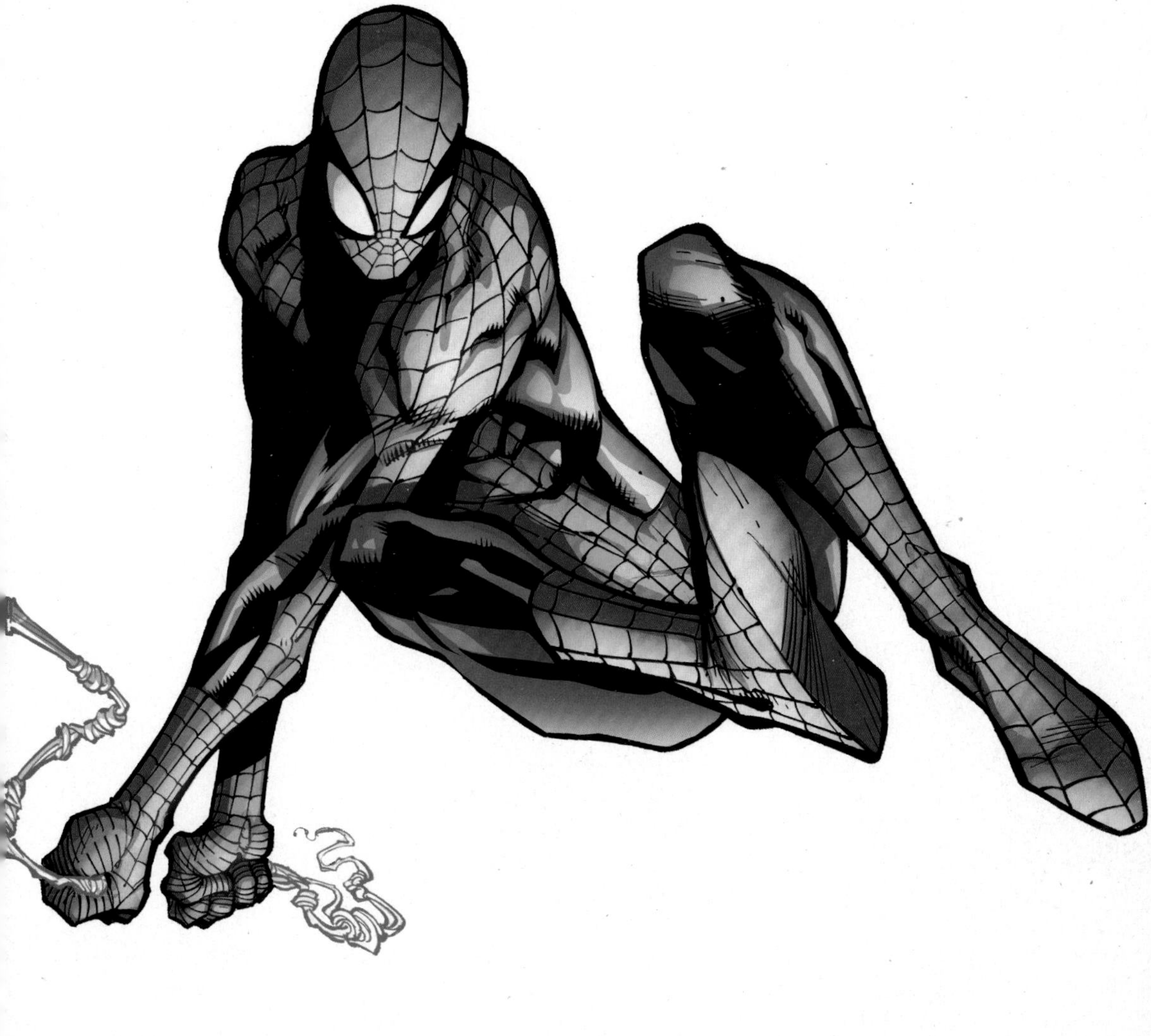

The AMAZING SPIDER-MAN

GRAVEYARD SHIFT

Collection Editor: **Jennifer Grünwald**
Assistant Editor: **Sarah Brunstad**
Associate Managing Editor: **Alex Starbuck**
Editor, Special Projects: **Mark D. Beazley**
Senior Editor, Special Projects: **Jeff Youngquist**
SVP Print, Sales & Marketing: **David Gabriel**
Book Designer: **Adam Del Re**

Editor in Chief: **Axel Alonso**
Chief Creative Officer: **Joe Quesada**
Publisher: **Dan Buckley**
Executive Producer: **Alan Fine**

AMAZING SPIDER-MAN VOL. 4: GRAVEYARD SHIFT. Contains material originally published in magazine form as AMAZING SPIDER-MAN #16-18 and ANNUAL #1. First printing 2015. ISBN# 978-0-7851-9338-8. Published by MARVEL WORLDWIDE, INC., a subsidiary of MARVEL ENTERTAINMENT, LLC. OFFICE OF PUBLICATION: 135 West 50th Street, New York, NY 10020. **Printed in Canada.** ALAN FINE, President, Marvel Entertainment; DAN BUCKLEY, President, TV, Publishing and Brand Management; JOE QUESADA, Chief Creative Officer; TOM BREVOORT, SVP of Publishing; DAVID BOGART, SVP of Operations & Procurement, Publishing; C.B. CEBULSKI, VP of International Development & Brand Management; DAVID GABRIEL, SVP Print, Sales & Marketing; JIM O'KEEFE, VP of Operations & Logistics; DAN CARR, Executive Director of Publishing Technology; SUSAN CRESPI, Editorial Operations Manager; ALEX MORALES, Publishing Operations Manager; STAN LEE, Chairman Emeritus. For information regarding advertising in Marvel Comics or on Marvel.com, please contact Jonathan Rheingold, VP of Custom Solutions & Ad Sales, at jrheingold@marvel.com. For Marvel subscription inquiries, please call 800-217-9158. **Manufactured between 7/3/2015 and 8/10/2015 by SOLISCO PRINTERS, SCOTT, QC, CANADA.**

10 9 8 7 6 5 4 3 2 1

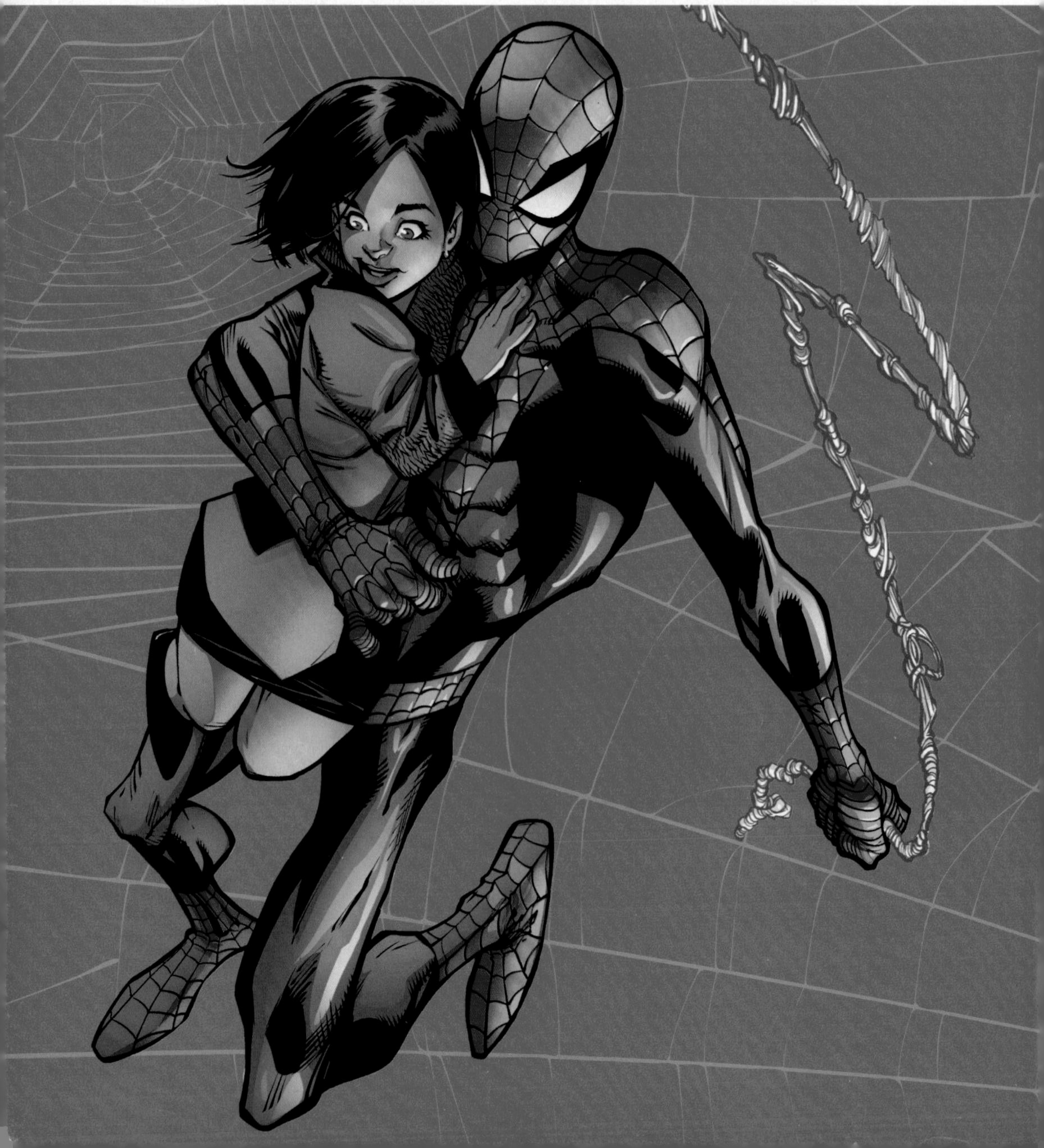

The AMAZING SPIDER-MAN

GRAVEYARD SHIFT

WRITERS:
DAN SLOTT
& CHRISTOS GAGE

PENCILER:
HUMBERTO RAMOS

INKER: **VICTOR OLAZABA**

COLORIST: **EDGAR DELGADO**

LETTERER: **CHRIS ELIOPOULOS**

COVER ART: **HUMBERTO RAMOS & EDGAR DELGADO**

ASSISTANT EDITOR: **DEVIN LEWIS**

ASSOCIATE EDITOR: **ELLIE PYLE**

EDITOR:
NICK LOWE

ANNUAL #1

"I CAN'T HELP MYSELF"
WRITER: **SEAN RYAN**
ARTIST: **BRANDON PETERSON**
COLOR ARTIST: **ANTONIO FABELA**

"THE A-MAY-ZING SPIDER-AUNT"
WRITER/ARTIST: **CALE ATKINSON**

"THE QUIET ROOM"
WRITER: **JAI NITZ**
ARTIST: **RON SALAS**
COLOR ARTIST: **RICO RENZI**

LETTERER: **TRAVIS LANHAM**
COVER ART: **BRANDON PETERSON**
ASSOCIATE EDITOR: **ELLIE PYLE**
EDITOR: **NICK LOWE**

SPIDER-MAN CREATED BY STAN LEE & STEVE DITKO

WHEN A MURDEROUS FAMILY OF INTERDIMENSIONAL CREATURES CALLED **THE INHERITORS** BEGAN HUNTING AND FEASTING ON THE LIFE FORCE OF SPIDER-PEOPLE FROM ACROSS THE MULTIVERSE, IT FELL TO PETER PARKER, **THE AMAZING SPIDER-MAN**, TO LEAD THOSE WHO SURVIVED IN A DANGEROUS FIGHT FOR THEIR OWN SURVIVAL.

ONE OF THE INHERITORS, AN OLD FOE OF SPIDER-MAN'S NAMED **MORLUN**, MANAGED TO LEECH SOME OF SPIDER-MAN'S LIFE FORCE BEFORE SPIDEY AND THE REST OF THE SPIDER-PEOPLE WERE ABLE TO DEFEAT THE INHERITORS FOR GOOD. AS A RESULT, PETER IS PHYSICALLY DRAINED, AND FEELS THE EFFECTS OF EVERY BATTLE EXHAUST HIM MORE THAN EVER.

MENTALLY, THOUGH, PETER'S SPIRITS COULDN'T BE HIGHER. AFTER LITERALLY LEADING AN ARMY AGAINST CERTAIN DOOM, HE'S CERTAIN HE CAN LEAD HIS COMPANY, **PARKER INDUSTRIES**, TO A SUCCESSFUL FUTURE.

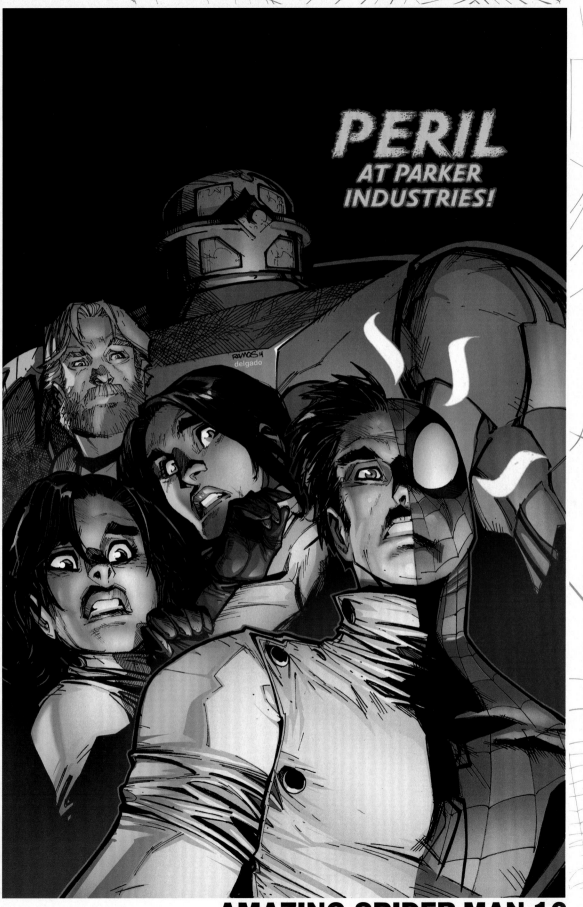

PERIL
AT PARKER
INDUSTRIES!

AMAZING SPIDER-MAN 16
GRAVEYARD SHIFT, PART ONE: THE LATE, LATE MR. PARKER

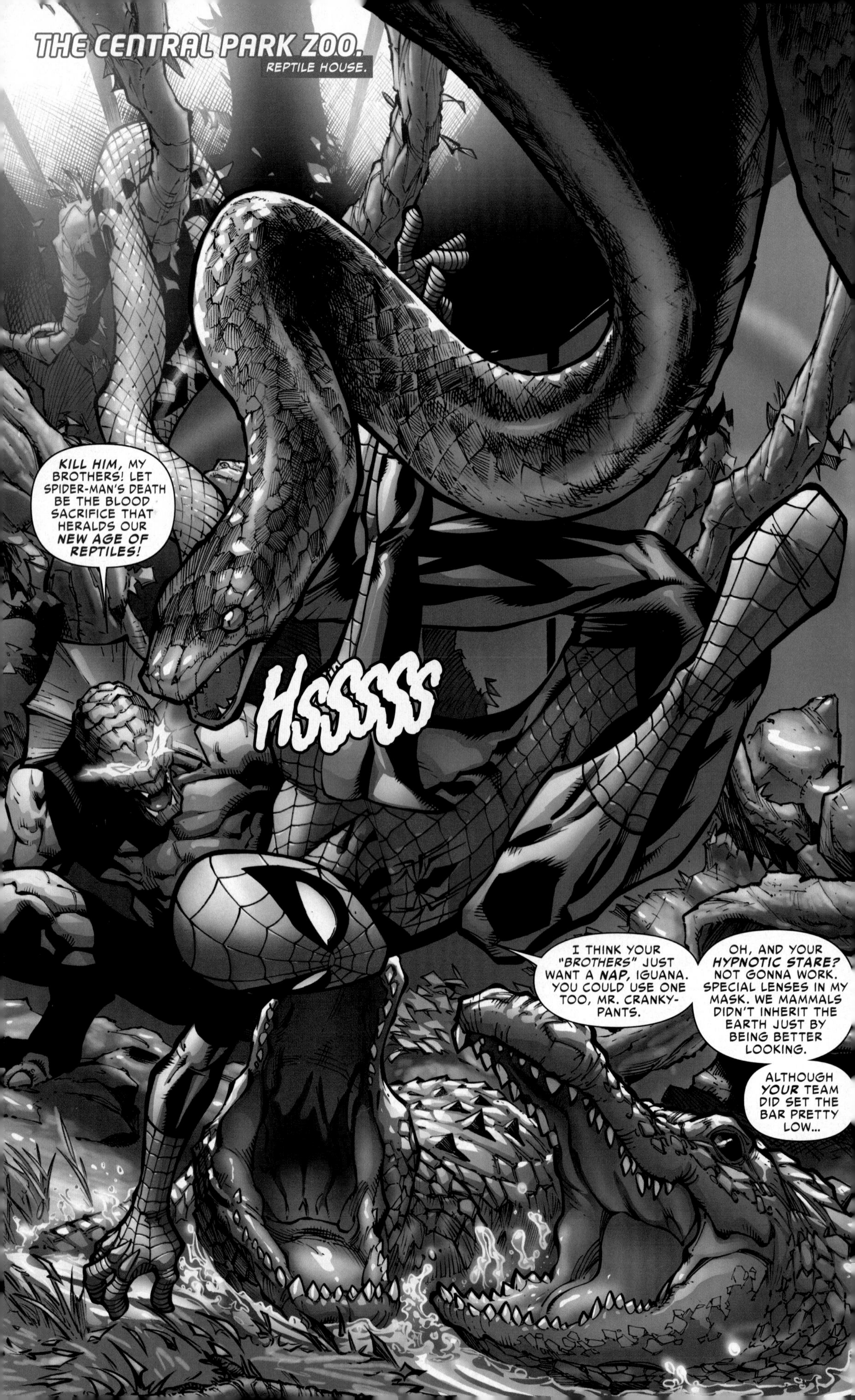
THE CENTRAL PARK ZOO.
REPTILE HOUSE.
KILL HIM, MY BROTHERS! LET SPIDER-MAN'S DEATH BE THE BLOOD SACRIFICE THAT HERALDS OUR NEW AGE OF REPTILES!
HSSSSS
I THINK YOUR "BROTHERS" JUST WANT A NAP, IGUANA. YOU COULD USE ONE TOO, MR. CRANKY-PANTS.
OH, AND YOUR HYPNOTIC STARE? NOT GONNA WORK. SPECIAL LENSES IN MY MASK. WE MAMMALS DIDN'T INHERIT THE EARTH JUST BY BEING BETTER LOOKING.
ALTHOUGH YOUR TEAM DID SET THE BAR PRETTY LOW...

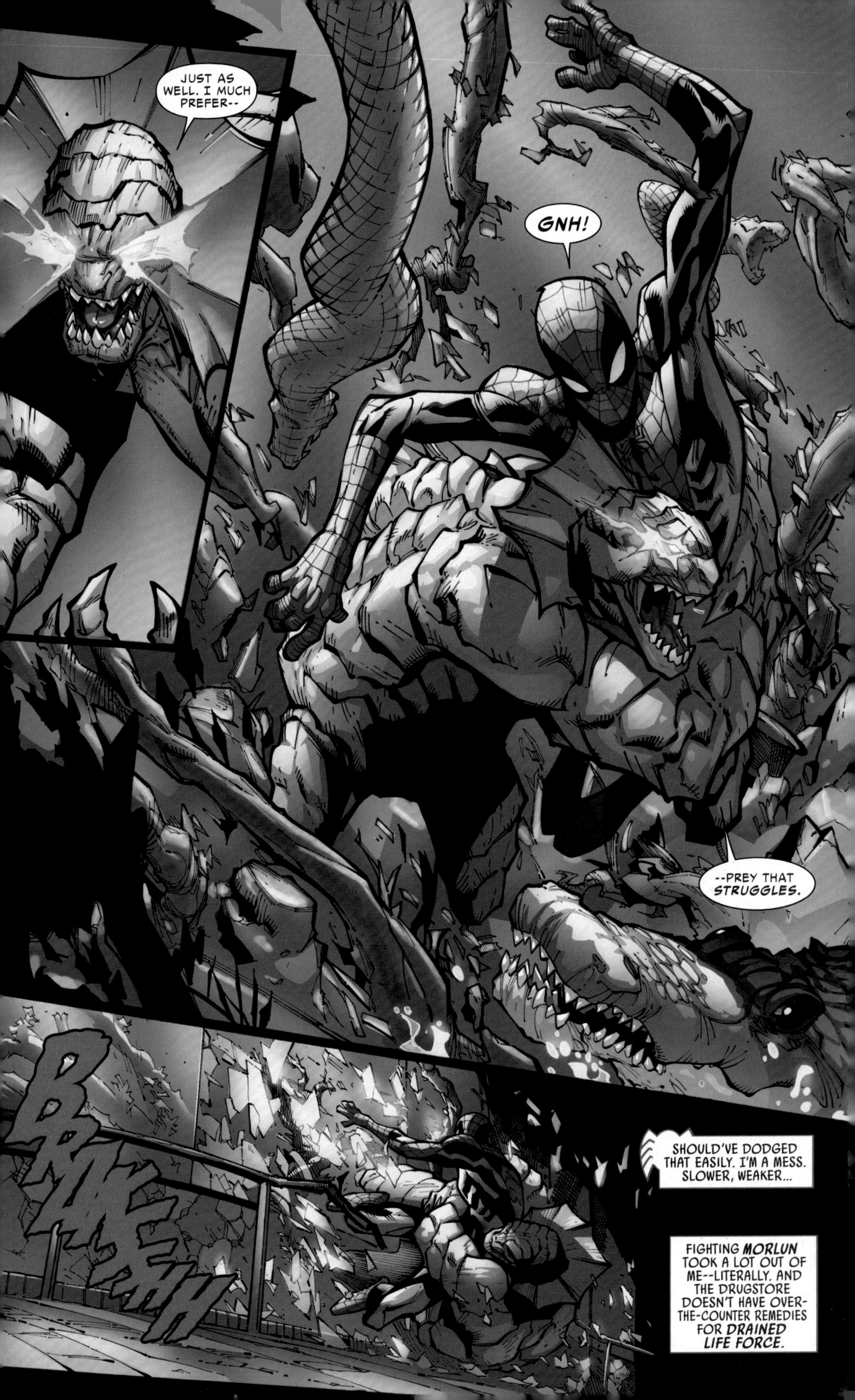
JUST AS WELL. I MUCH PREFER--
GNH!
--PREY THAT STRUGGLES.
BRAKASHH
SHOULD'VE DODGED THAT EASILY. I'M A MESS. SLOWER, WEAKER...
FIGHTING MORLUN TOOK A LOT OUT OF ME--LITERALLY. AND THE DRUGSTORE DOESN'T HAVE OVER-THE-COUNTER REMEDIES FOR DRAINED LIFE FORCE.

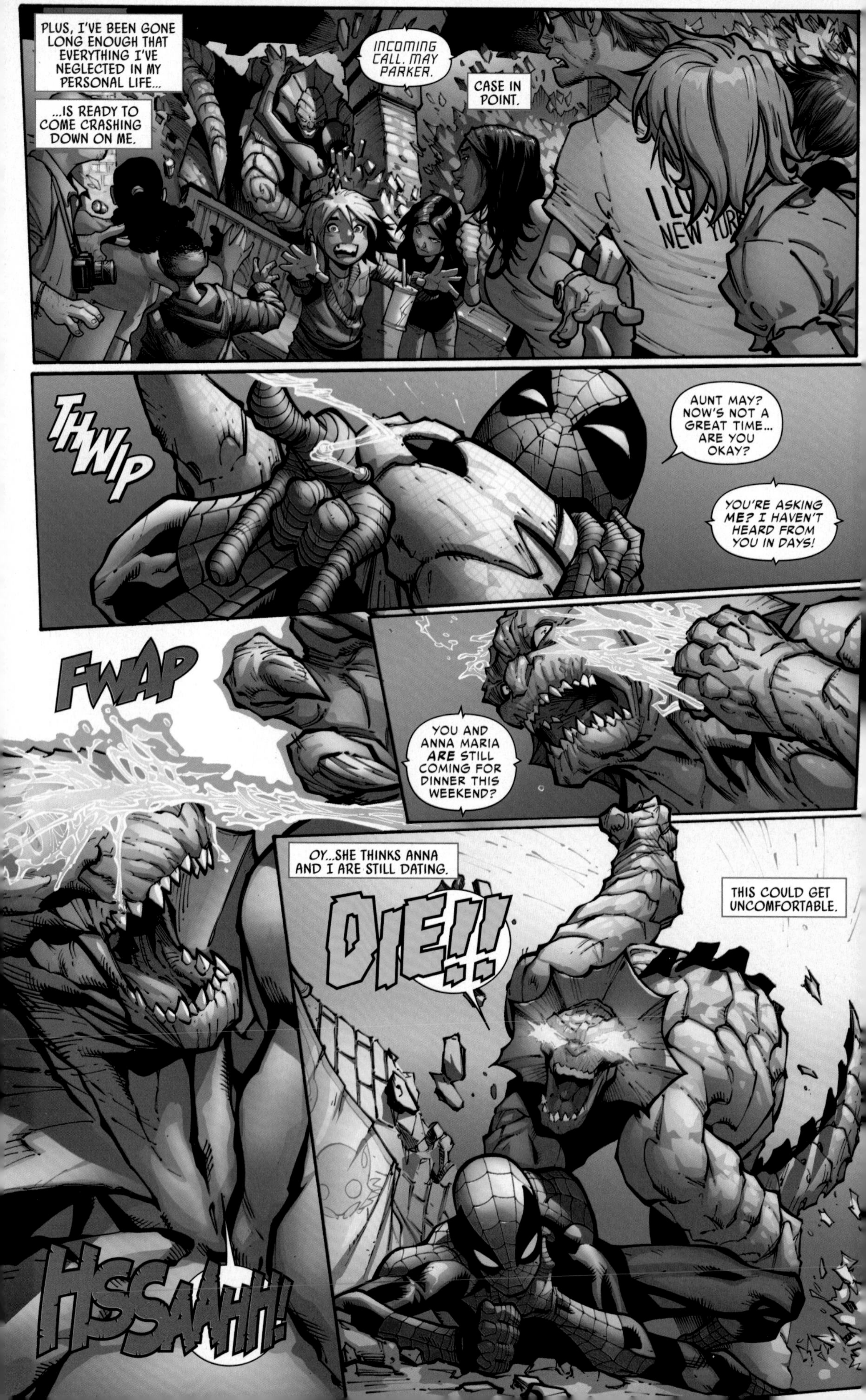
PLUS, I'VE BEEN GONE LONG ENOUGH THAT EVERYTHING I'VE NEGLECTED IN MY PERSONAL LIFE...
...IS READY TO COME CRASHING DOWN ON ME.
INCOMING CALL. MAY PARKER.
CASE IN POINT.
I LO NEW YOR
THWIP
AUNT MAY? NOW'S NOT A GREAT TIME... ARE YOU OKAY?
YOU'RE ASKING ME? I HAVEN'T HEARD FROM YOU IN DAYS!
FWAP
YOU AND ANNA MARIA ARE STILL COMING FOR DINNER THIS WEEKEND?
OY...SHE THINKS ANNA AND I ARE STILL DATING.
THIS COULD GET UNCOMFORTABLE.
DIE!!
HSSAAHH!

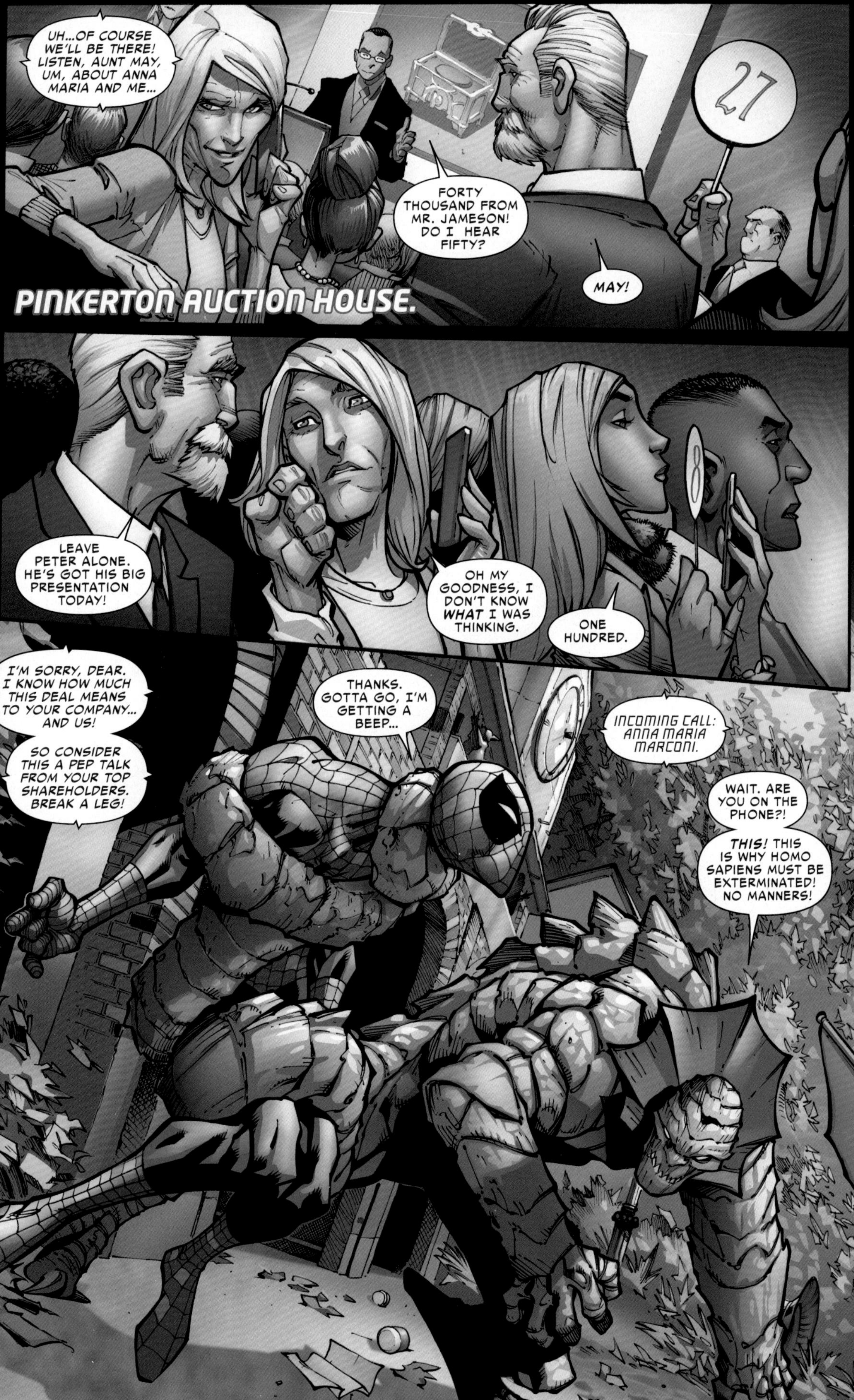
UH...OF COURSE WE'LL BE THERE! LISTEN, AUNT MAY, UM, ABOUT ANNA MARIA AND ME...
FORTY THOUSAND FROM MR. JAMESON! DO I HEAR FIFTY?
27
MAY!
PINKERTON AUCTION HOUSE.
LEAVE PETER ALONE. HE'S GOT HIS BIG PRESENTATION TODAY!
OH MY GOODNESS, I DON'T KNOW WHAT I WAS THINKING.
8
ONE HUNDRED.
I'M SORRY, DEAR. I KNOW HOW MUCH THIS DEAL MEANS TO YOUR COMPANY... AND US!
SO CONSIDER THIS A PEP TALK FROM YOUR TOP SHAREHOLDERS. BREAK A LEG!
THANKS. GOTTA GO, I'M GETTING A BEEP...
INCOMING CALL: ANNA MARIA MARCONI.
WAIT. ARE YOU ON THE PHONE?!
THIS! THIS IS WHY HOMO SAPIENS MUST BE EXTERMINATED! NO MANNERS!

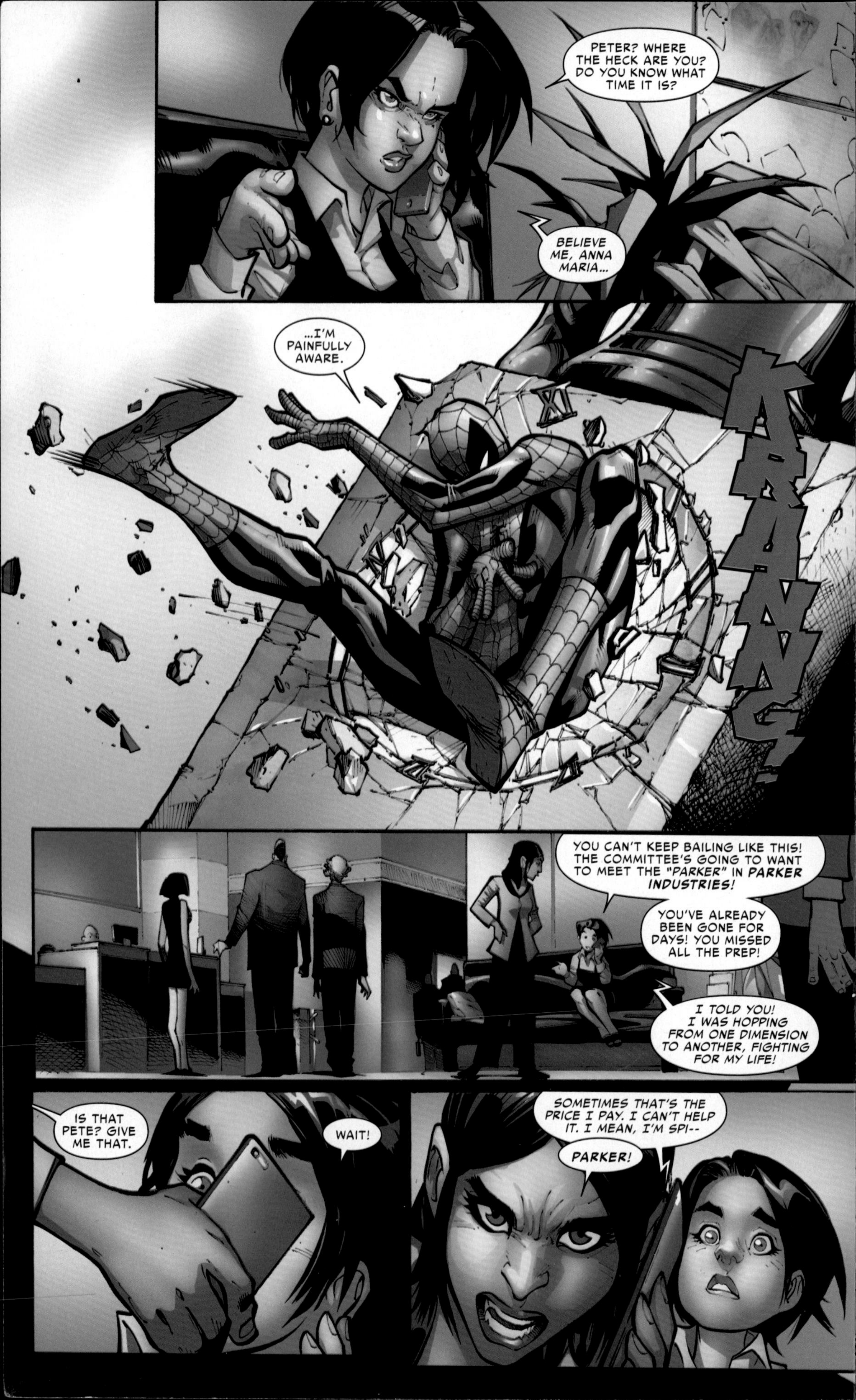
PETER? WHERE THE HECK ARE YOU? DO YOU KNOW WHAT TIME IT IS?
BELIEVE ME, ANNA MARIA...
...I'M PAINFULLY AWARE.
KRANG
YOU CAN'T KEEP BAILING LIKE THIS! THE COMMITTEE'S GOING TO WANT TO MEET THE "PARKER" IN PARKER INDUSTRIES!
YOU'VE ALREADY BEEN GONE FOR DAYS! YOU MISSED ALL THE PREP!
I TOLD YOU! I WAS HOPPING FROM ONE DIMENSION TO ANOTHER, FIGHTING FOR MY LIFE!
IS THAT PETE? GIVE ME THAT.
WAIT!
SOMETIMES THAT'S THE PRICE I PAY. I CAN'T HELP IT. I MEAN, I'M SPI--
PARKER!

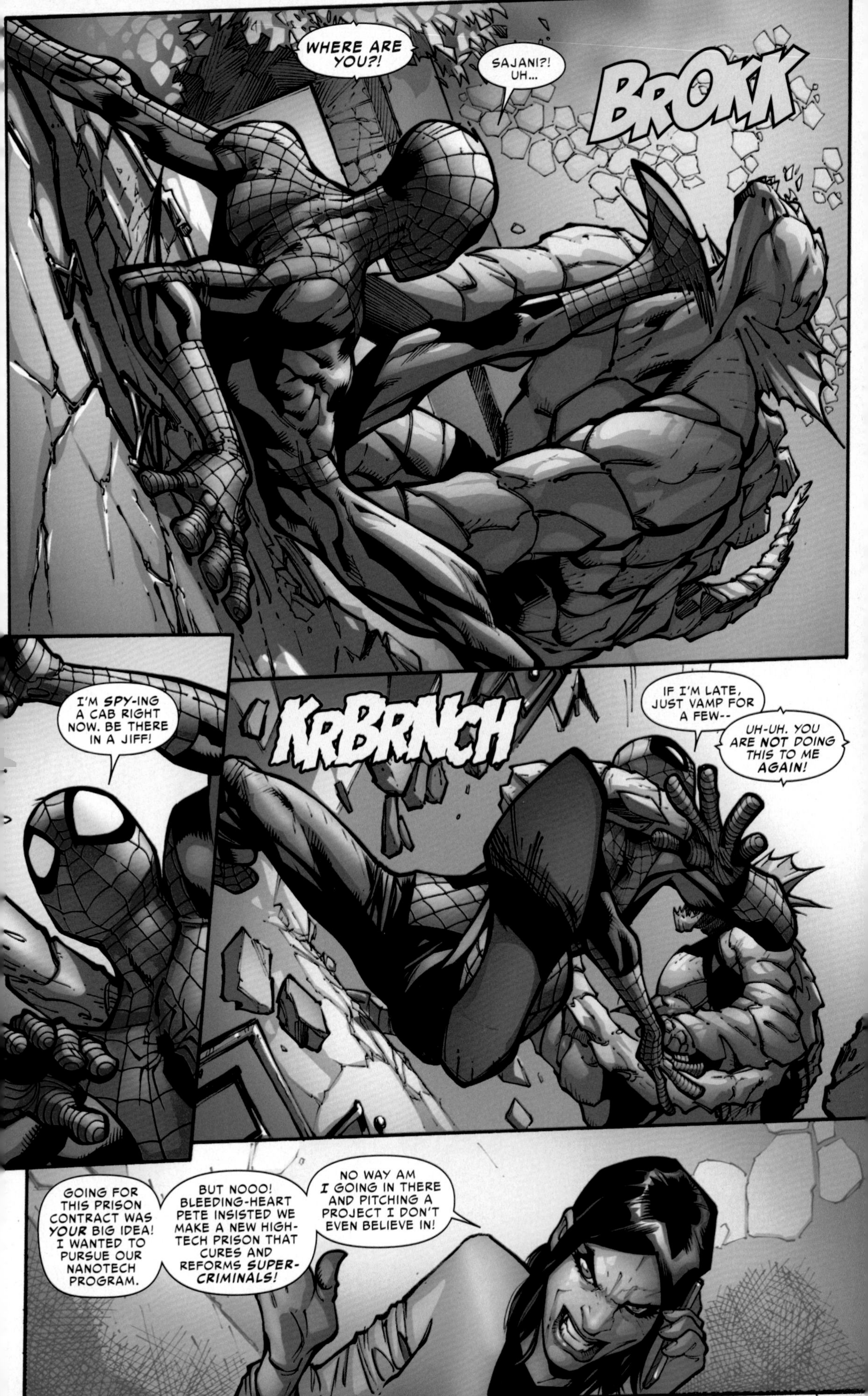
WHERE ARE YOU?!
SAJANI?! UH...
BROKK
I'M SPY-ING A CAB RIGHT NOW. BE THERE IN A JIFF!
KRBRNCH
IF I'M LATE, JUST VAMP FOR A FEW--
UH-UH. YOU ARE NOT DOING THIS TO ME AGAIN!
GOING FOR THIS PRISON CONTRACT WAS YOUR BIG IDEA! I WANTED TO PURSUE OUR NANOTECH PROGRAM.
BUT NOOO! BLEEDING-HEART PETE INSISTED WE MAKE A NEW HIGH-TECH PRISON THAT CURES AND REFORMS SUPER-CRIMINALS!
NO WAY AM I GOING IN THERE AND PITCHING A PROJECT I DON'T EVEN BELIEVE IN!

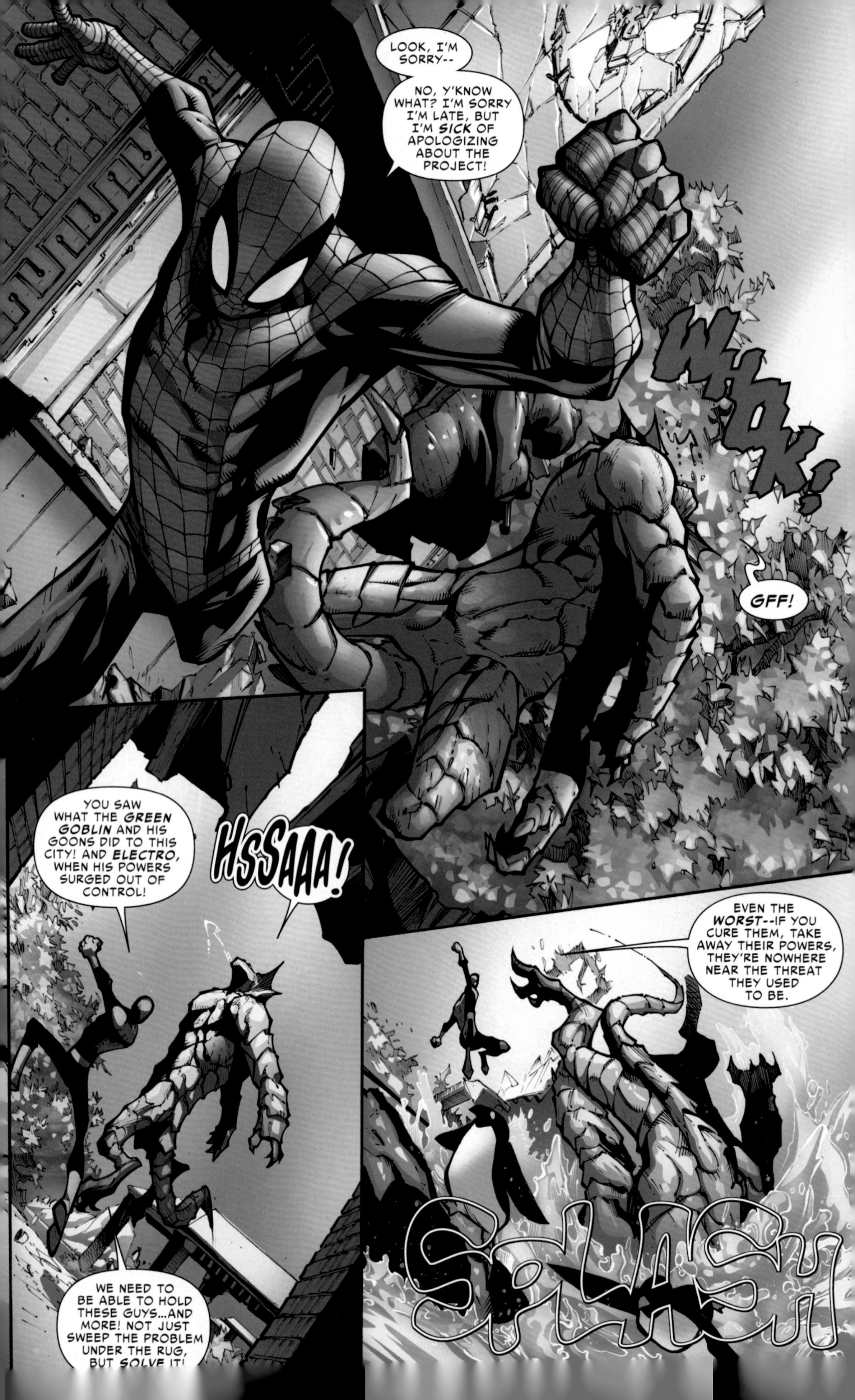

LOOK, I'M SORRY--
NO, Y'KNOW WHAT? I'M SORRY I'M LATE, BUT I'M SICK OF APOLOGIZING ABOUT THE PROJECT!
WHOK!
GFF!
YOU SAW WHAT THE GREEN GOBLIN AND HIS GOONS DID TO THIS CITY! AND ELECTRO, WHEN HIS POWERS SURGED OUT OF CONTROL!
HSSAAA!
WE NEED TO BE ABLE TO HOLD THESE GUYS...AND MORE! NOT JUST SWEEP THE PROBLEM UNDER THE RUG, BUT SOLVE IT!
EVEN THE WORST--IF YOU CURE THEM, TAKE AWAY THEIR POWERS, THEY'RE NOWHERE NEAR THE THREAT THEY USED TO BE.
SPLASH

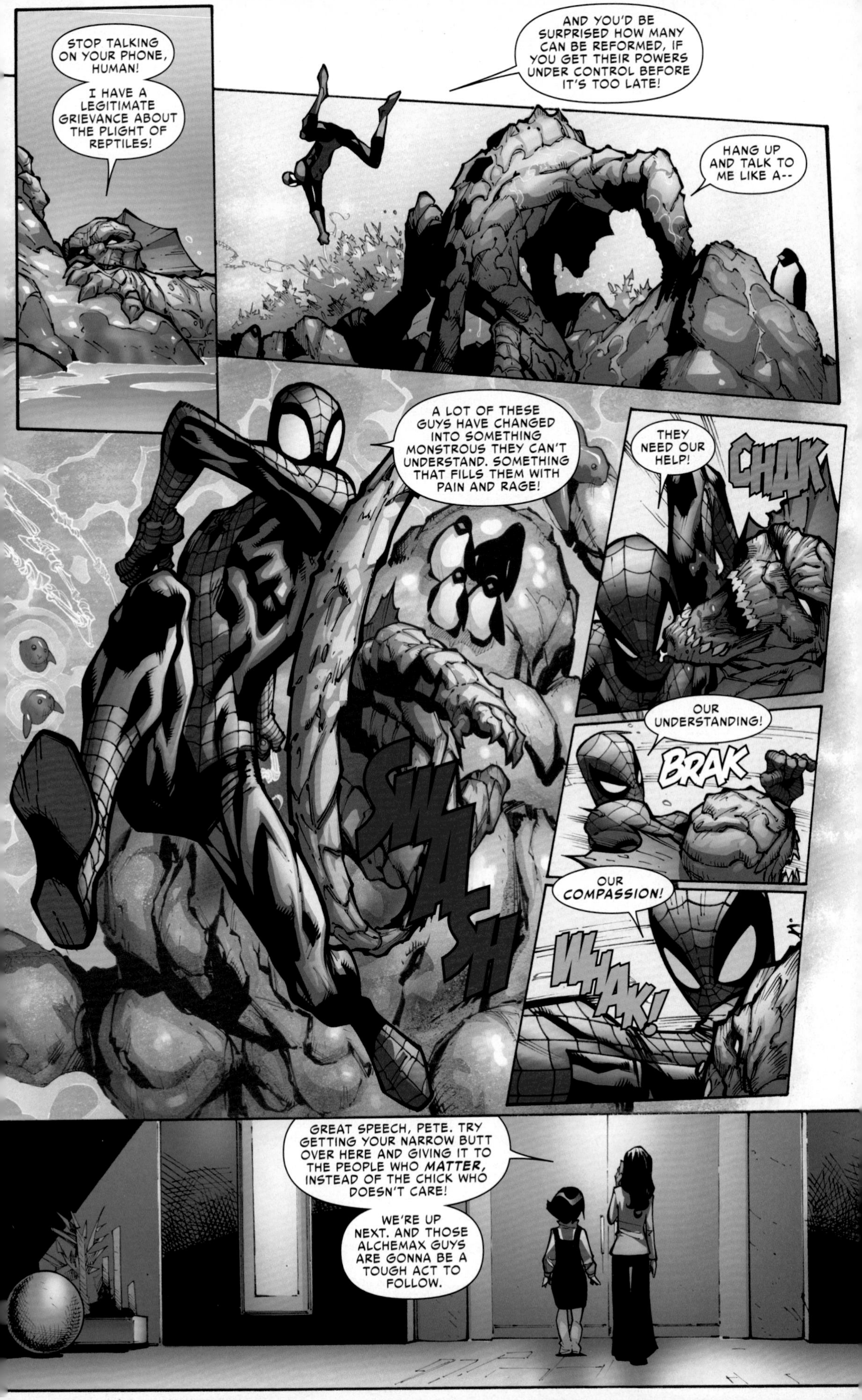
STOP TALKING ON YOUR PHONE, HUMAN!
I HAVE A LEGITIMATE GRIEVANCE ABOUT THE PLIGHT OF REPTILES!
AND YOU'D BE SURPRISED HOW MANY CAN BE REFORMED, IF YOU GET THEIR POWERS UNDER CONTROL BEFORE IT'S TOO LATE!
HANG UP AND TALK TO ME LIKE A--
A LOT OF THESE GUYS HAVE CHANGED INTO SOMETHING MONSTROUS THEY CAN'T UNDERSTAND. SOMETHING THAT FILLS THEM WITH PAIN AND RAGE!
THEY NEED OUR HELP!
CHAK
OUR UNDERSTANDING!
BRAK
OUR COMPASSION!
WHAK!
GREAT SPEECH, PETE. TRY GETTING YOUR NARROW BUTT OVER HERE AND GIVING IT TO THE PEOPLE WHO *MATTER*, INSTEAD OF THE CHICK WHO DOESN'T CARE!
WE'RE UP NEXT. AND THOSE ALCHEMAX GUYS ARE GONNA BE A TOUGH ACT TO FOLLOW.

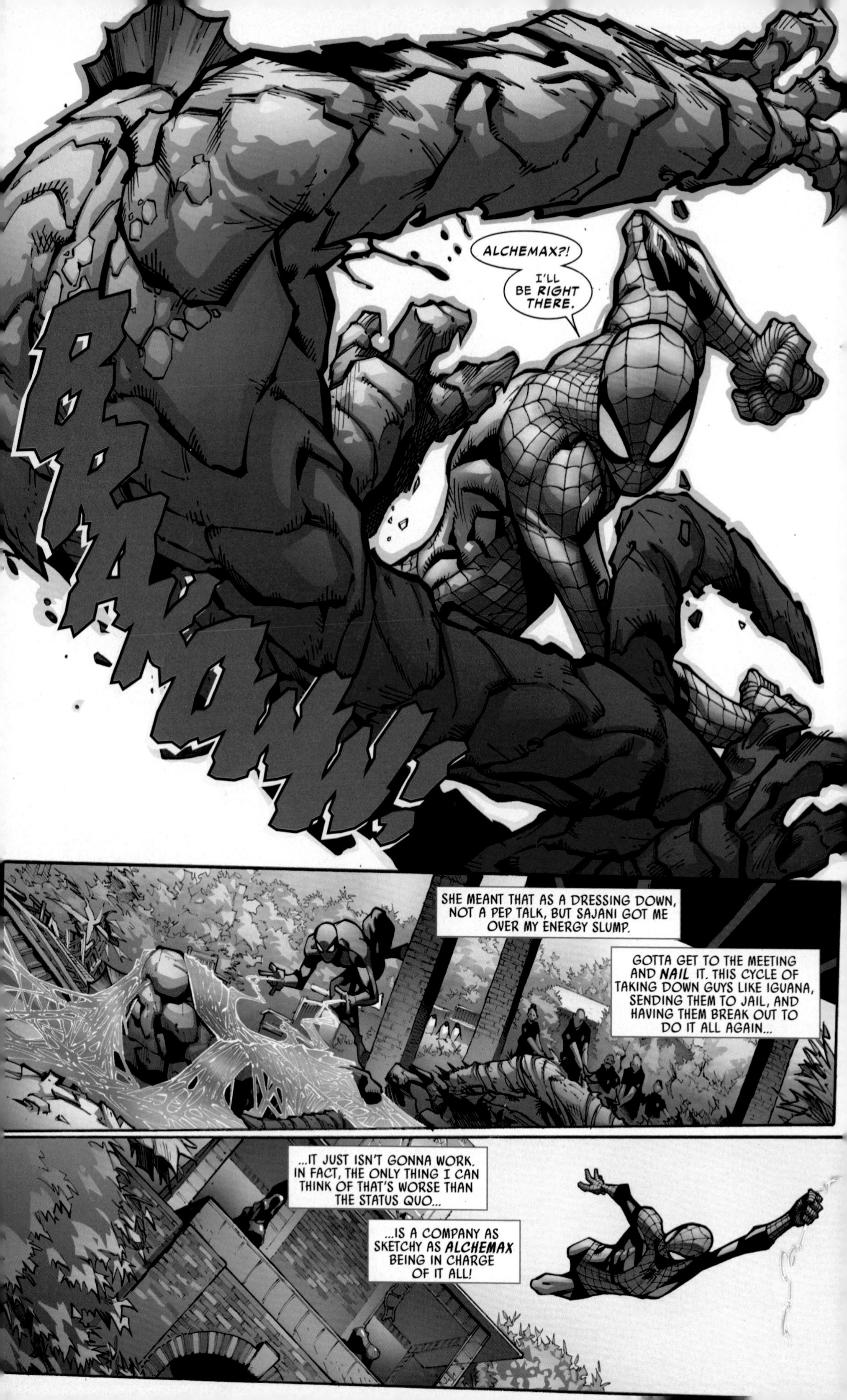
ALCHEMAX?!
I'LL BE RIGHT THERE.
SHE MEANT THAT AS A DRESSING DOWN, NOT A PEP TALK, BUT SAJANI GOT ME OVER MY ENERGY SLUMP.
GOTTA GET TO THE MEETING AND NAIL IT. THIS CYCLE OF TAKING DOWN GUYS LIKE IGUANA, SENDING THEM TO JAIL, AND HAVING THEM BREAK OUT TO DO IT ALL AGAIN...
...IT JUST ISN'T GONNA WORK. IN FACT, THE ONLY THING I CAN THINK OF THAT'S WORSE THAN THE STATUS QUO...
...IS A COMPANY AS SKETCHY AS ALCHEMAX BEING IN CHARGE OF IT ALL!

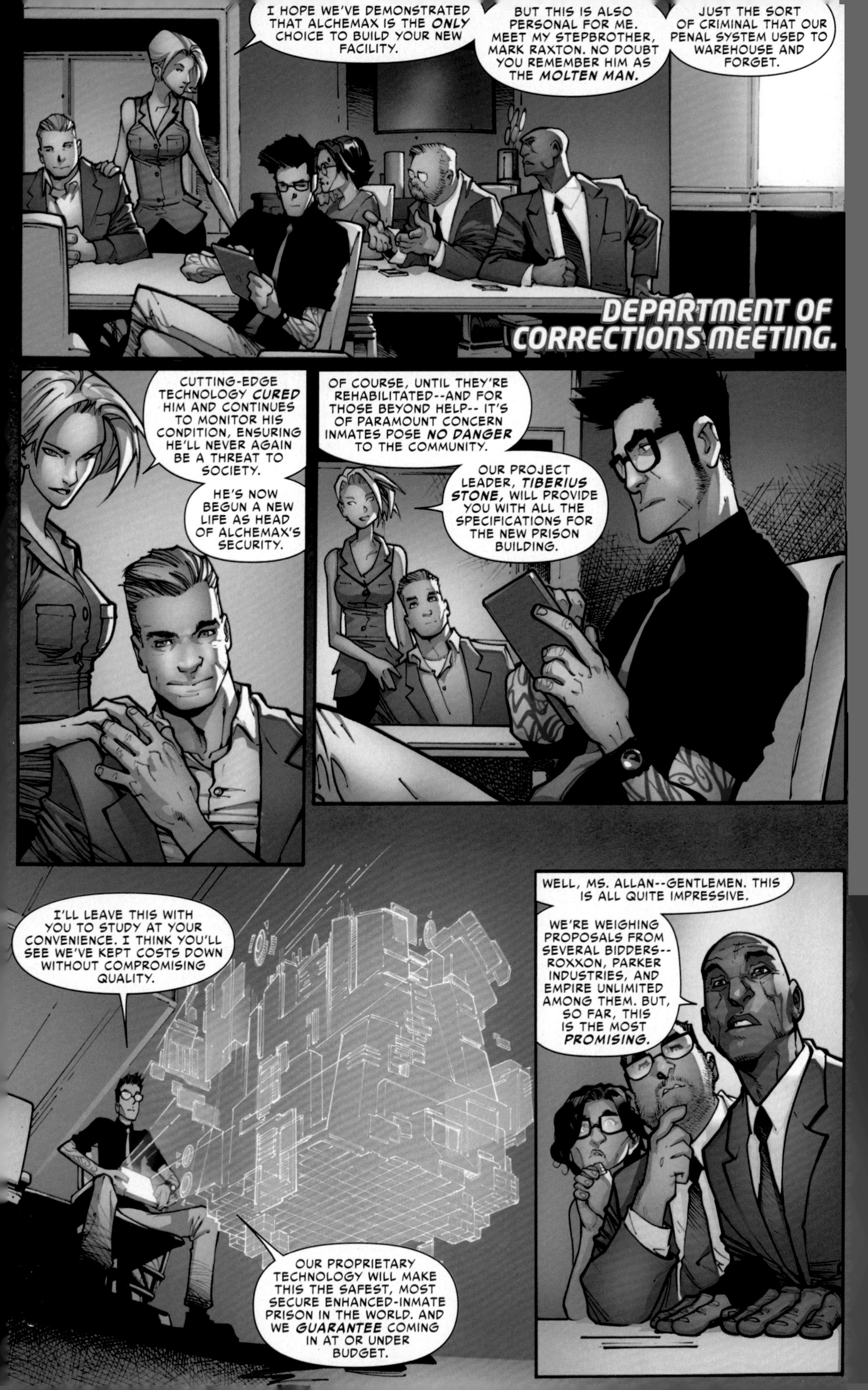

I HOPE WE'VE DEMONSTRATED THAT ALCHEMAX IS THE ONLY CHOICE TO BUILD YOUR NEW FACILITY.
BUT THIS IS ALSO PERSONAL FOR ME. MEET MY STEPBROTHER, MARK RAXTON. NO DOUBT YOU REMEMBER HIM AS THE MOLTEN MAN.
JUST THE SORT OF CRIMINAL THAT OUR PENAL SYSTEM USED TO WAREHOUSE AND FORGET.
DEPARTMENT OF CORRECTIONS MEETING.
CUTTING-EDGE TECHNOLOGY CURED HIM AND CONTINUES TO MONITOR HIS CONDITION, ENSURING HE'LL NEVER AGAIN BE A THREAT TO SOCIETY.
HE'S NOW BEGUN A NEW LIFE AS HEAD OF ALCHEMAX'S SECURITY.
OF COURSE, UNTIL THEY'RE REHABILITATED--AND FOR THOSE BEYOND HELP-- IT'S OF PARAMOUNT CONCERN INMATES POSE NO DANGER TO THE COMMUNITY.
OUR PROJECT LEADER, TIBERIUS STONE, WILL PROVIDE YOU WITH ALL THE SPECIFICATIONS FOR THE NEW PRISON BUILDING.
I'LL LEAVE THIS WITH YOU TO STUDY AT YOUR CONVENIENCE. I THINK YOU'LL SEE WE'VE KEPT COSTS DOWN WITHOUT COMPROMISING QUALITY.
OUR PROPRIETARY TECHNOLOGY WILL MAKE THIS THE SAFEST, MOST SECURE ENHANCED-INMATE PRISON IN THE WORLD. AND WE GUARANTEE COMING IN AT OR UNDER BUDGET.
WELL, MS. ALLAN--GENTLEMEN. THIS IS ALL QUITE IMPRESSIVE.
WE'RE WEIGHING PROPOSALS FROM SEVERAL BIDDERS--ROXXON, PARKER INDUSTRIES, AND EMPIRE UNLIMITED AMONG THEM. BUT, SO FAR, THIS IS THE MOST PROMISING.

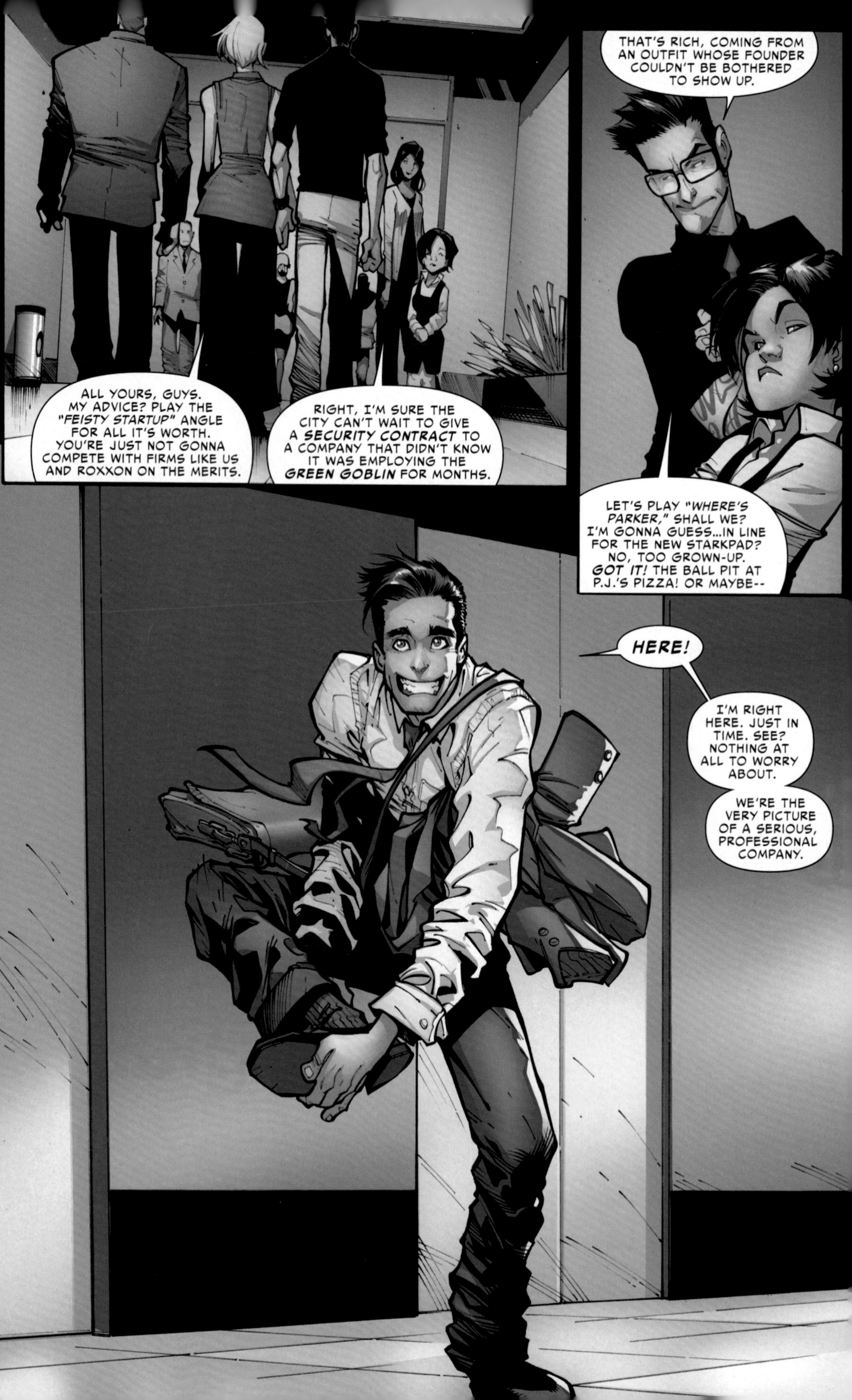
ALL YOURS, GUYS. MY ADVICE? PLAY THE "FEISTY STARTUP" ANGLE FOR ALL IT'S WORTH. YOU'RE JUST NOT GONNA COMPETE WITH FIRMS LIKE US AND ROXXON ON THE MERITS.
RIGHT, I'M SURE THE CITY CAN'T WAIT TO GIVE A SECURITY CONTRACT TO A COMPANY THAT DIDN'T KNOW IT WAS EMPLOYING THE GREEN GOBLIN FOR MONTHS.
THAT'S RICH, COMING FROM AN OUTFIT WHOSE FOUNDER COULDN'T BE BOTHERED TO SHOW UP.
LET'S PLAY "WHERE'S PARKER," SHALL WE? I'M GONNA GUESS...IN LINE FOR THE NEW STARKPAD? NO, TOO GROWN-UP. GOT IT! THE BALL PIT AT P.J.'S PIZZA! OR MAYBE--
HERE!
I'M RIGHT HERE. JUST IN TIME. SEE? NOTHING AT ALL TO WORRY ABOUT.
WE'RE THE VERY PICTURE OF A SERIOUS, PROFESSIONAL COMPANY.

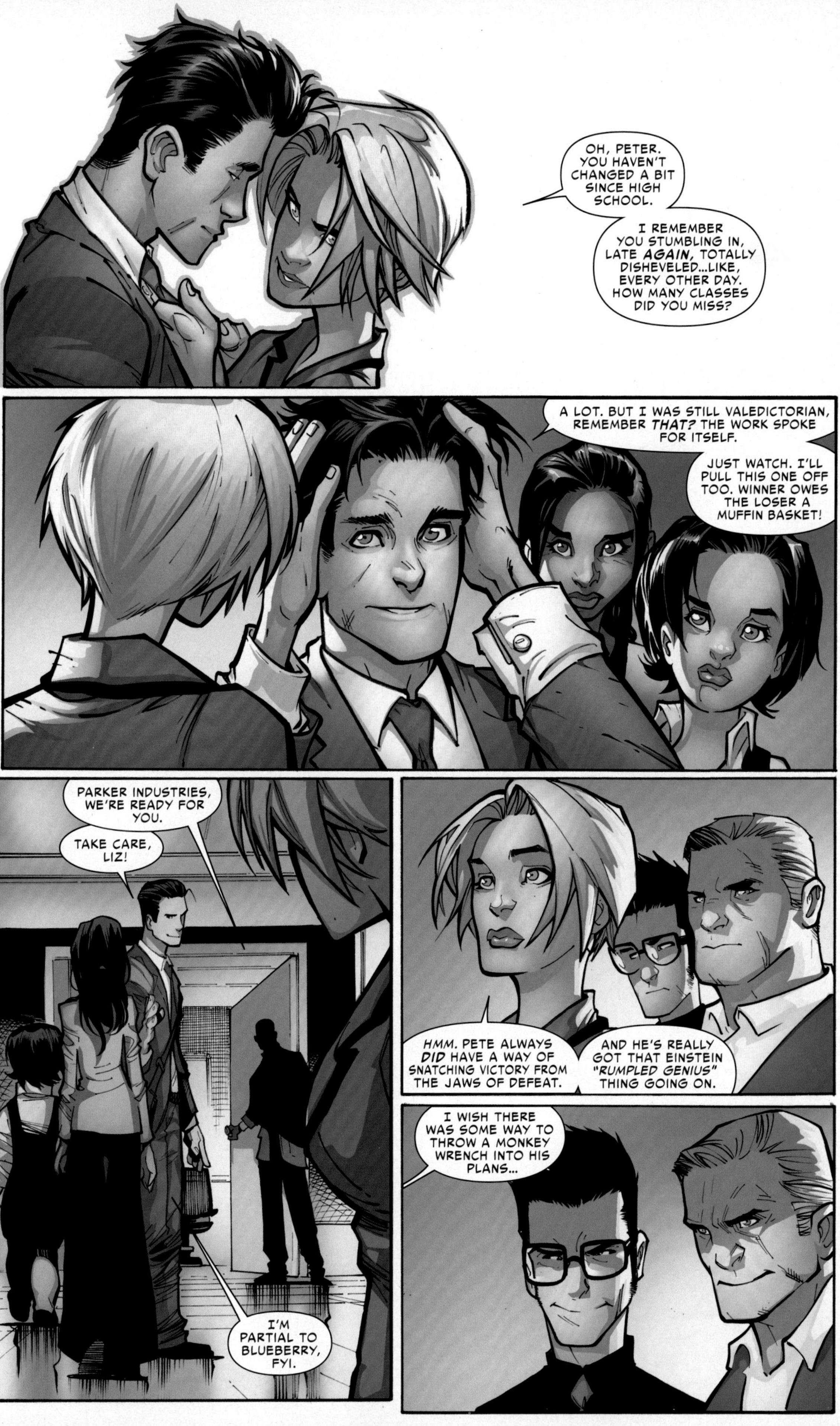

OH, PETER. YOU HAVEN'T CHANGED A BIT SINCE HIGH SCHOOL.
I REMEMBER YOU STUMBLING IN, LATE AGAIN, TOTALLY DISHEVELED...LIKE, EVERY OTHER DAY. HOW MANY CLASSES DID YOU MISS?
A LOT. BUT I WAS STILL VALEDICTORIAN, REMEMBER THAT? THE WORK SPOKE FOR ITSELF.
JUST WATCH. I'LL PULL THIS ONE OFF TOO. WINNER OWES THE LOSER A MUFFIN BASKET!
PARKER INDUSTRIES, WE'RE READY FOR YOU.
TAKE CARE, LIZ!
I'M PARTIAL TO BLUEBERRY, FYI.
HMM. PETE ALWAYS DID HAVE A WAY OF SNATCHING VICTORY FROM THE JAWS OF DEFEAT.
AND HE'S REALLY GOT THAT EINSTEIN "RUMPLED GENIUS" THING GOING ON.
I WISH THERE WAS SOME WAY TO THROW A MONKEY WRENCH INTO HIS PLANS...

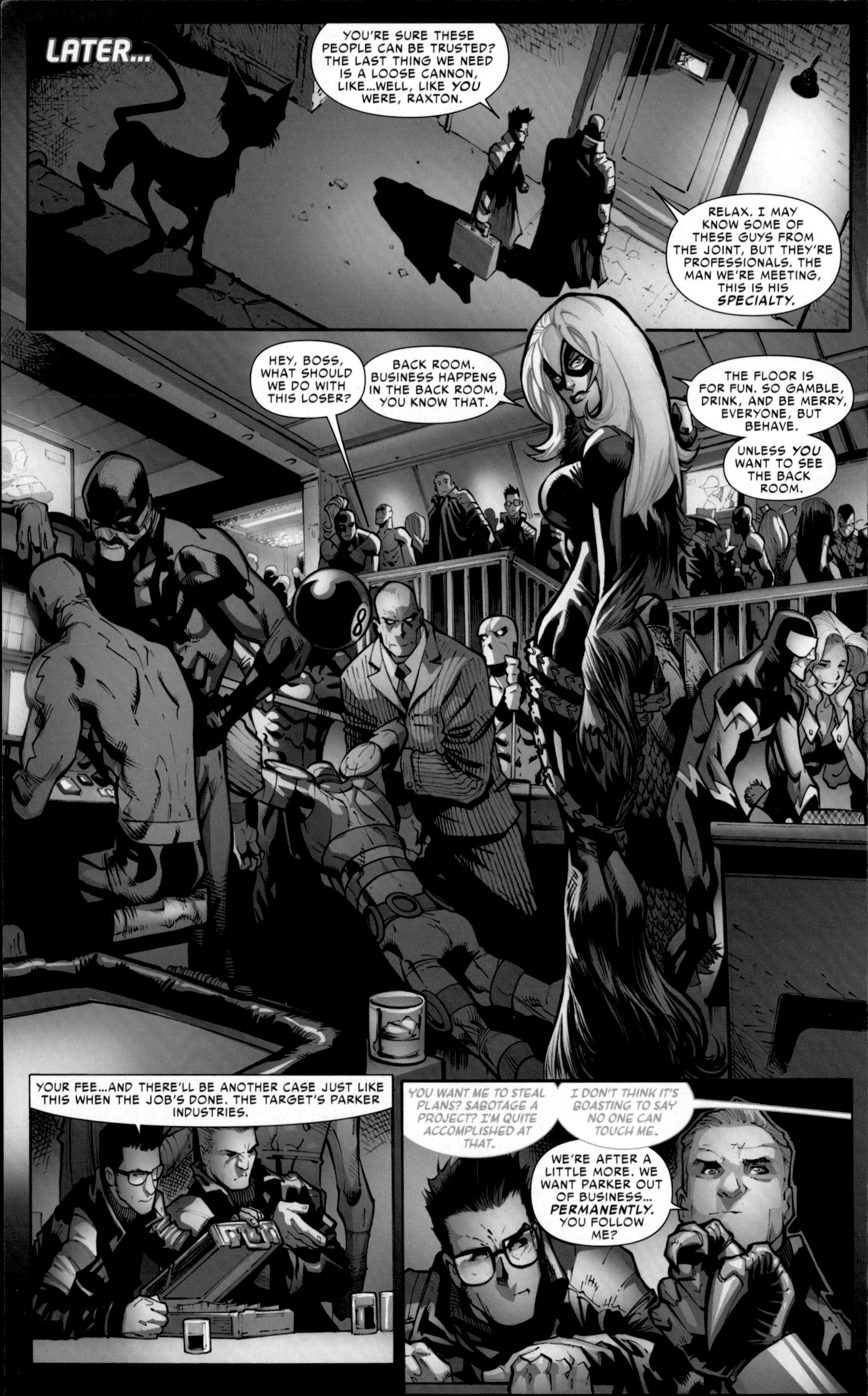
LATER...
YOU'RE SURE THESE PEOPLE CAN BE TRUSTED? THE LAST THING WE NEED IS A LOOSE CANNON, LIKE...WELL, LIKE YOU WERE, RAXTON.
RELAX. I MAY KNOW SOME OF THESE GUYS FROM THE JOINT, BUT THEY'RE PROFESSIONALS. THE MAN WE'RE MEETING, THIS IS HIS SPECIALTY.
HEY, BOSS, WHAT SHOULD WE DO WITH THIS LOSER?
BACK ROOM. BUSINESS HAPPENS IN THE BACK ROOM, YOU KNOW THAT.
THE FLOOR IS FOR FUN. SO GAMBLE, DRINK, AND BE MERRY, EVERYONE, BUT BEHAVE.
UNLESS YOU WANT TO SEE THE BACK ROOM.
YOUR FEE...AND THERE'LL BE ANOTHER CASE JUST LIKE THIS WHEN THE JOB'S DONE. THE TARGET'S PARKER INDUSTRIES.
YOU WANT ME TO STEAL PLANS? SABOTAGE A PROJECT? I'M QUITE ACCOMPLISHED AT THAT.
I DON'T THINK IT'S BOASTING TO SAY NO ONE CAN TOUCH ME.
WE'RE AFTER A LITTLE MORE. WE WANT PARKER OUT OF BUSINESS... PERMANENTLY. YOU FOLLOW ME?

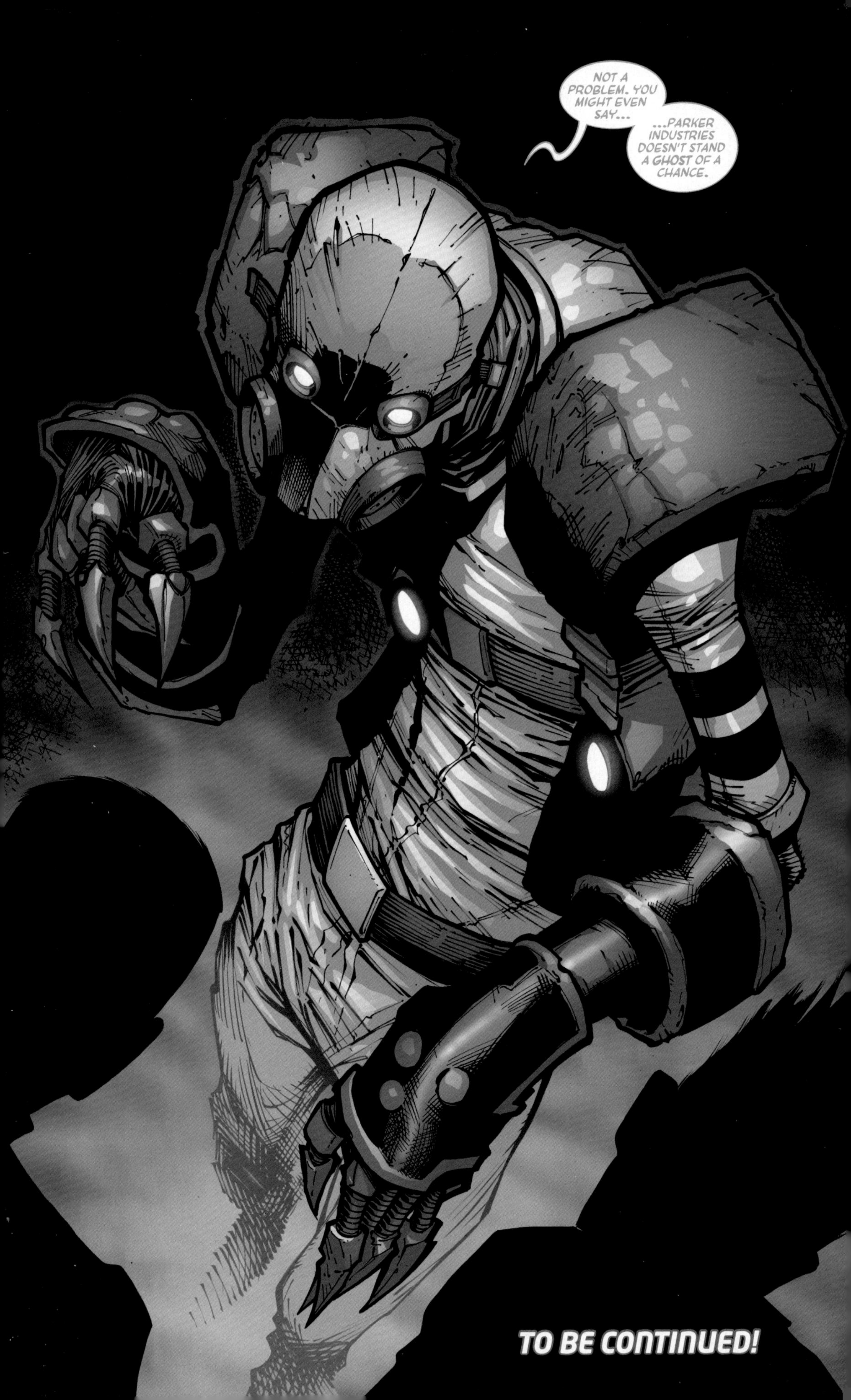
NOT A PROBLEM. YOU MIGHT EVEN SAY...
...PARKER INDUSTRIES DOESN'T STAND A GHOST OF A CHANCE.
TO BE CONTINUED!

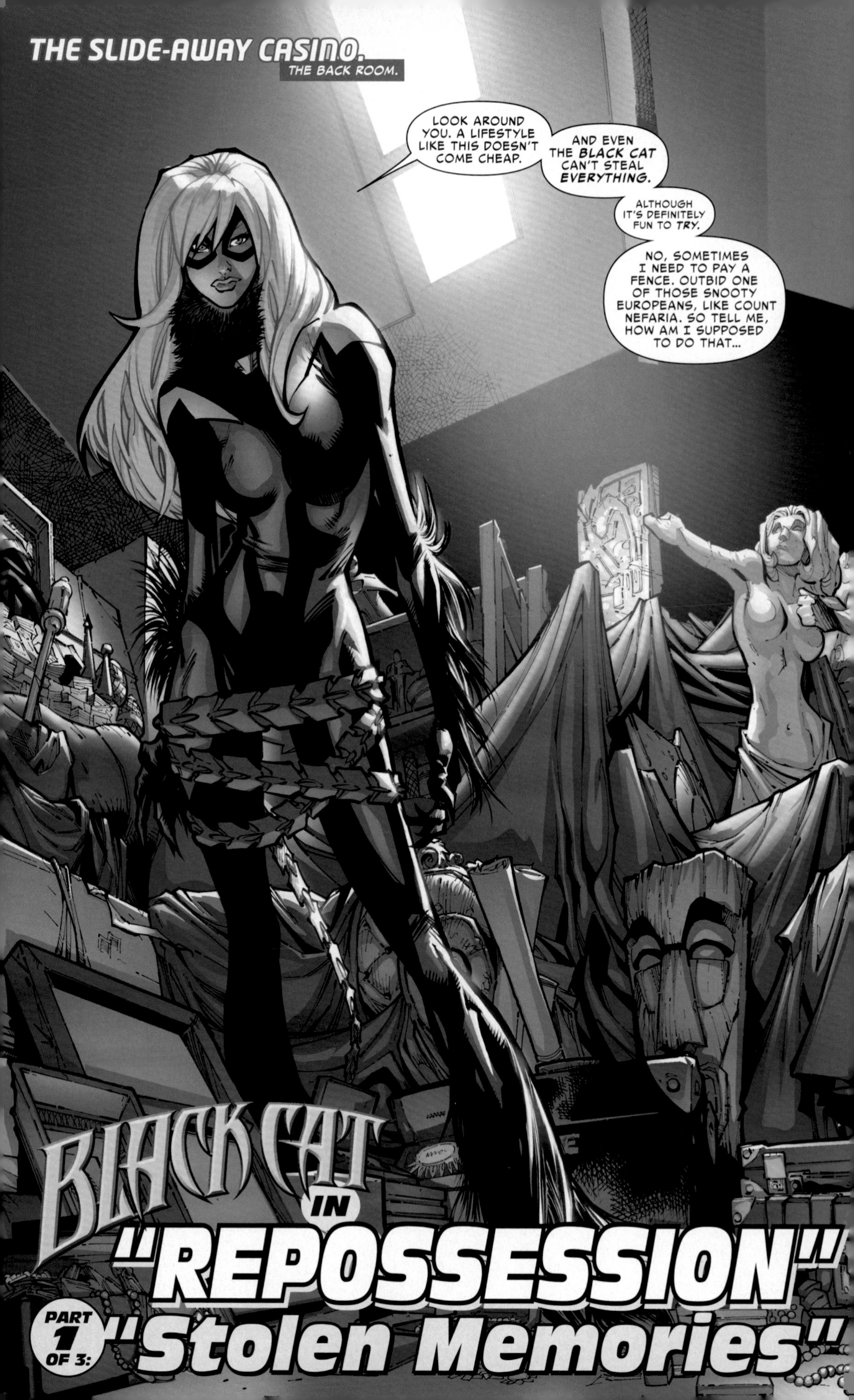
THE SLIDE-AWAY CASINO.
THE BACK ROOM.
LOOK AROUND YOU. A LIFESTYLE LIKE THIS DOESN'T COME CHEAP.
AND EVEN THE BLACK CAT CAN'T STEAL EVERYTHING.
ALTHOUGH IT'S DEFINITELY FUN TO TRY.
NO, SOMETIMES I NEED TO PAY A FENCE. OUTBID ONE OF THOSE SNOOTY EUROPEANS, LIKE COUNT NEFARIA. SO TELL ME, HOW AM I SUPPOSED TO DO THAT...
BLACK CAT
IN
"REPOSSESSION"
PART 1 OF 3: "Stolen Memories"

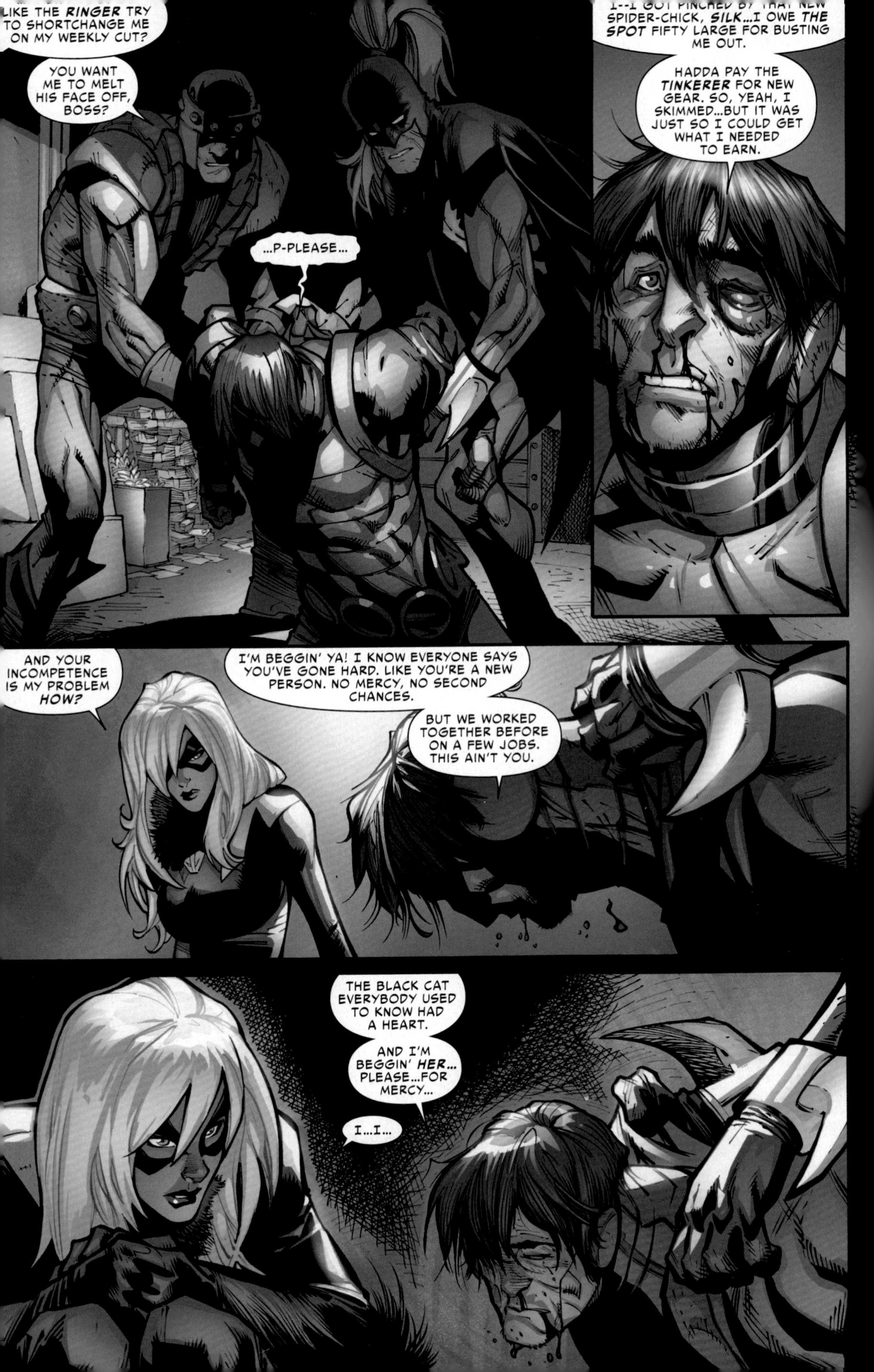
LIKE THE RINGER TRY TO SHORTCHANGE ME ON MY WEEKLY CUT?
YOU WANT ME TO MELT HIS FACE OFF, BOSS?
...P-PLEASE...
I--I GOT PINCHED BY THAT NEW SPIDER-CHICK, SILK...I OWE THE SPOT FIFTY LARGE FOR BUSTING ME OUT.
HADDA PAY THE TINKERER FOR NEW GEAR. SO, YEAH, I SKIMMED...BUT IT WAS JUST SO I COULD GET WHAT I NEEDED TO EARN.
AND YOUR INCOMPETENCE IS MY PROBLEM HOW?
I'M BEGGIN' YA! I KNOW EVERYONE SAYS YOU'VE GONE HARD. LIKE YOU'RE A NEW PERSON. NO MERCY, NO SECOND CHANCES.
BUT WE WORKED TOGETHER BEFORE ON A FEW JOBS. THIS AIN'T YOU.
THE BLACK CAT EVERYBODY USED TO KNOW HAD A HEART.
AND I'M BEGGIN' HER... PLEASE...FOR MERCY...
I...I...

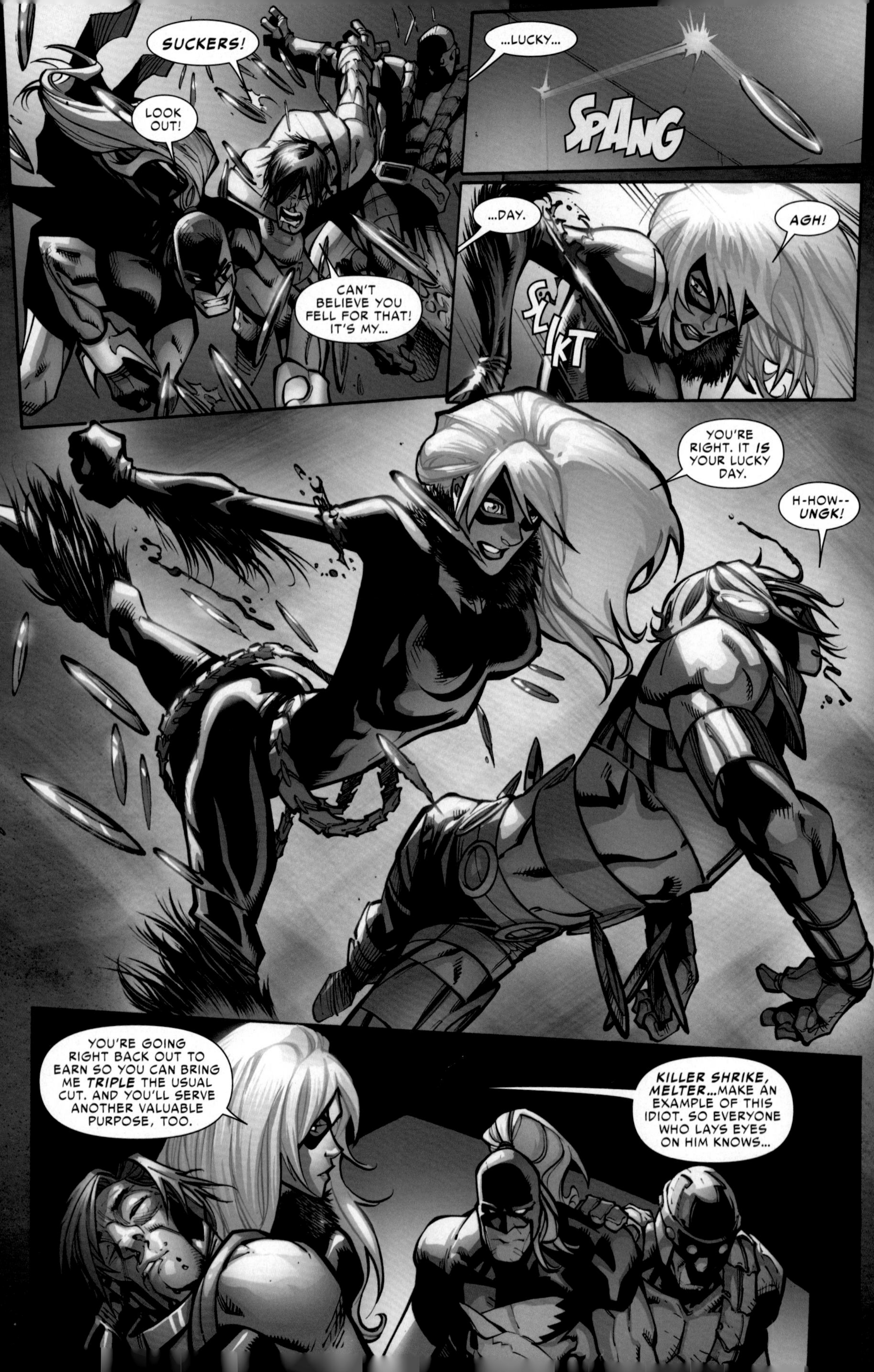
SUCKERS!
LOOK OUT!
CAN'T BELIEVE YOU FELL FOR THAT! IT'S MY...
...LUCKY...
SPANG
...DAY.
AGH!
SLIKT
YOU'RE RIGHT. IT IS YOUR LUCKY DAY.
H-HOW-- UNGK!
YOU'RE GOING RIGHT BACK OUT TO EARN SO YOU CAN BRING ME TRIPLE THE USUAL CUT. AND YOU'LL SERVE ANOTHER VALUABLE PURPOSE, TOO.
KILLER SHRIKE, MELTER...MAKE AN EXAMPLE OF THIS IDIOT. SO EVERYONE WHO LAYS EYES ON HIM KNOWS...

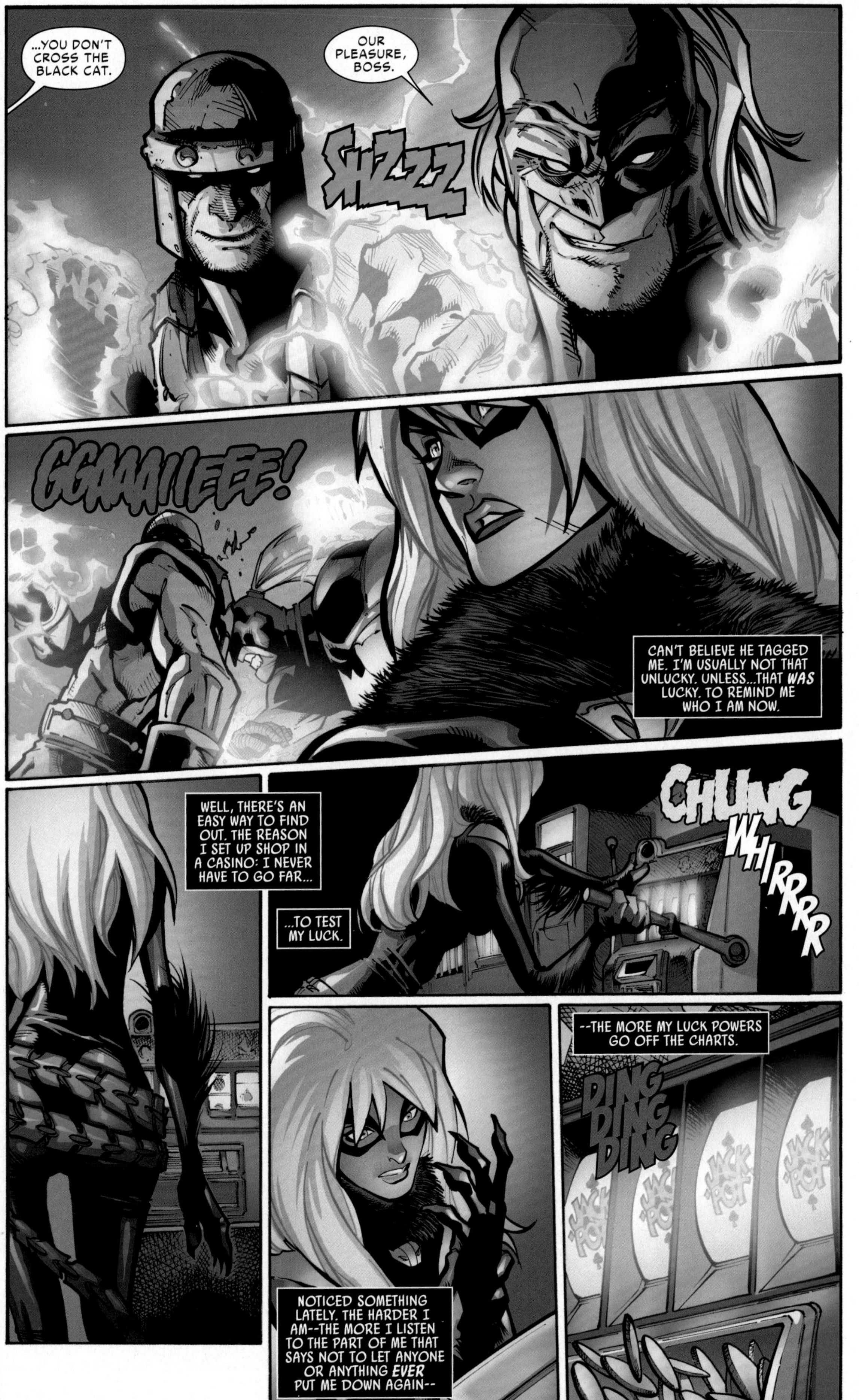
...YOU DON'T CROSS THE BLACK CAT.
OUR PLEASURE, BOSS.
SHZZZ
GGAAAIIEEE!
CAN'T BELIEVE HE TAGGED ME. I'M USUALLY NOT THAT UNLUCKY. UNLESS...THAT WAS LUCKY. TO REMIND ME WHO I AM NOW.
WELL, THERE'S AN EASY WAY TO FIND OUT. THE REASON I SET UP SHOP IN A CASINO: I NEVER HAVE TO GO FAR...
...TO TEST MY LUCK.
CHUNG
WHIRRRR
NOTICED SOMETHING LATELY. THE HARDER I AM--THE MORE I LISTEN TO THE PART OF ME THAT SAYS NOT TO LET ANYONE OR ANYTHING EVER PUT ME DOWN AGAIN--
--THE MORE MY LUCK POWERS GO OFF THE CHARTS.
DING DING DING
JACK POT
JACK POT
JACK POT
JACK POT

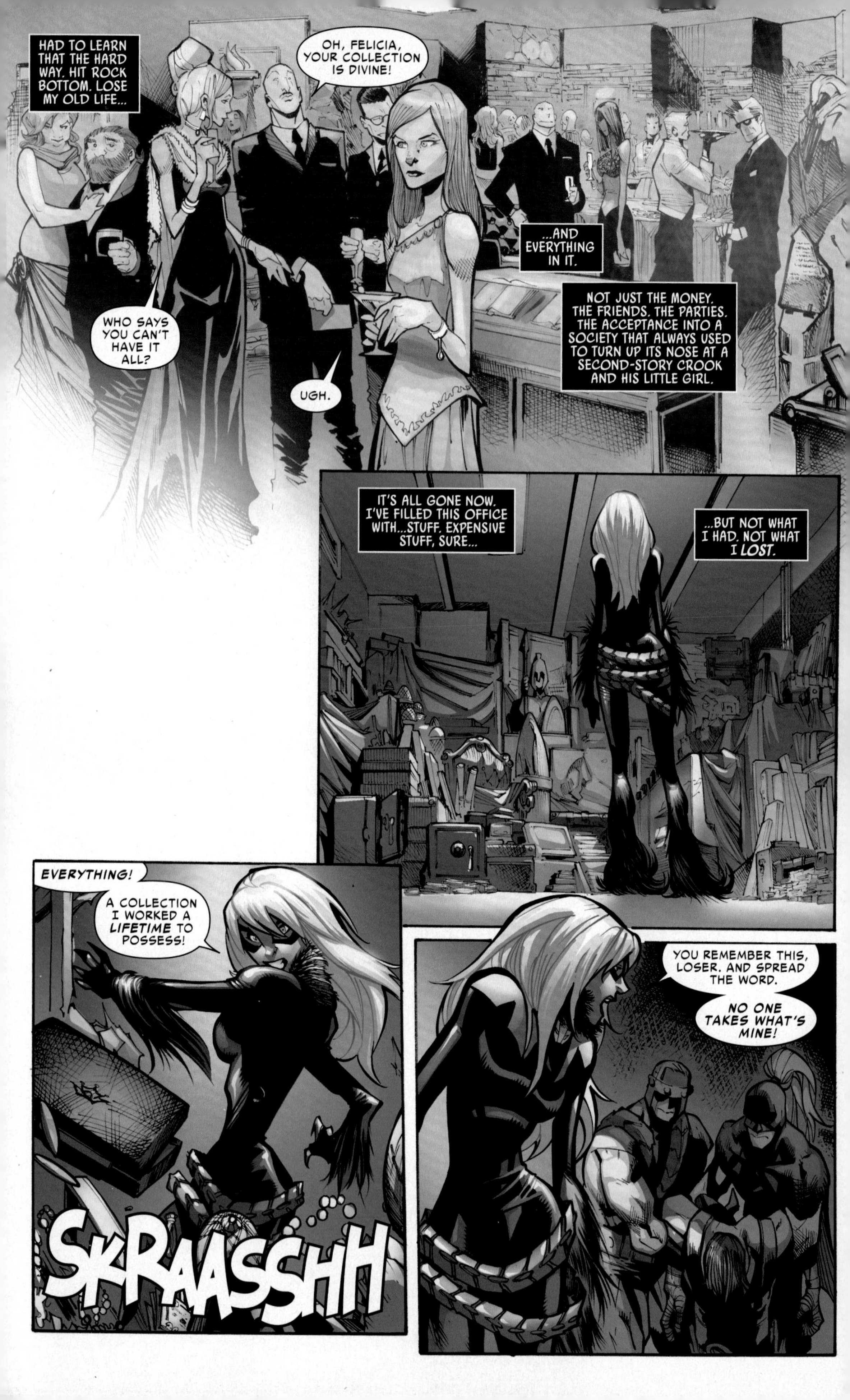

HAD TO LEARN THAT THE HARD WAY. HIT ROCK BOTTOM. LOSE MY OLD LIFE...
OH, FELICIA, YOUR COLLECTION IS DIVINE!
...AND EVERYTHING IN IT.
NOT JUST THE MONEY. THE FRIENDS. THE PARTIES. THE ACCEPTANCE INTO A SOCIETY THAT ALWAYS USED TO TURN UP ITS NOSE AT A SECOND-STORY CROOK AND HIS LITTLE GIRL.
WHO SAYS YOU CAN'T HAVE IT ALL?
UGH.
IT'S ALL GONE NOW. I'VE FILLED THIS OFFICE WITH...STUFF. EXPENSIVE STUFF, SURE...
...BUT NOT WHAT I HAD. NOT WHAT I LOST.
EVERYTHING!
A COLLECTION I WORKED A LIFETIME TO POSSESS!
SKRAASSHH
YOU REMEMBER THIS, LOSER. AND SPREAD THE WORD.
NO ONE TAKES WHAT'S MINE!

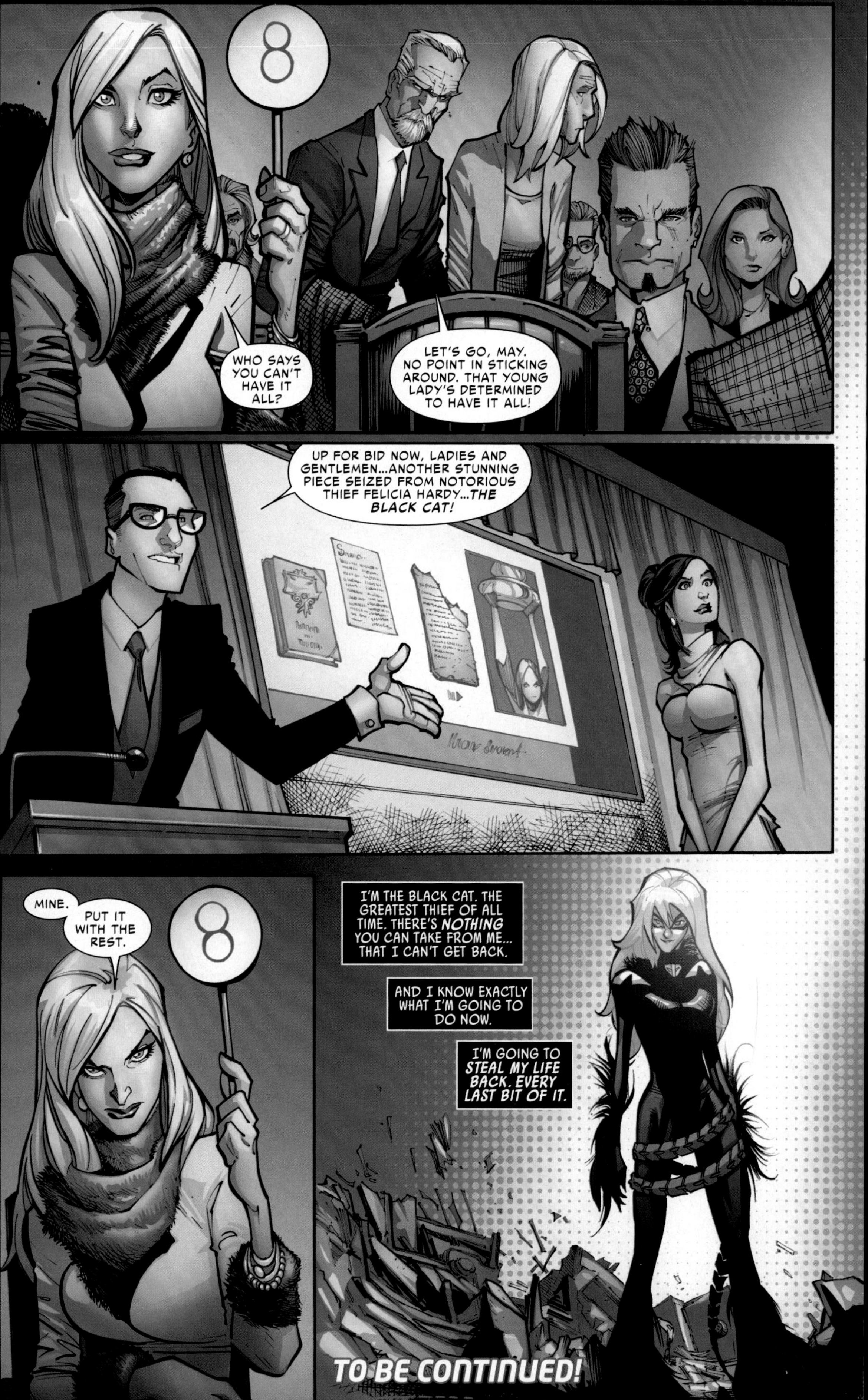
8
WHO SAYS YOU CAN'T HAVE IT ALL?
LET'S GO, MAY. NO POINT IN STICKING AROUND. THAT YOUNG LADY'S DETERMINED TO HAVE IT ALL!
UP FOR BID NOW, LADIES AND GENTLEMEN...ANOTHER STUNNING PIECE SEIZED FROM NOTORIOUS THIEF FELICIA HARDY...*THE BLACK CAT!*
MINE.
PUT IT WITH THE REST.
8
I'M THE BLACK CAT. THE GREATEST THIEF OF ALL TIME. THERE'S *NOTHING* YOU CAN TAKE FROM ME... THAT I CAN'T GET BACK.
AND I KNOW EXACTLY WHAT I'M GOING TO DO NOW.
I'M GOING TO *STEAL MY LIFE BACK. EVERY LAST BIT OF IT.*
TO BE CONTINUED!

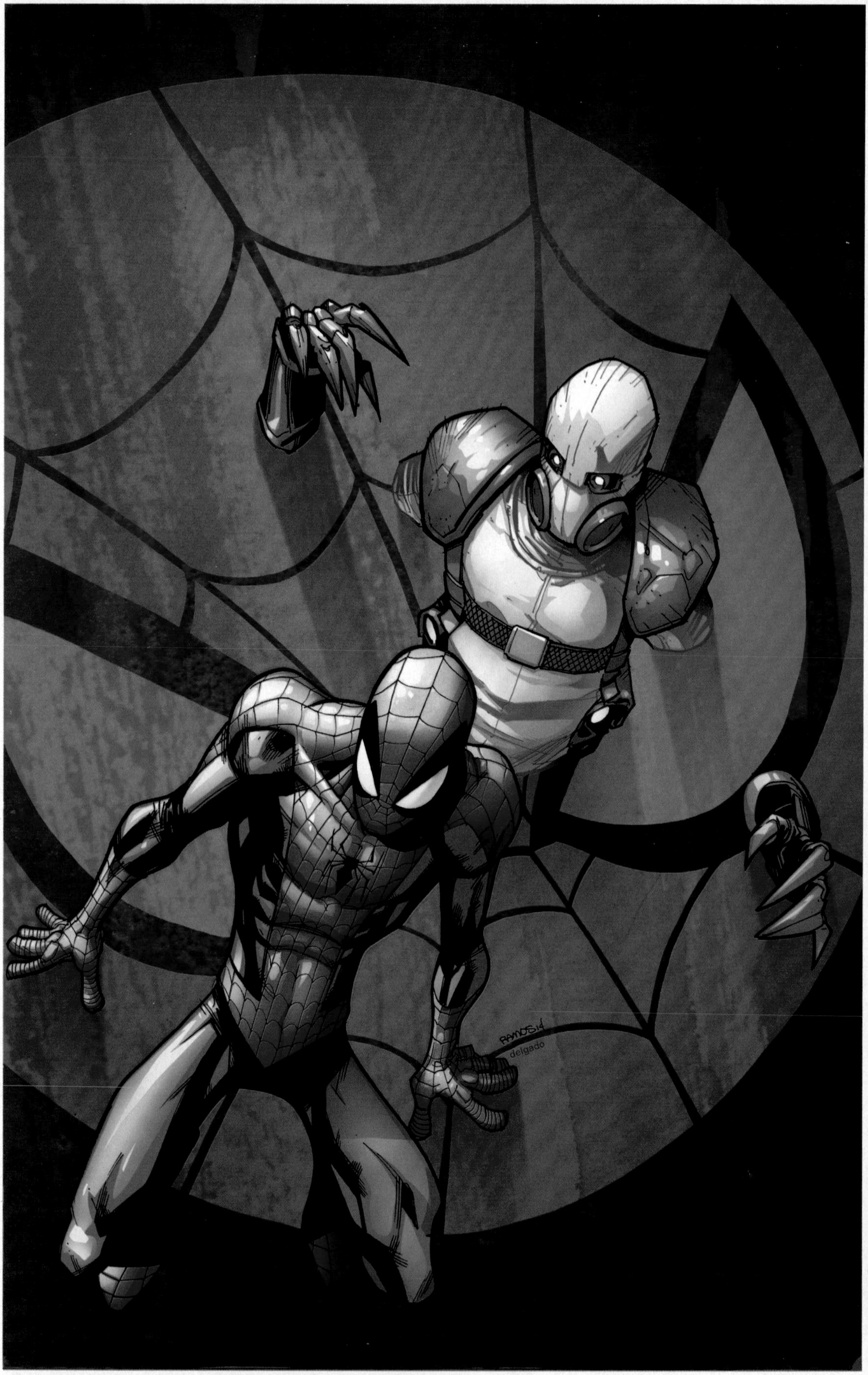

AMAZING SPIDER-MAN 17

GRAVEYARD SHIFT, PART TWO: TRUST ISSUES

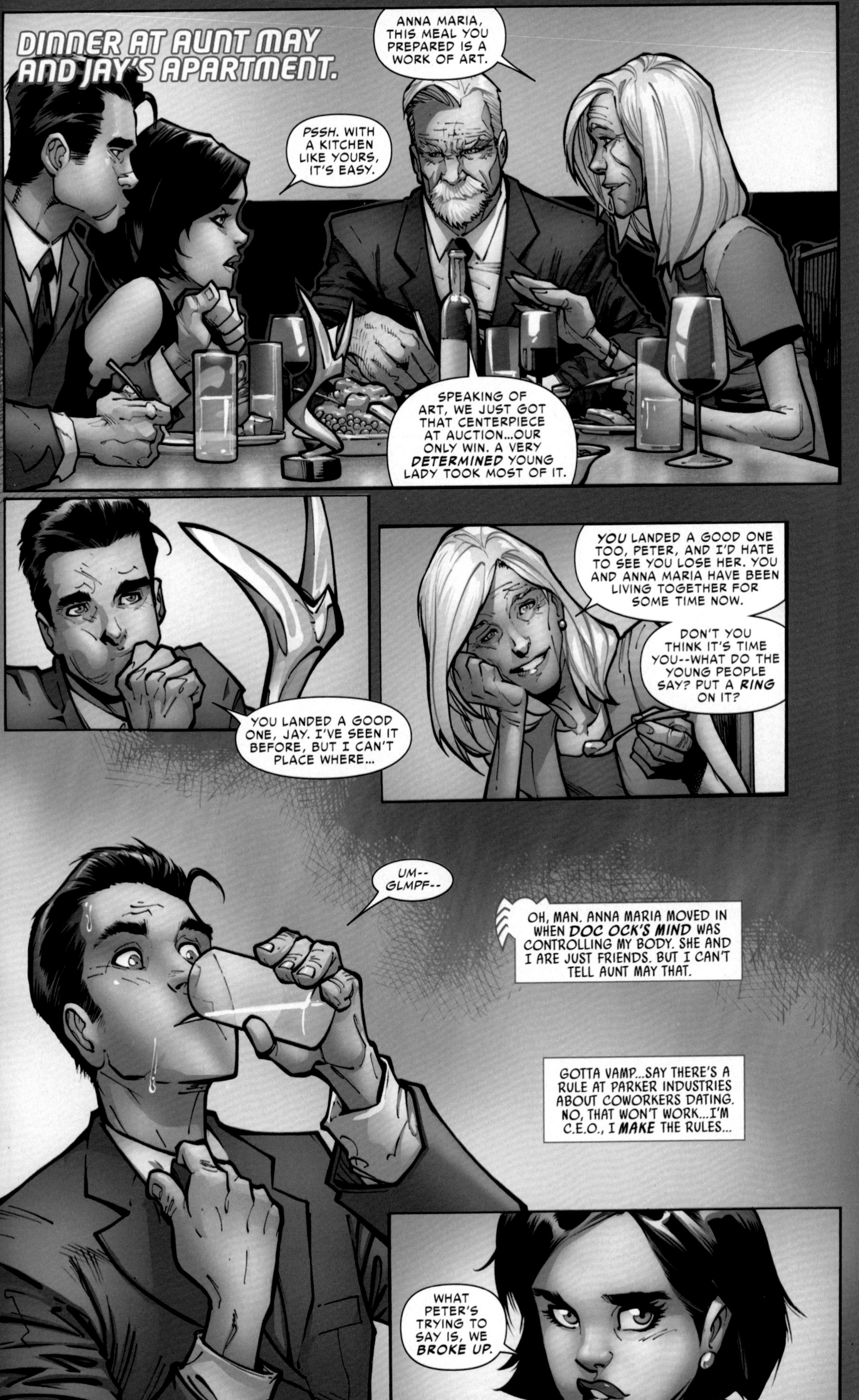
DINNER AT AUNT MAY AND JAY'S APARTMENT.
ANNA MARIA, THIS MEAL YOU PREPARED IS A WORK OF ART.
PSSH. WITH A KITCHEN LIKE YOURS, IT'S EASY.
SPEAKING OF ART, WE JUST GOT THAT CENTERPIECE AT AUCTION...OUR ONLY WIN. A VERY DETERMINED YOUNG LADY TOOK MOST OF IT.
YOU LANDED A GOOD ONE, JAY. I'VE SEEN IT BEFORE, BUT I CAN'T PLACE WHERE...
YOU LANDED A GOOD ONE TOO, PETER, AND I'D HATE TO SEE YOU LOSE HER. YOU AND ANNA MARIA HAVE BEEN LIVING TOGETHER FOR SOME TIME NOW.
DON'T YOU THINK IT'S TIME YOU--WHAT DO THE YOUNG PEOPLE SAY? PUT A RING ON IT?
UM-- GLMPF--
OH, MAN. ANNA MARIA MOVED IN WHEN DOC OCK'S MIND WAS CONTROLLING MY BODY. SHE AND I ARE JUST FRIENDS. BUT I CAN'T TELL AUNT MAY THAT.
GOTTA VAMP...SAY THERE'S A RULE AT PARKER INDUSTRIES ABOUT COWORKERS DATING. NO, THAT WON'T WORK...I'M C.E.O., I MAKE THE RULES...
WHAT PETER'S TRYING TO SAY IS, WE BROKE UP.

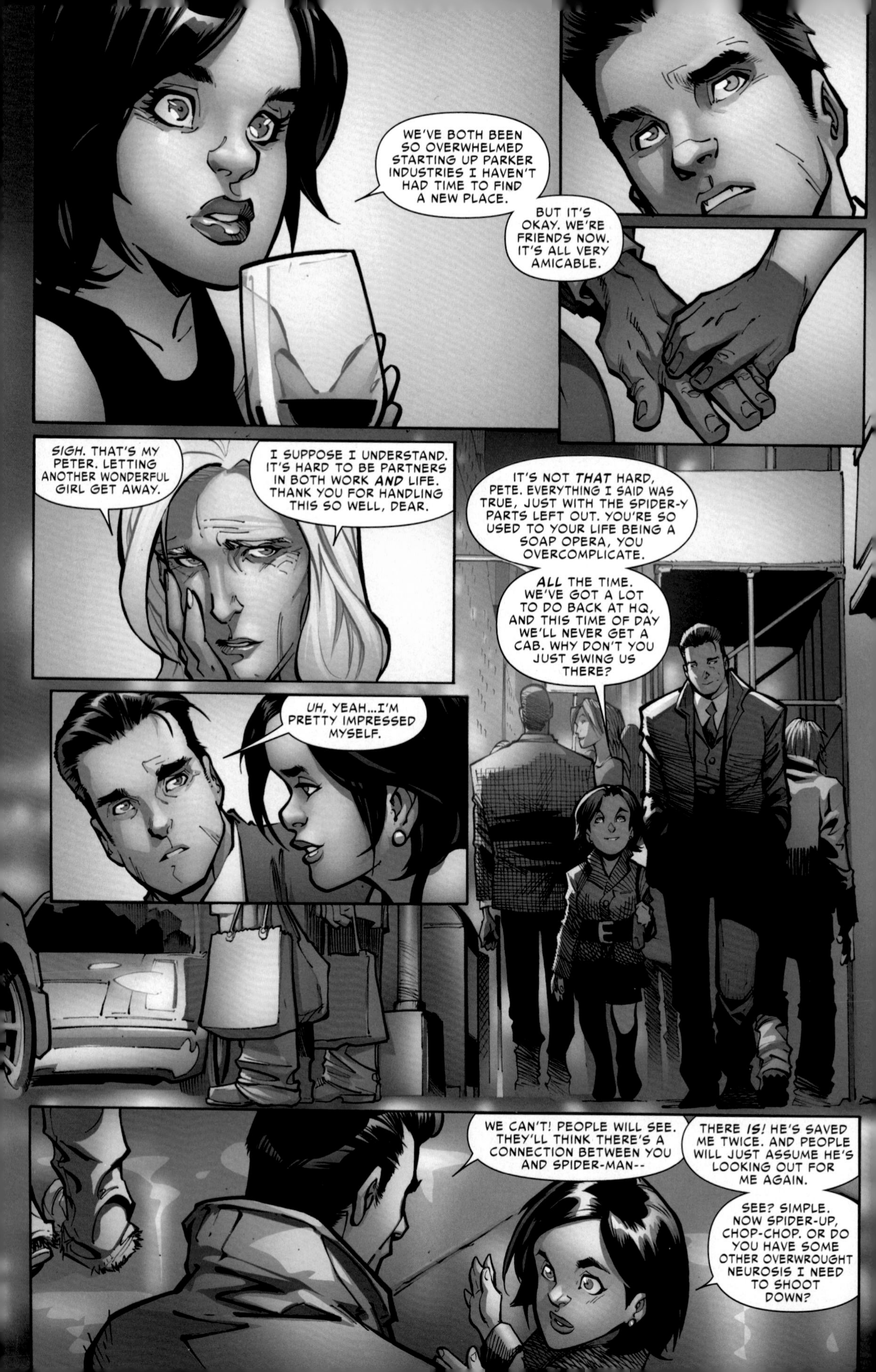
WE'VE BOTH BEEN SO OVERWHELMED STARTING UP PARKER INDUSTRIES I HAVEN'T HAD TIME TO FIND A NEW PLACE.
BUT IT'S OKAY. WE'RE FRIENDS NOW. IT'S ALL VERY AMICABLE.
SIGH. THAT'S MY PETER. LETTING ANOTHER WONDERFUL GIRL GET AWAY.
I SUPPOSE I UNDERSTAND. IT'S HARD TO BE PARTNERS IN BOTH WORK AND LIFE. THANK YOU FOR HANDLING THIS SO WELL, DEAR.
UH, YEAH...I'M PRETTY IMPRESSED MYSELF.
IT'S NOT THAT HARD, PETE. EVERYTHING I SAID WAS TRUE, JUST WITH THE SPIDER-Y PARTS LEFT OUT. YOU'RE SO USED TO YOUR LIFE BEING A SOAP OPERA, YOU OVERCOMPLICATE.
ALL THE TIME. WE'VE GOT A LOT TO DO BACK AT HQ, AND THIS TIME OF DAY WE'LL NEVER GET A CAB. WHY DON'T YOU JUST SWING US THERE?
WE CAN'T! PEOPLE WILL SEE. THEY'LL THINK THERE'S A CONNECTION BETWEEN YOU AND SPIDER-MAN--
THERE IS! HE'S SAVED ME TWICE. AND PEOPLE WILL JUST ASSUME HE'S LOOKING OUT FOR ME AGAIN.
SEE? SIMPLE. NOW SPIDER-UP, CHOP-CHOP. OR DO YOU HAVE SOME OTHER OVERWROUGHT NEUROSIS I NEED TO SHOOT DOWN?

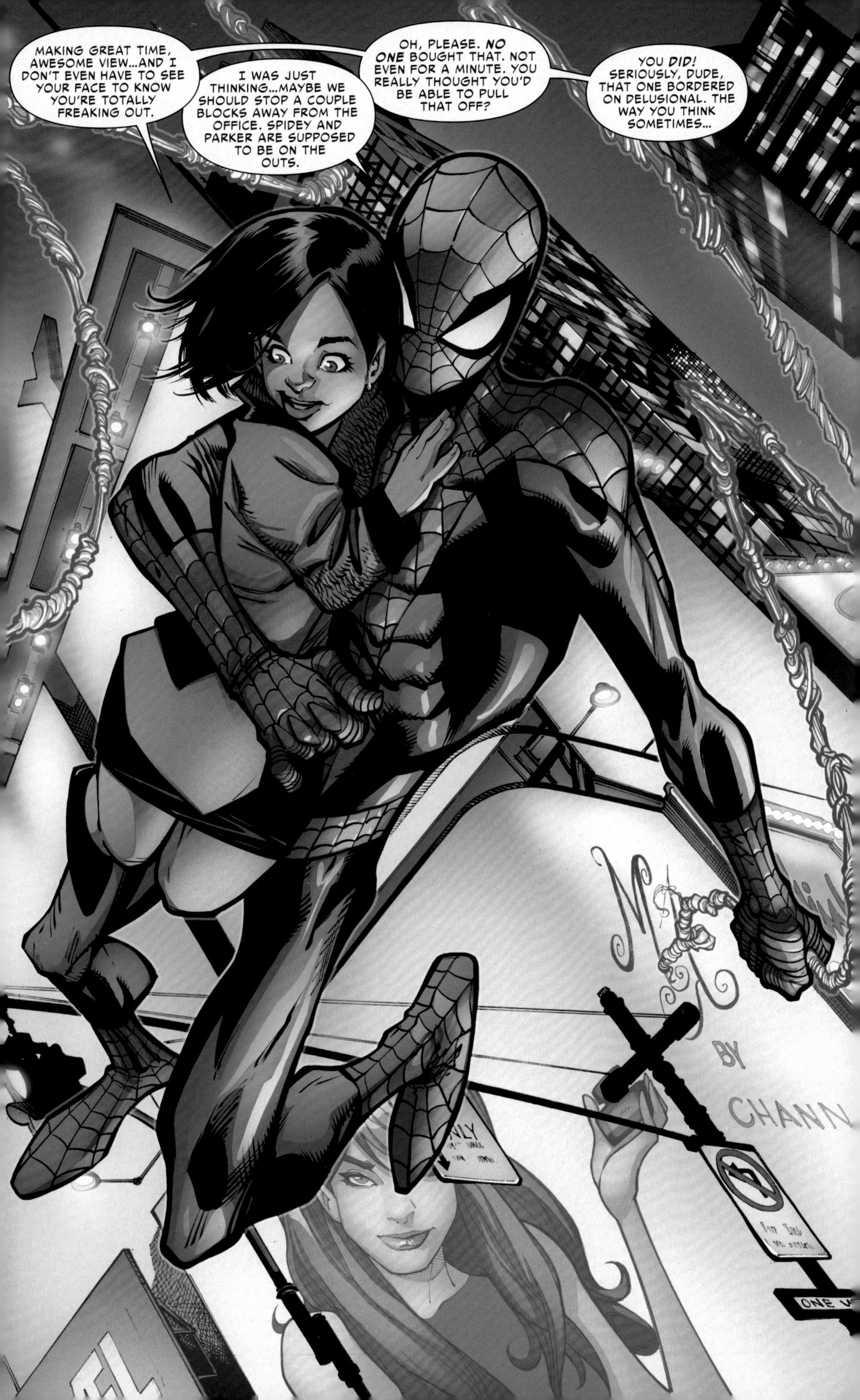
MAKING GREAT TIME, AWESOME VIEW...AND I DON'T EVEN HAVE TO SEE YOUR FACE TO KNOW YOU'RE TOTALLY FREAKING OUT.
I WAS JUST THINKING...MAYBE WE SHOULD STOP A COUPLE BLOCKS AWAY FROM THE OFFICE. SPIDEY AND PARKER ARE SUPPOSED TO BE ON THE OUTS.
OH, PLEASE. NO ONE BOUGHT THAT. NOT EVEN FOR A MINUTE. YOU REALLY THOUGHT YOU'D BE ABLE TO PULL THAT OFF?
YOU DID! SERIOUSLY, DUDE, THAT ONE BORDERED ON DELUSIONAL. THE WAY YOU THINK SOMETIMES...
BY
CHANN
ONE

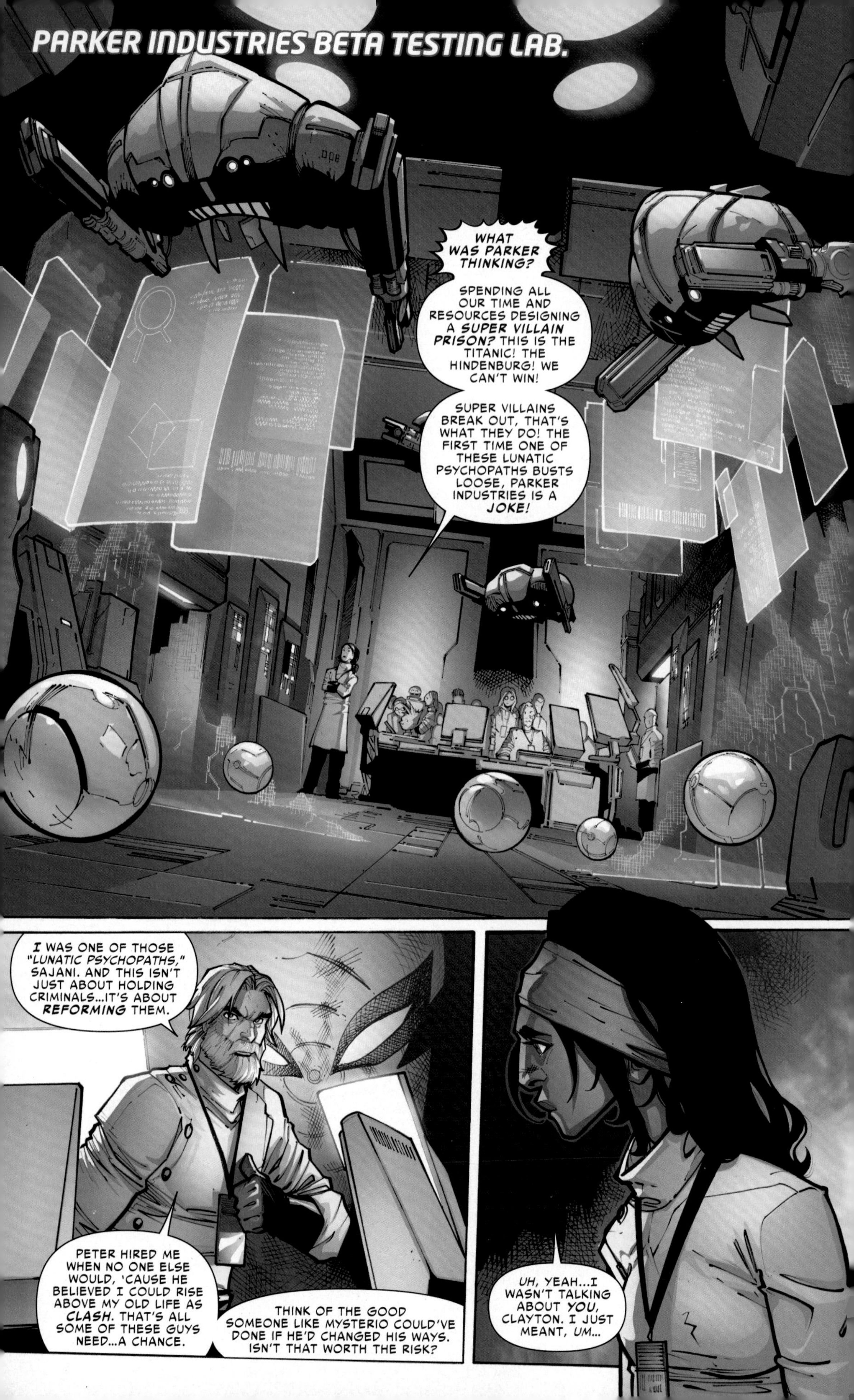
PARKER INDUSTRIES BETA TESTING LAB.
WHAT WAS PARKER THINKING?
SPENDING ALL OUR TIME AND RESOURCES DESIGNING A SUPER VILLAIN PRISON? THIS IS THE TITANIC! THE HINDENBURG! WE CAN'T WIN!
SUPER VILLAINS BREAK OUT, THAT'S WHAT THEY DO! THE FIRST TIME ONE OF THESE LUNATIC PSYCHOPATHS BUSTS LOOSE, PARKER INDUSTRIES IS A JOKE!
I WAS ONE OF THOSE "LUNATIC PSYCHOPATHS," SAJANI. AND THIS ISN'T JUST ABOUT HOLDING CRIMINALS...IT'S ABOUT REFORMING THEM.
PETER HIRED ME WHEN NO ONE ELSE WOULD, 'CAUSE HE BELIEVED I COULD RISE ABOVE MY OLD LIFE AS CLASH. THAT'S ALL SOME OF THESE GUYS NEED...A CHANCE.
THINK OF THE GOOD SOMEONE LIKE MYSTERIO COULD'VE DONE IF HE'D CHANGED HIS WAYS. ISN'T THAT WORTH THE RISK?
UH, YEAH...I WASN'T TALKING ABOUT YOU, CLAYTON. I JUST MEANT, UM...

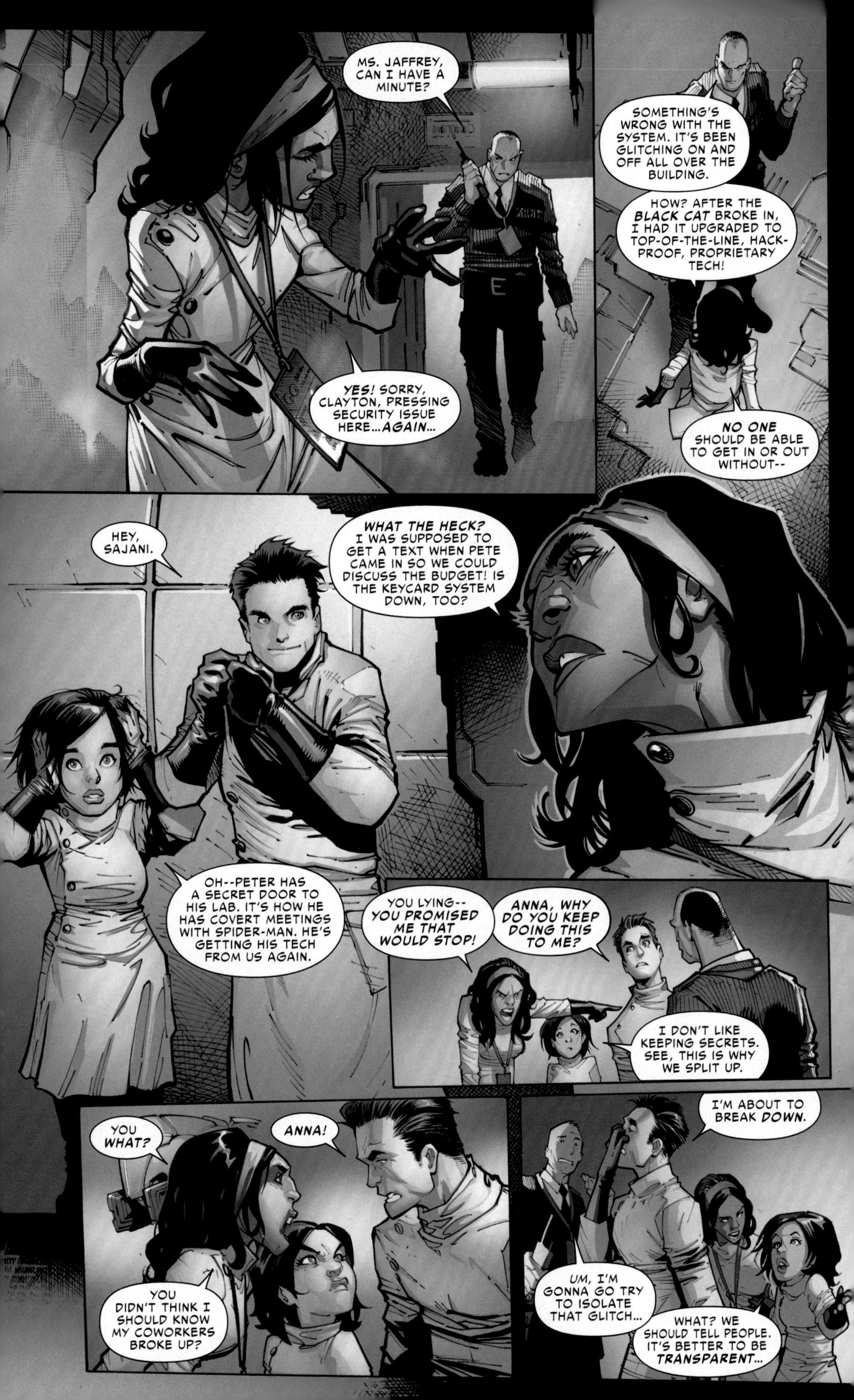
MS. JAFFREY, CAN I HAVE A MINUTE?
YES! SORRY, CLAYTON, PRESSING SECURITY ISSUE HERE...AGAIN...
SOMETHING'S WRONG WITH THE SYSTEM. IT'S BEEN GLITCHING ON AND OFF ALL OVER THE BUILDING.
HOW? AFTER THE BLACK CAT BROKE IN, I HAD IT UPGRADED TO TOP-OF-THE-LINE, HACK-PROOF, PROPRIETARY TECH!
NO ONE SHOULD BE ABLE TO GET IN OR OUT WITHOUT--
HEY, SAJANI.
WHAT THE HECK? I WAS SUPPOSED TO GET A TEXT WHEN PETE CAME IN SO WE COULD DISCUSS THE BUDGET! IS THE KEYCARD SYSTEM DOWN, TOO?
OH--PETER HAS A SECRET DOOR TO HIS LAB. IT'S HOW HE HAS COVERT MEETINGS WITH SPIDER-MAN. HE'S GETTING HIS TECH FROM US AGAIN.
YOU LYING-- YOU PROMISED ME THAT WOULD STOP!
ANNA, WHY DO YOU KEEP DOING THIS TO ME?
I DON'T LIKE KEEPING SECRETS. SEE, THIS IS WHY WE SPLIT UP.
YOU WHAT?
ANNA!
YOU DIDN'T THINK I SHOULD KNOW MY COWORKERS BROKE UP?
I'M ABOUT TO BREAK DOWN.
UM, I'M GONNA GO TRY TO ISOLATE THAT GLITCH...
WHAT? WE SHOULD TELL PEOPLE. IT'S BETTER TO BE TRANSPARENT...

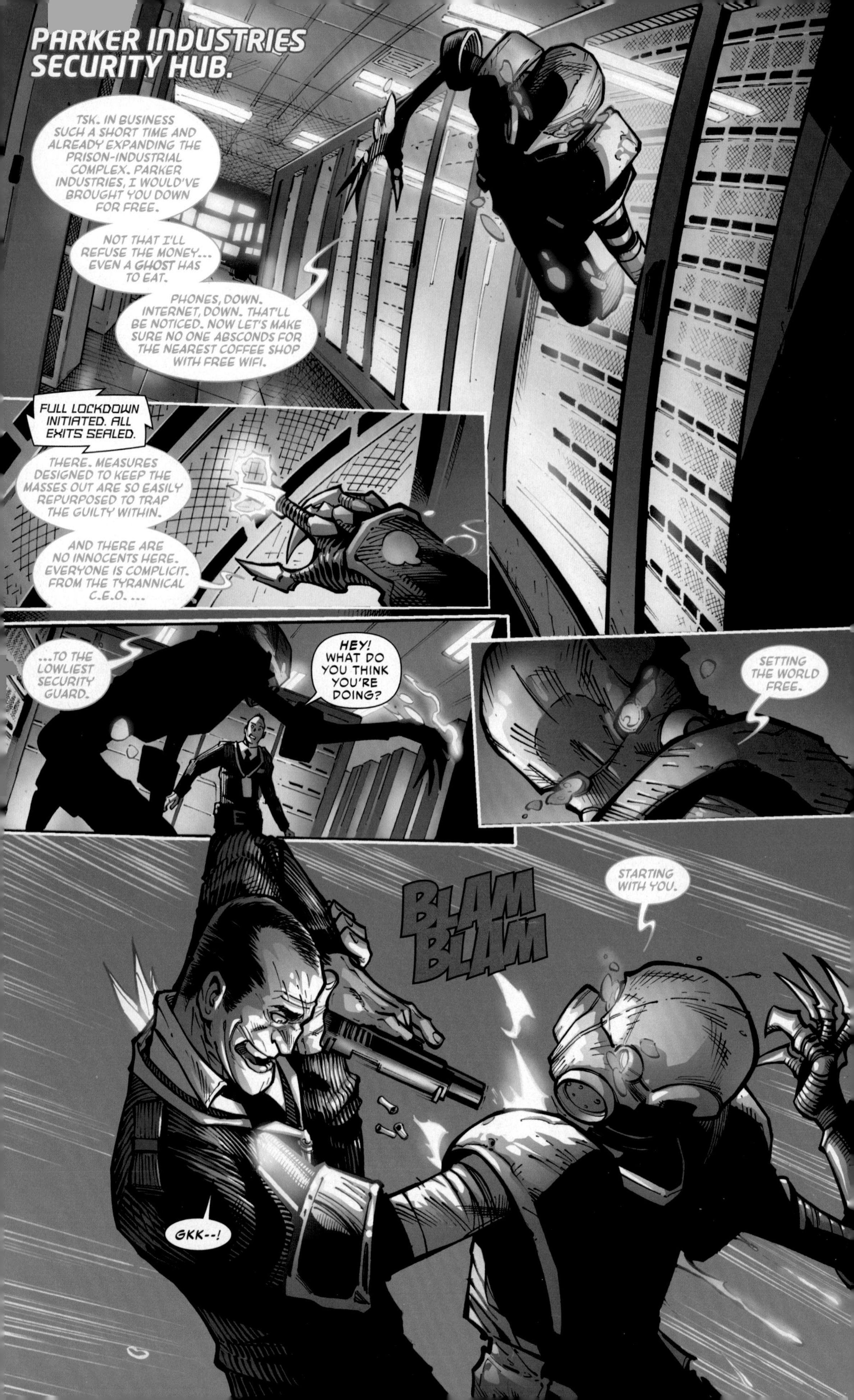
PARKER INDUSTRIES SECURITY HUB.
TSK. IN BUSINESS SUCH A SHORT TIME AND ALREADY EXPANDING THE PRISON-INDUSTRIAL COMPLEX. PARKER INDUSTRIES, I WOULD'VE BROUGHT YOU DOWN FOR FREE.
NOT THAT I'LL REFUSE THE MONEY... EVEN A GHOST HAS TO EAT.
PHONES, DOWN. INTERNET, DOWN. THAT'LL BE NOTICED. NOW LET'S MAKE SURE NO ONE ABSCONDS FOR THE NEAREST COFFEE SHOP WITH FREE WIFI.
FULL LOCKDOWN INITIATED. ALL EXITS SEALED.
THERE. MEASURES DESIGNED TO KEEP THE MASSES OUT ARE SO EASILY REPURPOSED TO TRAP THE GUILTY WITHIN.
AND THERE ARE NO INNOCENTS HERE. EVERYONE IS COMPLICIT. FROM THE TYRANNICAL C.E.O. ...
...TO THE LOWLIEST SECURITY GUARD.
HEY! WHAT DO YOU THINK YOU'RE DOING?
SETTING THE WORLD FREE.
BLAM BLAM
STARTING WITH YOU.
GKK--!

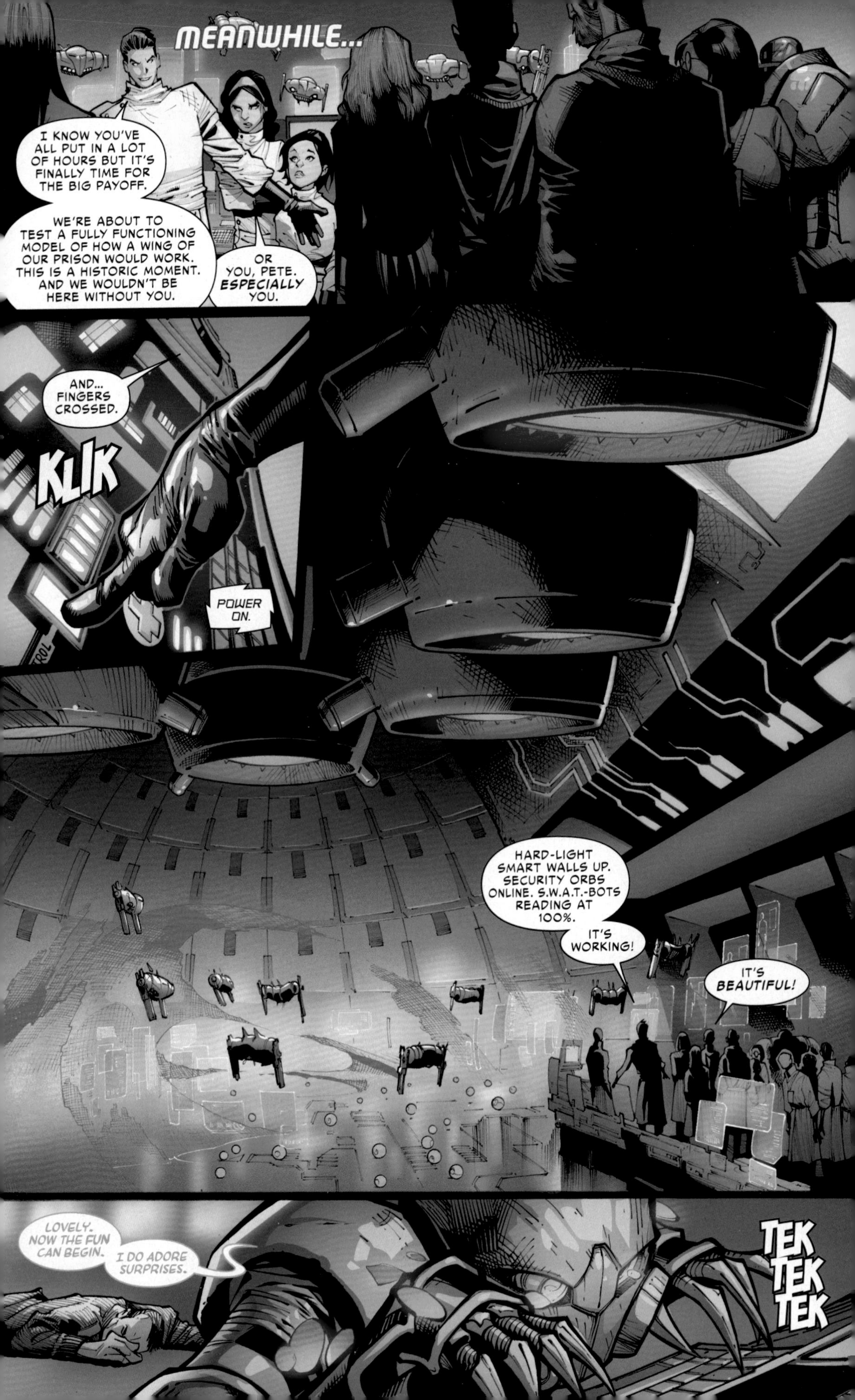
MEANWHILE...
I KNOW YOU'VE ALL PUT IN A LOT OF HOURS BUT IT'S FINALLY TIME FOR THE BIG PAYOFF.
WE'RE ABOUT TO TEST A FULLY FUNCTIONING MODEL OF HOW A WING OF OUR PRISON WOULD WORK. THIS IS A HISTORIC MOMENT. AND WE WOULDN'T BE HERE WITHOUT YOU.
OR YOU, PETE. ESPECIALLY YOU.
AND... FINGERS CROSSED.
KLIK
POWER ON.
HARD-LIGHT SMART WALLS UP. SECURITY ORBS ONLINE. S.W.A.T.-BOTS READING AT 100%.
IT'S WORKING!
IT'S BEAUTIFUL!
LOVELY. NOW THE FUN CAN BEGIN.
I DO ADORE SURPRISES.
TEK TEK TEK

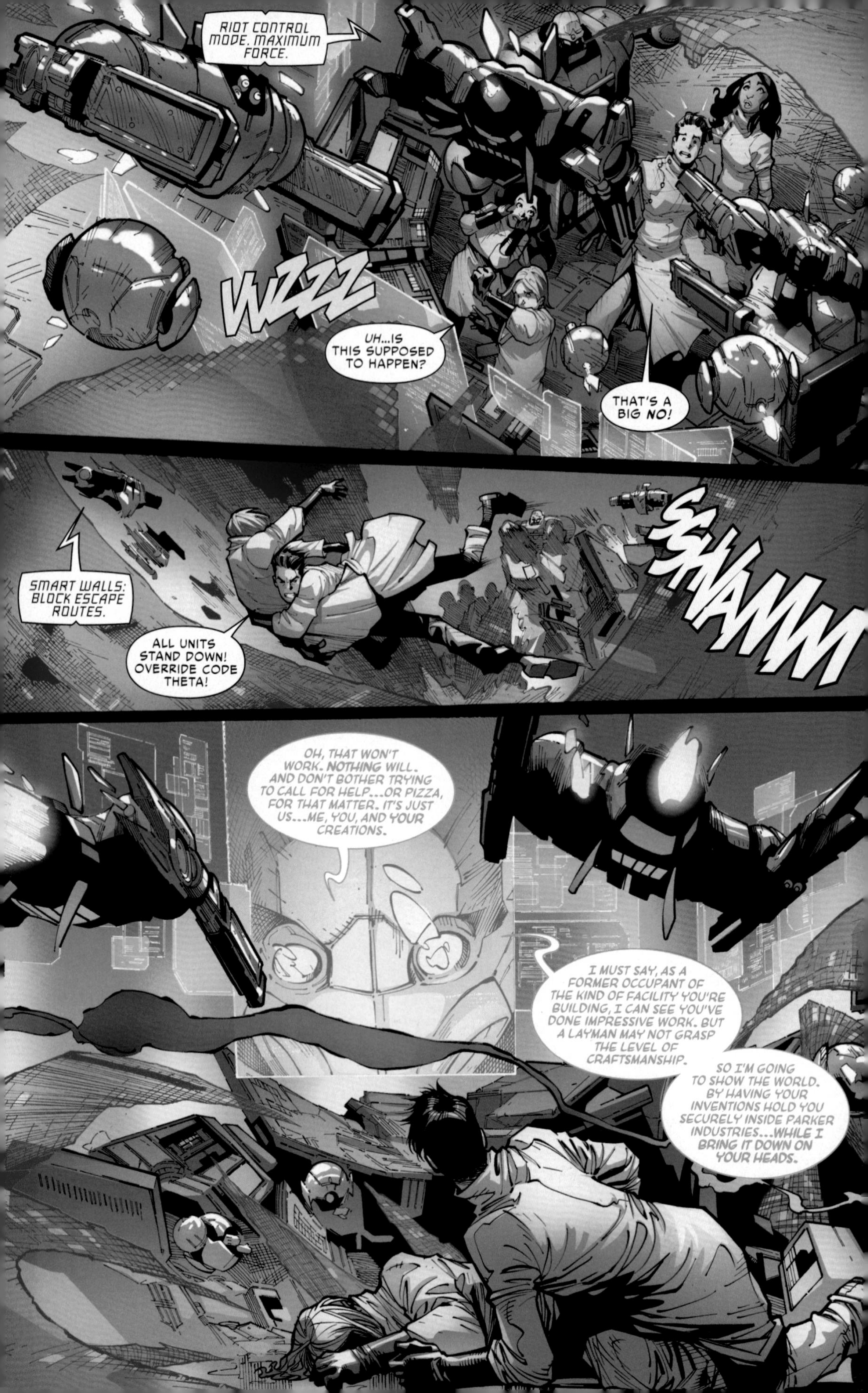
RIOT CONTROL MODE. MAXIMUM FORCE.
VVZZZ
UH...IS THIS SUPPOSED TO HAPPEN?
THAT'S A BIG NO!
SMART WALLS: BLOCK ESCAPE ROUTES.
ALL UNITS STAND DOWN! OVERRIDE CODE THETA!
SCHWAMM
OH, THAT WON'T WORK. NOTHING WILL. AND DON'T BOTHER TRYING TO CALL FOR HELP...OR PIZZA, FOR THAT MATTER. IT'S JUST US...ME, YOU, AND YOUR CREATIONS.
I MUST SAY, AS A FORMER OCCUPANT OF THE KIND OF FACILITY YOU'RE BUILDING, I CAN SEE YOU'VE DONE IMPRESSIVE WORK. BUT A LAYMAN MAY NOT GRASP THE LEVEL OF CRAFTSMANSHIP.
SO I'M GOING TO SHOW THE WORLD. BY HAVING YOUR INVENTIONS HOLD YOU SECURELY INSIDE PARKER INDUSTRIES...WHILE I BRING IT DOWN ON YOUR HEADS.

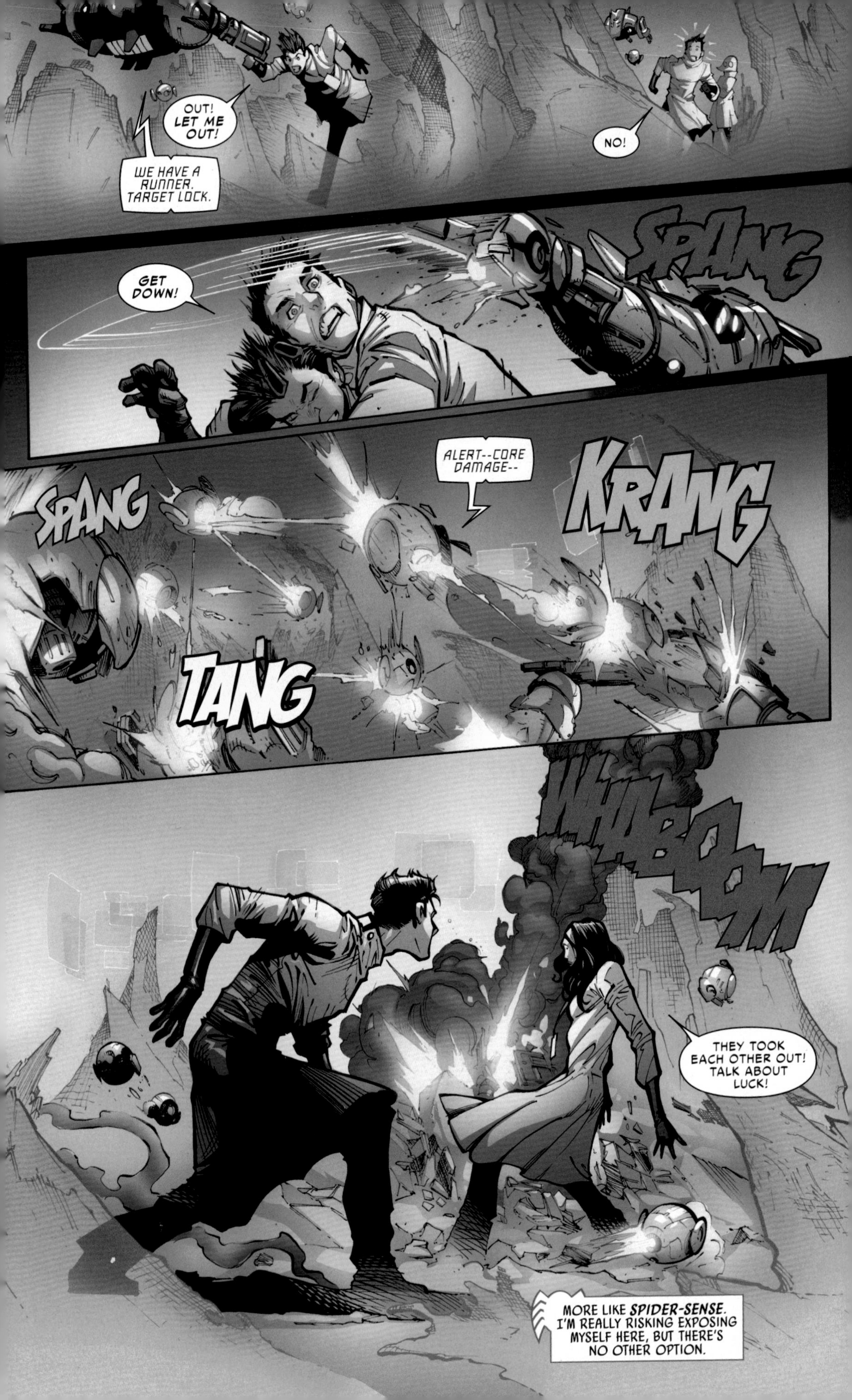
OUT! LET ME OUT!
WE HAVE A RUNNER. TARGET LOCK.
NO!
GET DOWN!
SPANG
ALERT--CORE DAMAGE--
SPANG
KRANG
TANG
WHABOOM
THEY TOOK EACH OTHER OUT! TALK ABOUT LUCK!
MORE LIKE SPIDER-SENSE. I'M REALLY RISKING EXPOSING MYSELF HERE, BUT THERE'S NO OTHER OPTION.

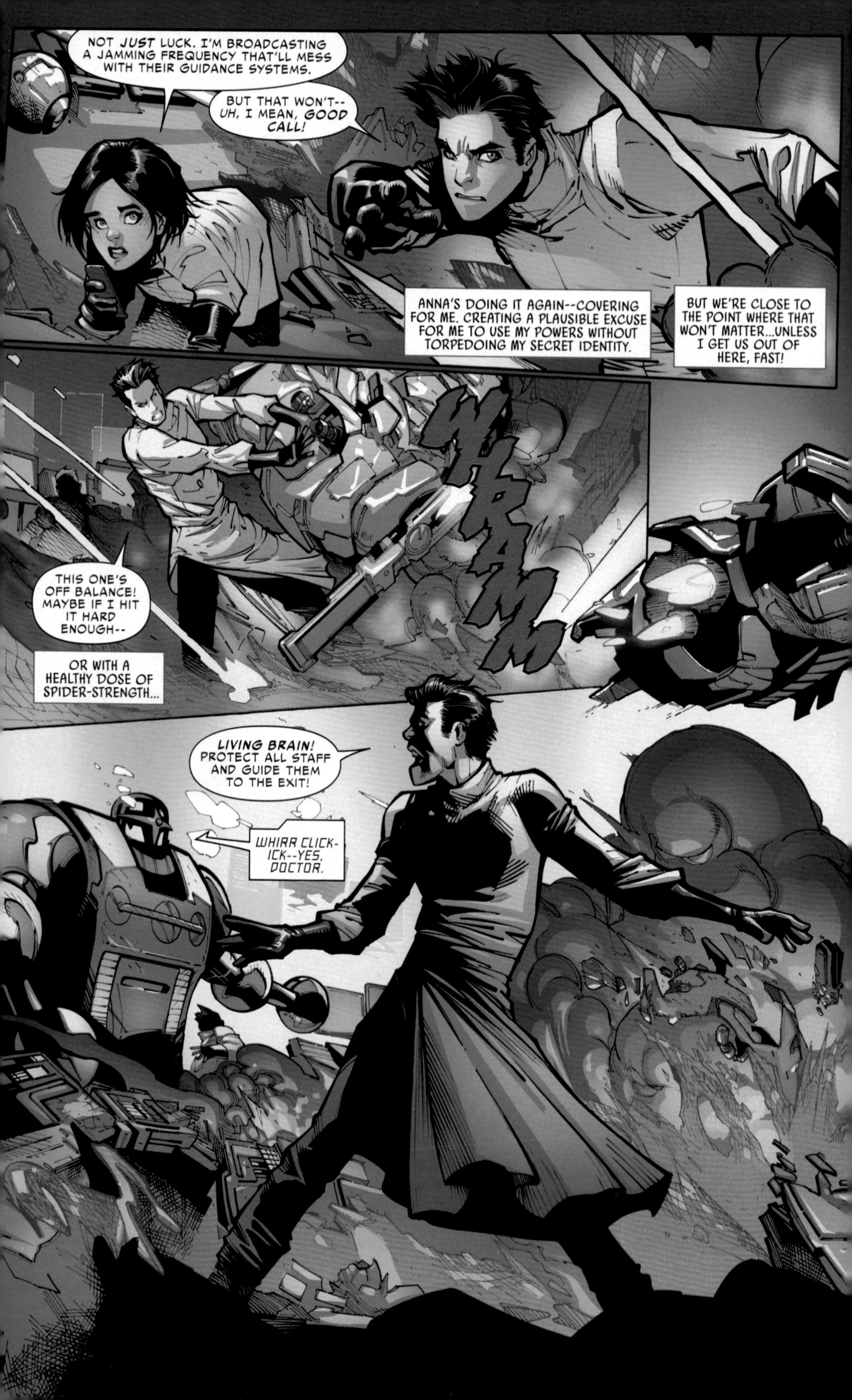
NOT JUST LUCK. I'M BROADCASTING A JAMMING FREQUENCY THAT'LL MESS WITH THEIR GUIDANCE SYSTEMS.
BUT THAT WON'T-- UH, I MEAN, GOOD CALL!
ANNA'S DOING IT AGAIN--COVERING FOR ME. CREATING A PLAUSIBLE EXCUSE FOR ME TO USE MY POWERS WITHOUT TORPEDOING MY SECRET IDENTITY.
BUT WE'RE CLOSE TO THE POINT WHERE THAT WON'T MATTER...UNLESS I GET US OUT OF HERE, FAST!
THIS ONE'S OFF BALANCE! MAYBE IF I HIT IT HARD ENOUGH--
OR WITH A HEALTHY DOSE OF SPIDER-STRENGTH...
WHRAMM
LIVING BRAIN! PROTECT ALL STAFF AND GUIDE THEM TO THE EXIT!
WHIRR CLICK-ICK--YES, DOCTOR.

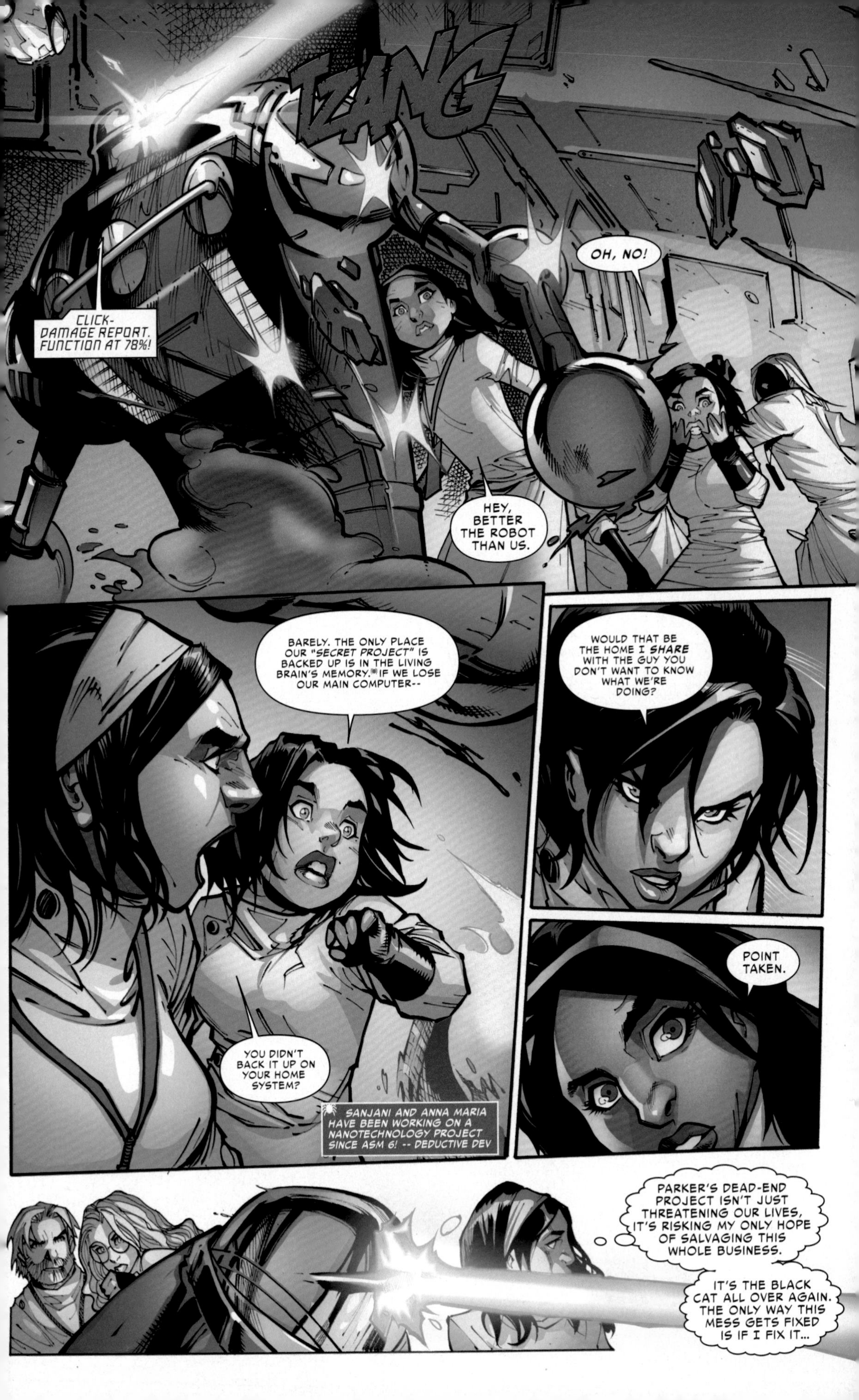
TZANG
CLICK- DAMAGE REPORT. FUNCTION AT 78%!
OH, NO!
HEY, BETTER THE ROBOT THAN US.
BARELY. THE ONLY PLACE OUR "SECRET PROJECT" IS BACKED UP IS IN THE LIVING BRAIN'S MEMORY.* IF WE LOSE OUR MAIN COMPUTER--
YOU DIDN'T BACK IT UP ON YOUR HOME SYSTEM?
SANJANI AND ANNA MARIA HAVE BEEN WORKING ON A NANOTECHNOLOGY PROJECT SINCE ASM 6! -- DEDUCTIVE DEV
WOULD THAT BE THE HOME I SHARE WITH THE GUY YOU DON'T WANT TO KNOW WHAT WE'RE DOING?
POINT TAKEN.
PARKER'S DEAD-END PROJECT ISN'T JUST THREATENING OUR LIVES, IT'S RISKING MY ONLY HOPE OF SALVAGING THIS WHOLE BUSINESS.
IT'S THE BLACK CAT ALL OVER AGAIN. THE ONLY WAY THIS MESS GETS FIXED IS IF I FIX IT...

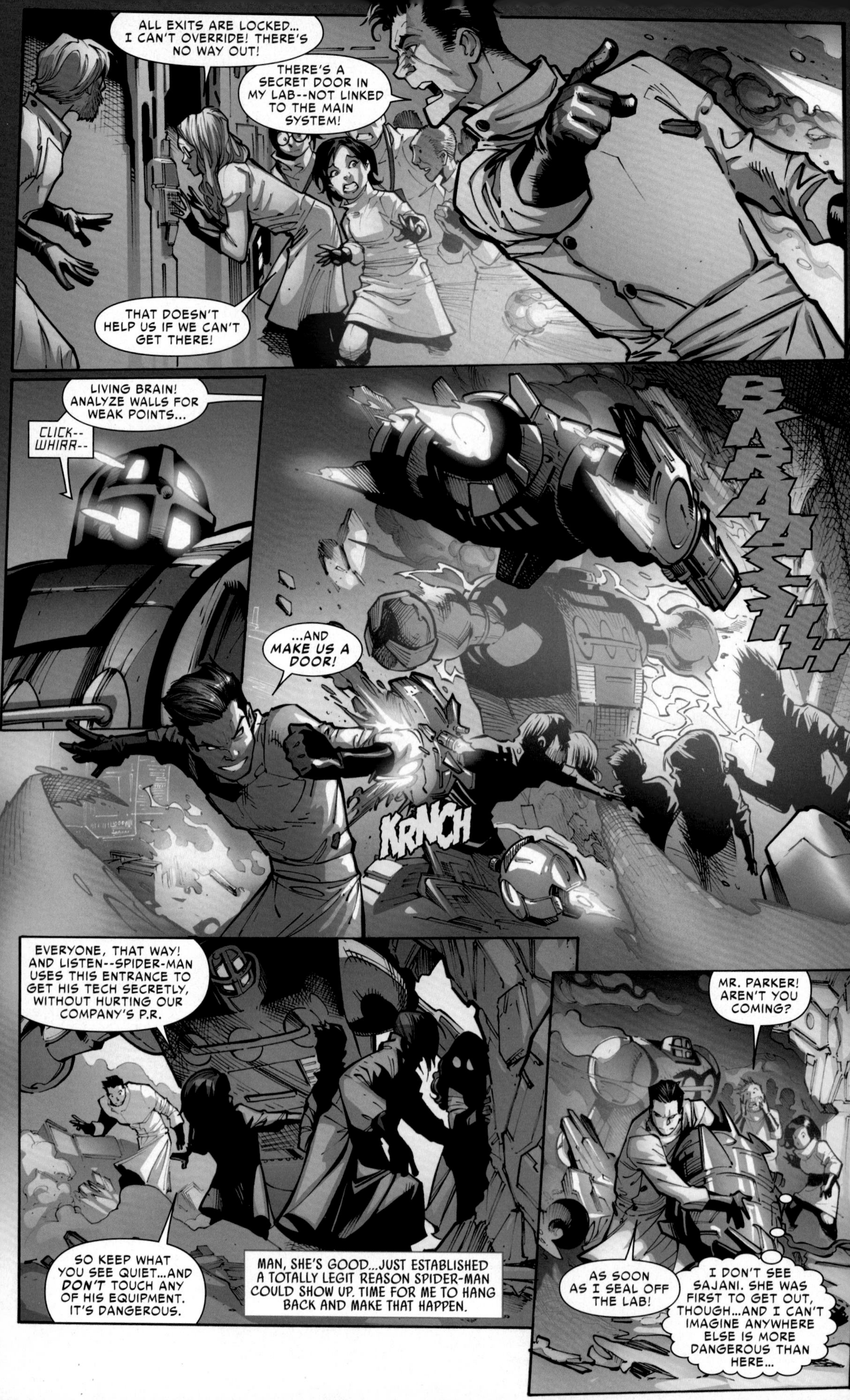

ALL EXITS ARE LOCKED... I CAN'T OVERRIDE! THERE'S NO WAY OUT!
THERE'S A SECRET DOOR IN MY LAB--NOT LINKED TO THE MAIN SYSTEM!
THAT DOESN'T HELP US IF WE CAN'T GET THERE!
LIVING BRAIN! ANALYZE WALLS FOR WEAK POINTS...
CLICK-- WHIRR--
...AND MAKE US A DOOR!
BRAASSHH
KRNCH
EVERYONE, THAT WAY! AND LISTEN--SPIDER-MAN USES THIS ENTRANCE TO GET HIS TECH SECRETLY, WITHOUT HURTING OUR COMPANY'S P.R.
SO KEEP WHAT YOU SEE QUIET...AND DON'T TOUCH ANY OF HIS EQUIPMENT. IT'S DANGEROUS.
MAN, SHE'S GOOD...JUST ESTABLISHED A TOTALLY LEGIT REASON SPIDER-MAN COULD SHOW UP. TIME FOR ME TO HANG BACK AND MAKE THAT HAPPEN.
MR. PARKER! AREN'T YOU COMING?
AS SOON AS I SEAL OFF THE LAB!
I DON'T SEE SAJANI. SHE WAS FIRST TO GET OUT, THOUGH...AND I CAN'T IMAGINE ANYWHERE ELSE IS MORE DANGEROUS THAN HERE...

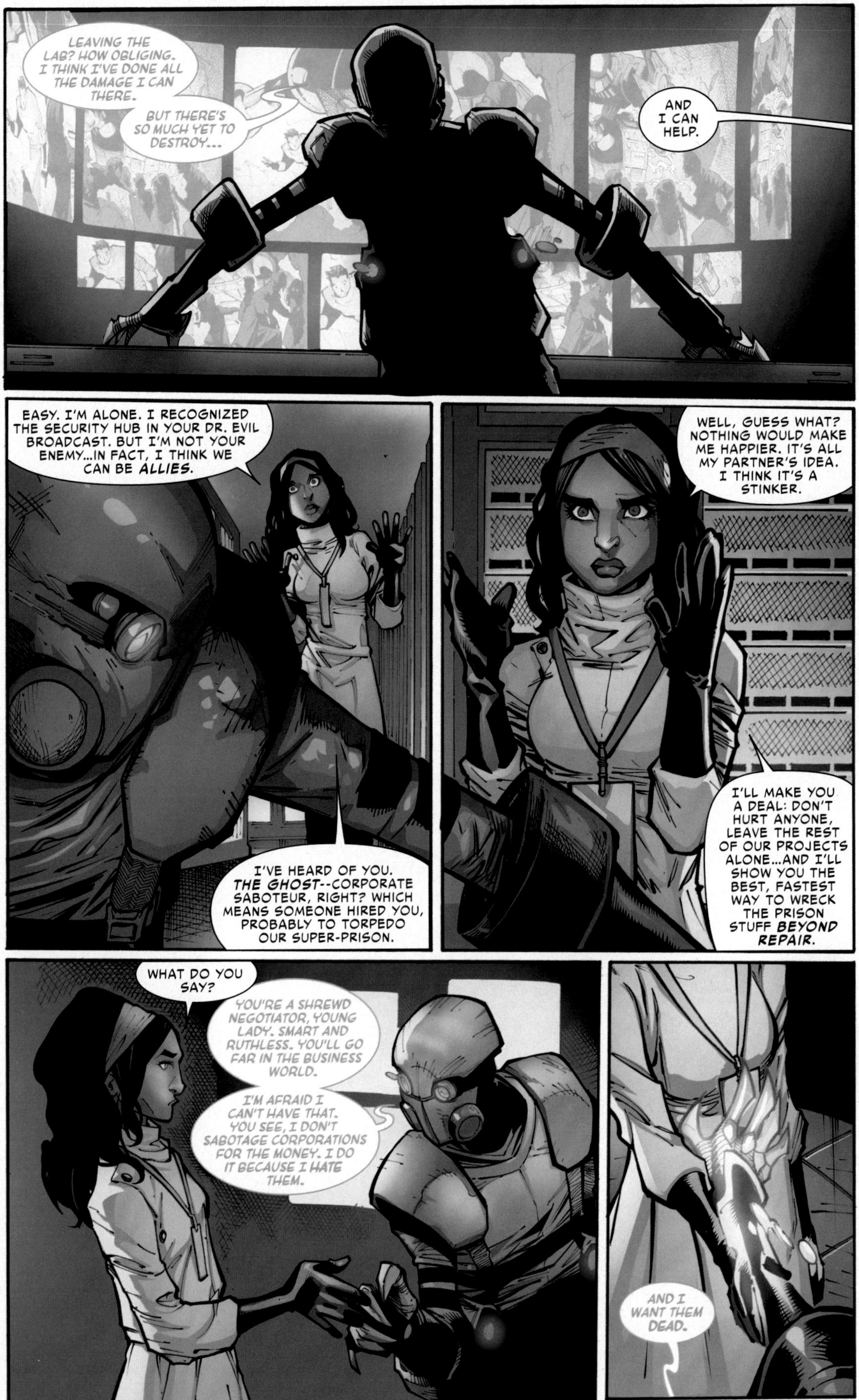
LEAVING THE LAB? HOW OBLIGING. I THINK I'VE DONE ALL THE DAMAGE I CAN THERE.
BUT THERE'S SO MUCH YET TO DESTROY...
AND I CAN HELP.
EASY. I'M ALONE. I RECOGNIZED THE SECURITY HUB IN YOUR DR. EVIL BROADCAST. BUT I'M NOT YOUR ENEMY...IN FACT, I THINK WE CAN BE ALLIES.
I'VE HEARD OF YOU. THE GHOST--CORPORATE SABOTEUR, RIGHT? WHICH MEANS SOMEONE HIRED YOU, PROBABLY TO TORPEDO OUR SUPER-PRISON.
WELL, GUESS WHAT? NOTHING WOULD MAKE ME HAPPIER. IT'S ALL MY PARTNER'S IDEA. I THINK IT'S A STINKER.
I'LL MAKE YOU A DEAL: DON'T HURT ANYONE, LEAVE THE REST OF OUR PROJECTS ALONE...AND I'LL SHOW YOU THE BEST, FASTEST WAY TO WRECK THE PRISON STUFF BEYOND REPAIR.
WHAT DO YOU SAY?
YOU'RE A SHREWD NEGOTIATOR, YOUNG LADY. SMART AND RUTHLESS. YOU'LL GO FAR IN THE BUSINESS WORLD.
I'M AFRAID I CAN'T HAVE THAT. YOU SEE, I DON'T SABOTAGE CORPORATIONS FOR THE MONEY. I DO IT BECAUSE I HATE THEM.
AND I WANT THEM DEAD.

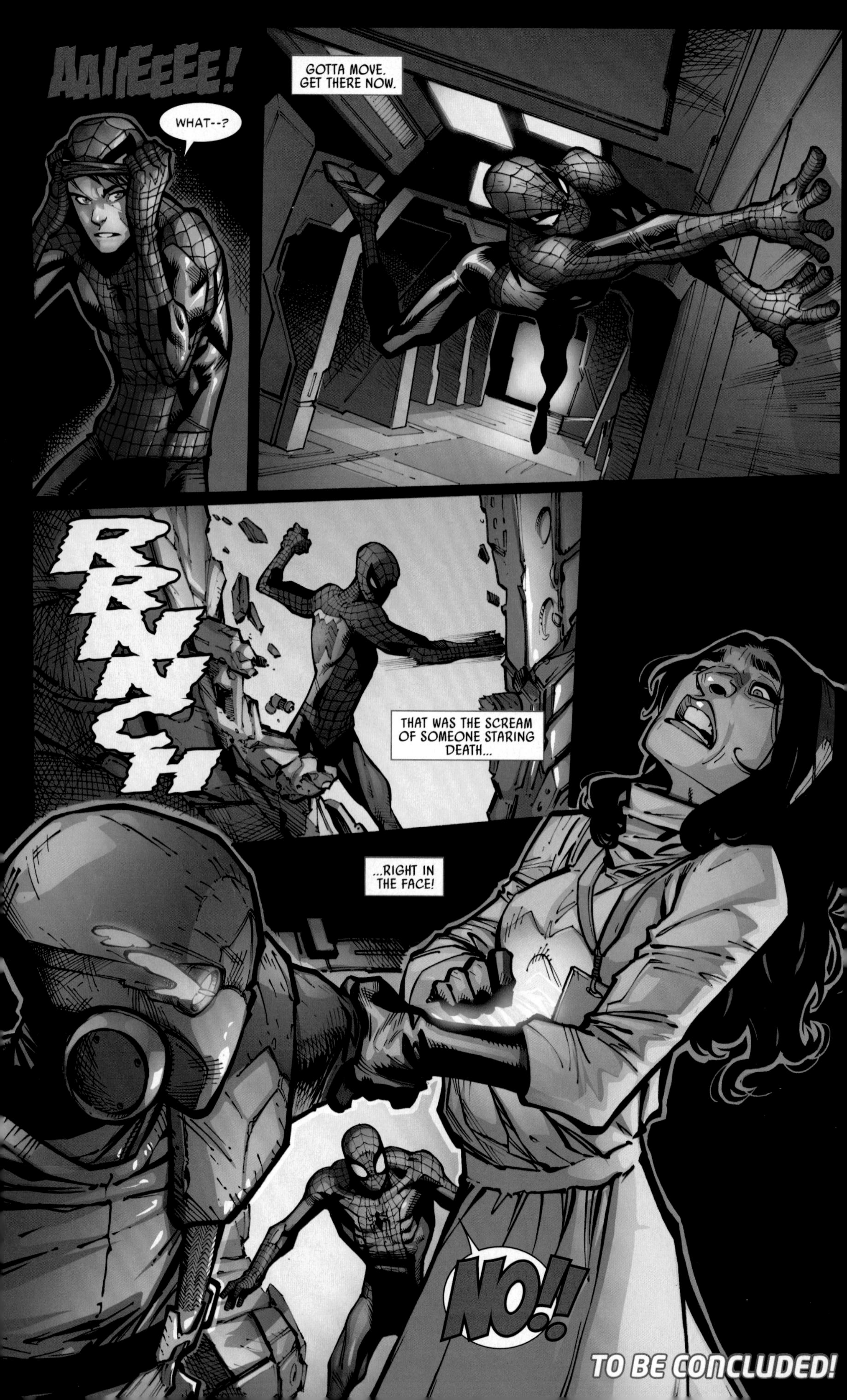
AAIIEEEE!
WHAT--?
GOTTA MOVE. GET THERE NOW.
RRNCH
THAT WAS THE SCREAM OF SOMEONE STARING DEATH...
...RIGHT IN THE FACE!
NO!!
TO BE CONCLUDED!

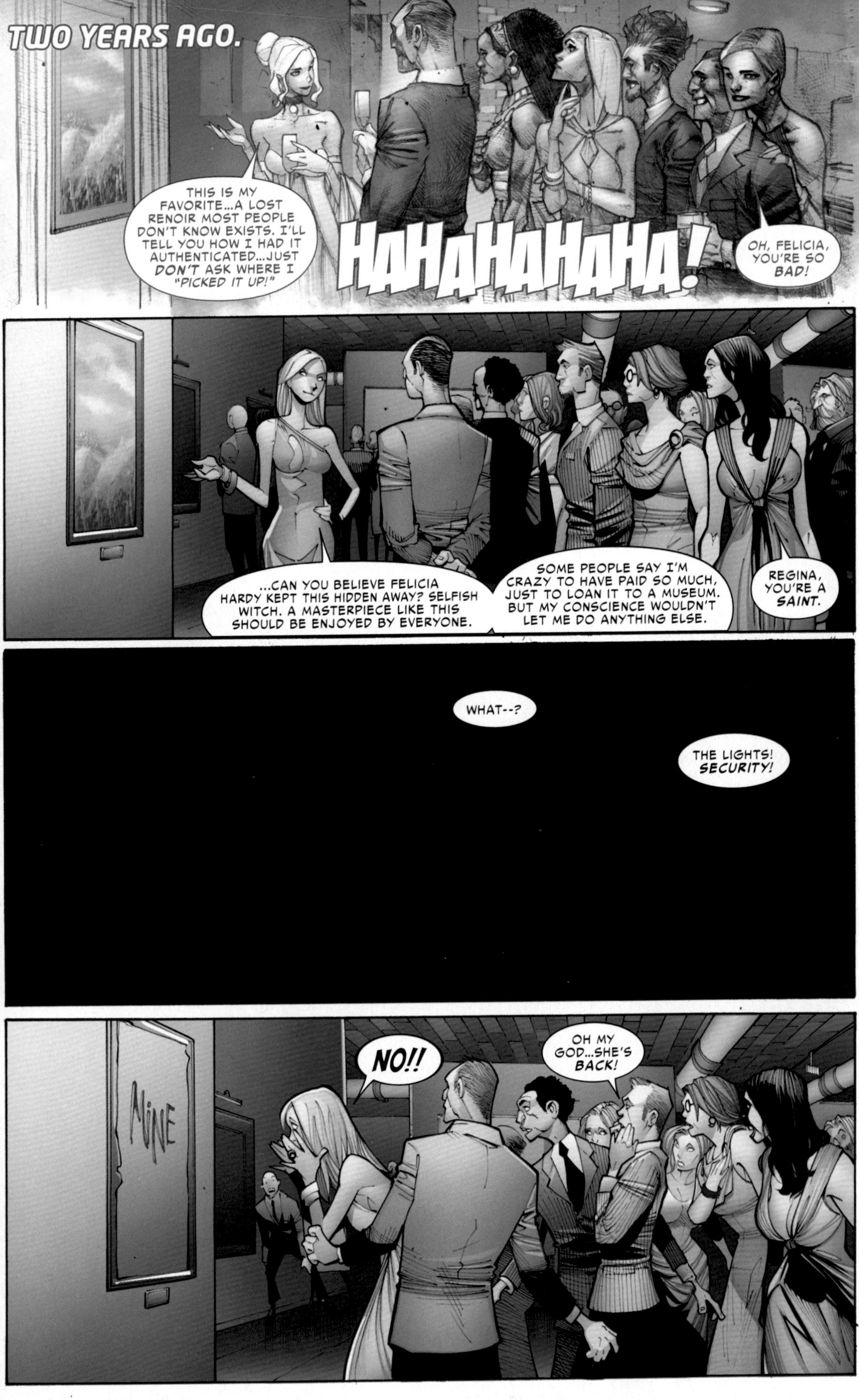
TWO YEARS AGO.
THIS IS MY FAVORITE...A LOST RENOIR MOST PEOPLE DON'T KNOW EXISTS. I'LL TELL YOU HOW I HAD IT AUTHENTICATED...JUST DON'T ASK WHERE I "PICKED IT UP!"
HAHAHAHAHAHA!
OH, FELICIA, YOU'RE SO BAD!
...CAN YOU BELIEVE FELICIA HARDY KEPT THIS HIDDEN AWAY? SELFISH WITCH. A MASTERPIECE LIKE THIS SHOULD BE ENJOYED BY EVERYONE.
SOME PEOPLE SAY I'M CRAZY TO HAVE PAID SO MUCH, JUST TO LOAN IT TO A MUSEUM. BUT MY CONSCIENCE WOULDN'T LET ME DO ANYTHING ELSE.
REGINA, YOU'RE A SAINT.
WHAT--?
THE LIGHTS! SECURITY!
NO!!
OH MY GOD...SHE'S BACK!
MINE

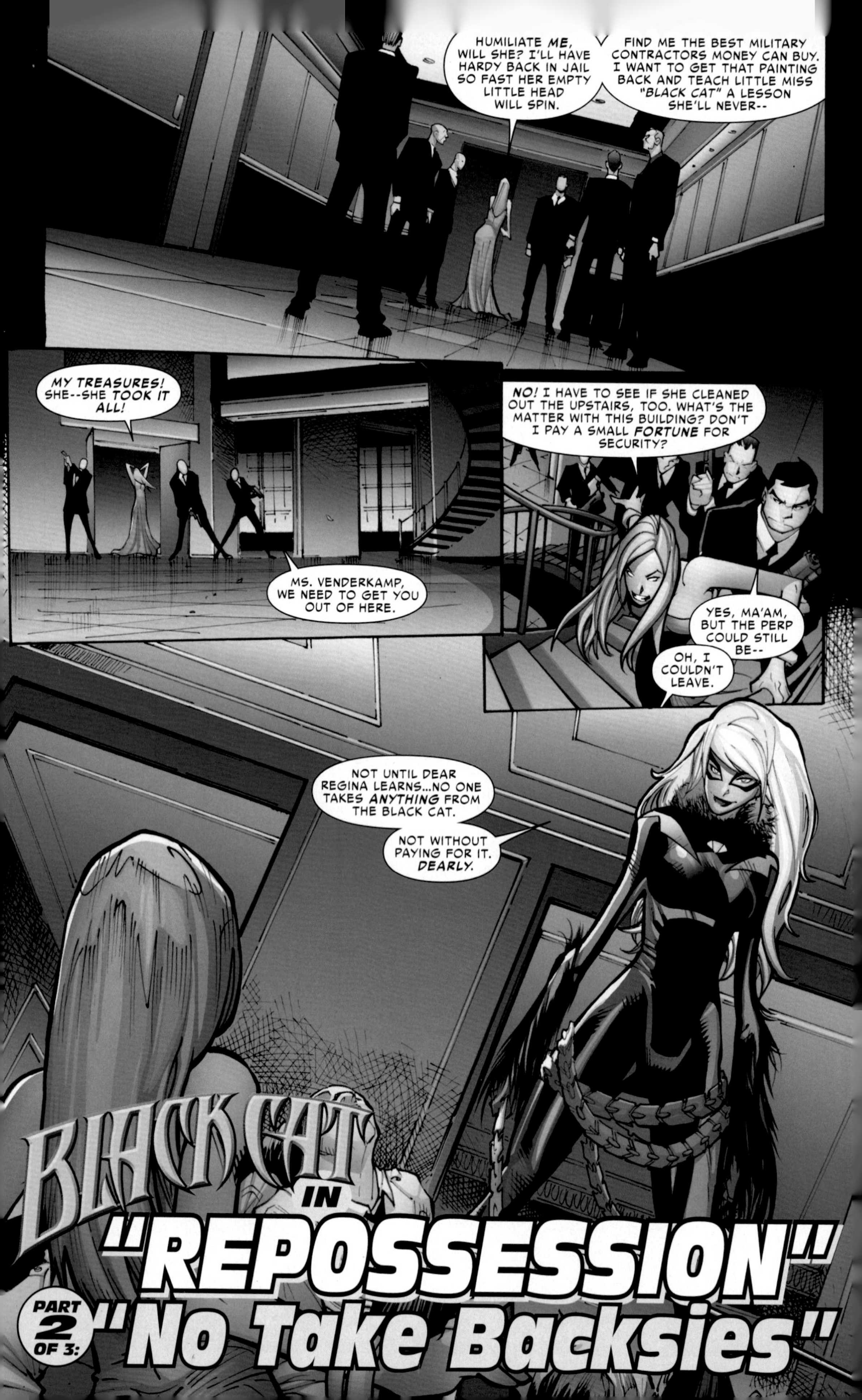
HUMILIATE ME, WILL SHE? I'LL HAVE HARDY BACK IN JAIL SO FAST HER EMPTY LITTLE HEAD WILL SPIN.
FIND ME THE BEST MILITARY CONTRACTORS MONEY CAN BUY. I WANT TO GET THAT PAINTING BACK AND TEACH LITTLE MISS "BLACK CAT" A LESSON SHE'LL NEVER--
MY TREASURES! SHE--SHE TOOK IT ALL!
MS. VENDERKAMP, WE NEED TO GET YOU OUT OF HERE.
NO! I HAVE TO SEE IF SHE CLEANED OUT THE UPSTAIRS, TOO. WHAT'S THE MATTER WITH THIS BUILDING? DON'T I PAY A SMALL FORTUNE FOR SECURITY?
YES, MA'AM, BUT THE PERP COULD STILL BE--
OH, I COULDN'T LEAVE.
NOT UNTIL DEAR REGINA LEARNS...NO ONE TAKES ANYTHING FROM THE BLACK CAT.
NOT WITHOUT PAYING FOR IT. DEARLY.
BLACK CAT IN
"REPOSSESSION"
PART 2 OF 3: "No Take Backsies"

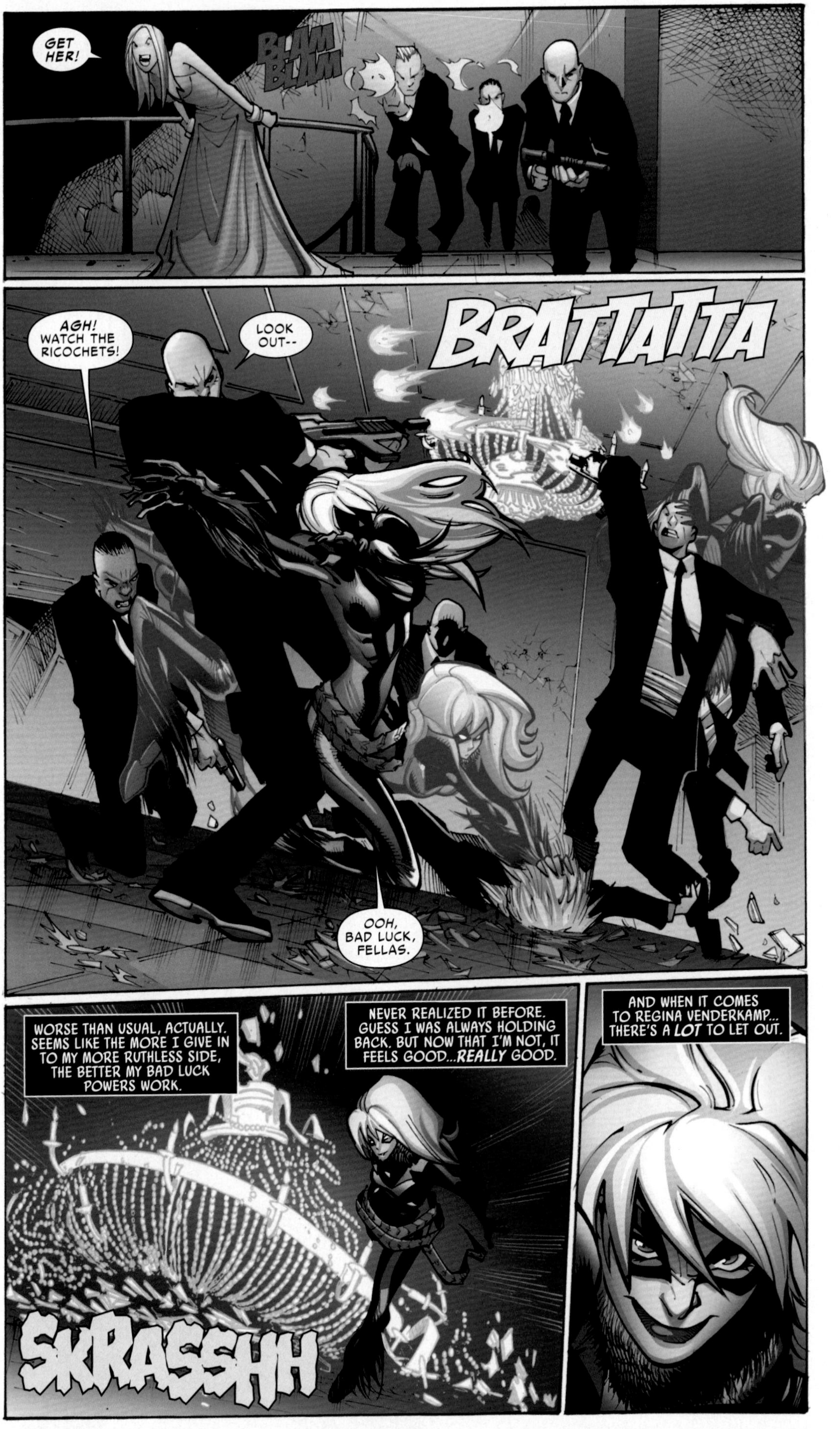
GET HER!
BLAM BLAM
AGH! WATCH THE RICOCHETS!
LOOK OUT--
BRATTATTA
OOH, BAD LUCK, FELLAS.
WORSE THAN USUAL, ACTUALLY. SEEMS LIKE THE MORE I GIVE IN TO MY MORE RUTHLESS SIDE, THE BETTER MY BAD LUCK POWERS WORK.
NEVER REALIZED IT BEFORE. GUESS I WAS ALWAYS HOLDING BACK. BUT NOW THAT I'M NOT, IT FEELS GOOD...REALLY GOOD.
SKRASSHH
AND WHEN IT COMES TO REGINA VENDERKAMP... THERE'S A LOT TO LET OUT.

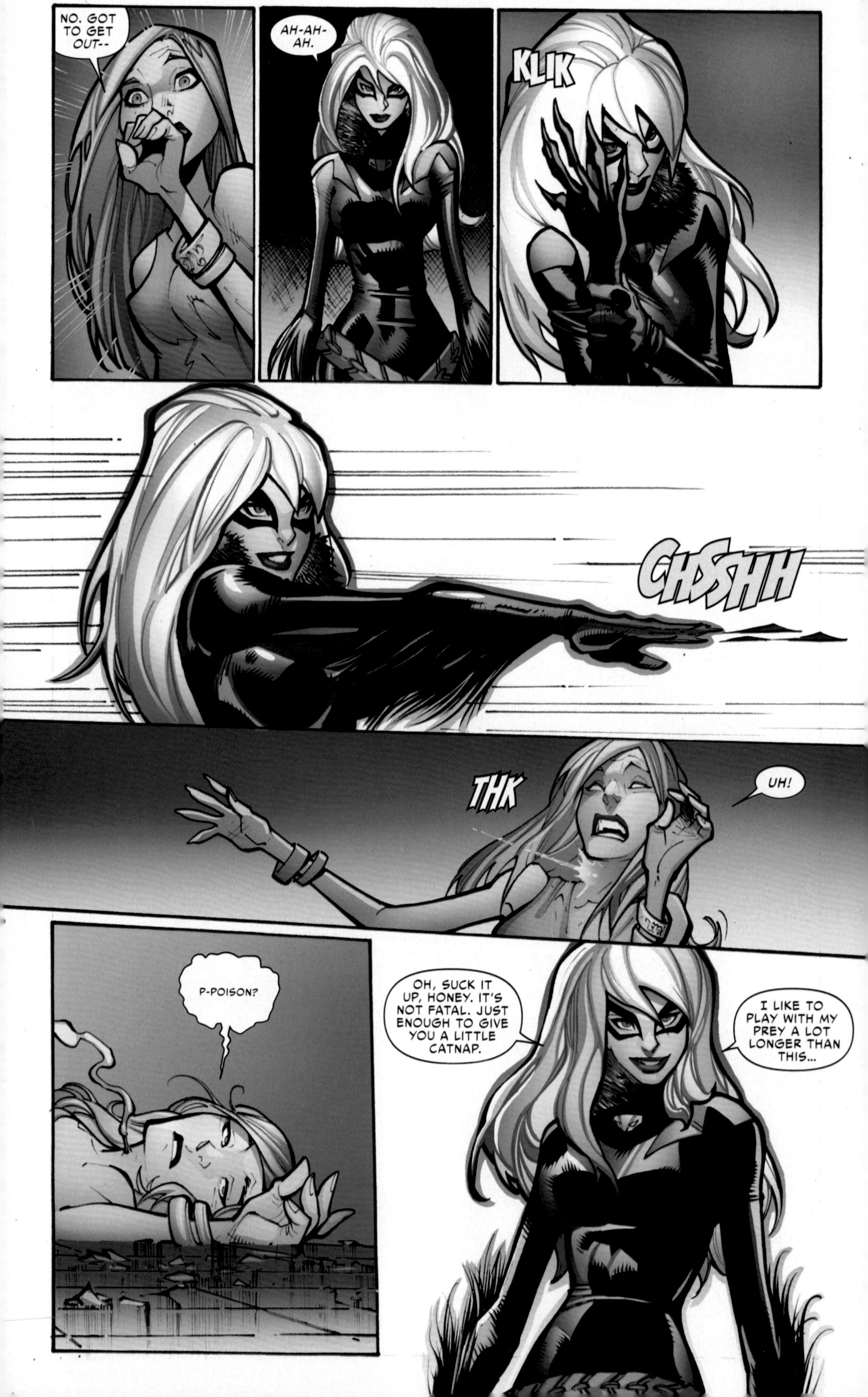
NO. GOT TO GET OUT--
AH-AH-AH.
KLIK
CHSHH
THK
UH!
P-POISON?
OH, SUCK IT UP, HONEY. IT'S NOT FATAL. JUST ENOUGH TO GIVE YOU A LITTLE CATNAP.
I LIKE TO PLAY WITH MY PREY A LOT LONGER THAN THIS...

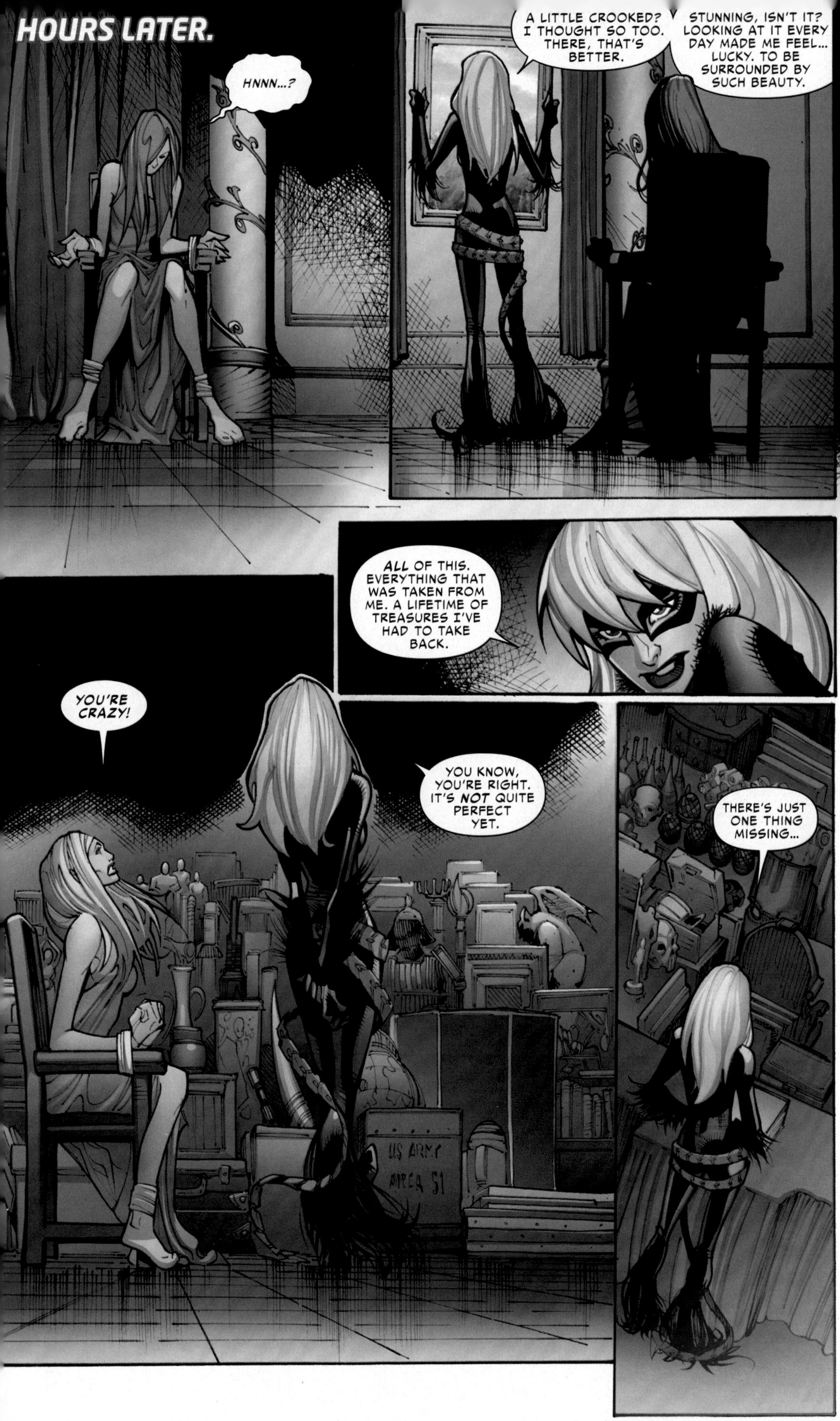
HOURS LATER.
HNNN...?
A LITTLE CROOKED? I THOUGHT SO TOO. THERE, THAT'S BETTER.
STUNNING, ISN'T IT? LOOKING AT IT EVERY DAY MADE ME FEEL... LUCKY. TO BE SURROUNDED BY SUCH BEAUTY.
ALL OF THIS. EVERYTHING THAT WAS TAKEN FROM ME. A LIFETIME OF TREASURES I'VE HAD TO TAKE BACK.
YOU'RE CRAZY!
YOU KNOW, YOU'RE RIGHT. IT'S NOT QUITE PERFECT YET.
US ARMY AREA 51
THERE'S JUST ONE THING MISSING...

THAT'S IT.

IT DOES LOOK NICE ON THE MANTEL, DOESN'T IT?

SO MUCH BETTER THAN THE TABLE. ALL THROUGH DINNER, I WORRIED PETER WOULD KNOCK IT OVER. I ADORE THAT BOY, BUT HE CAN BE A BIT KLUTZY.

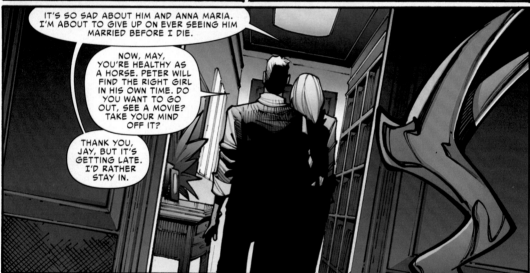

IT'S SO SAD ABOUT HIM AND ANNA MARIA. I'M ABOUT TO GIVE UP ON EVER SEEING HIM MARRIED BEFORE I DIE.

NOW, MAY, YOU'RE HEALTHY AS A HORSE. PETER WILL FIND THE RIGHT GIRL IN HIS OWN TIME. DO YOU WANT TO GO OUT, SEE A MOVIE? TAKE YOUR MIND OFF IT?

THANK YOU, JAY, BUT IT'S GETTING LATE. I'D RATHER STAY IN.

I'VE HAD ENOUGH EXCITEMENT FOR ONE NIGHT.

TO BE CONCLUDED!

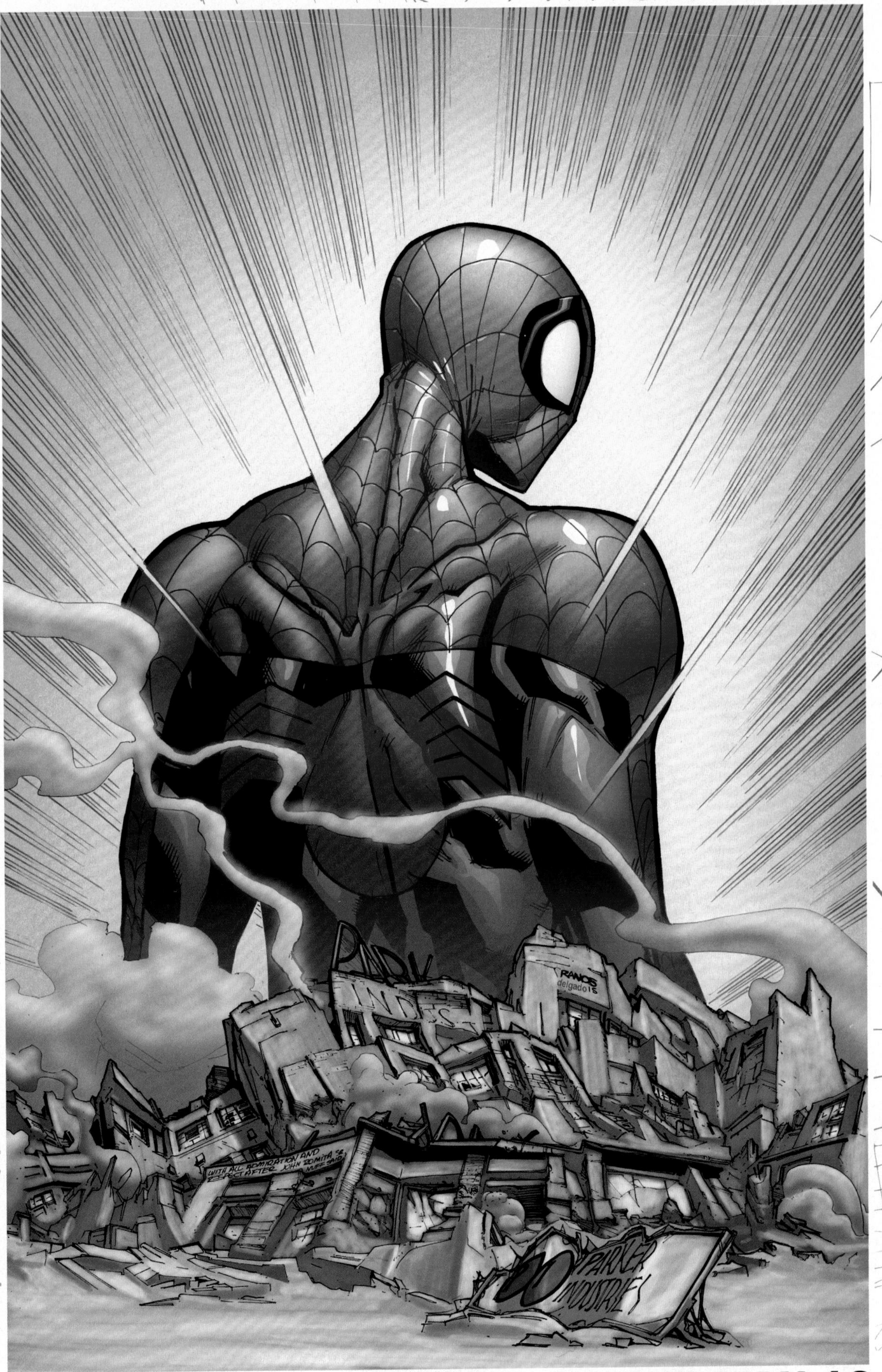
RAMOS
delgado 15
WITH ALL ADMIRATION AND RESPECT AFTER JOHN ROMITA SR. NUFF SAID

AMAZING SPIDER-MAN 18

GRAVEYARD SHIFT, PART THREE: TRADE SECRETS

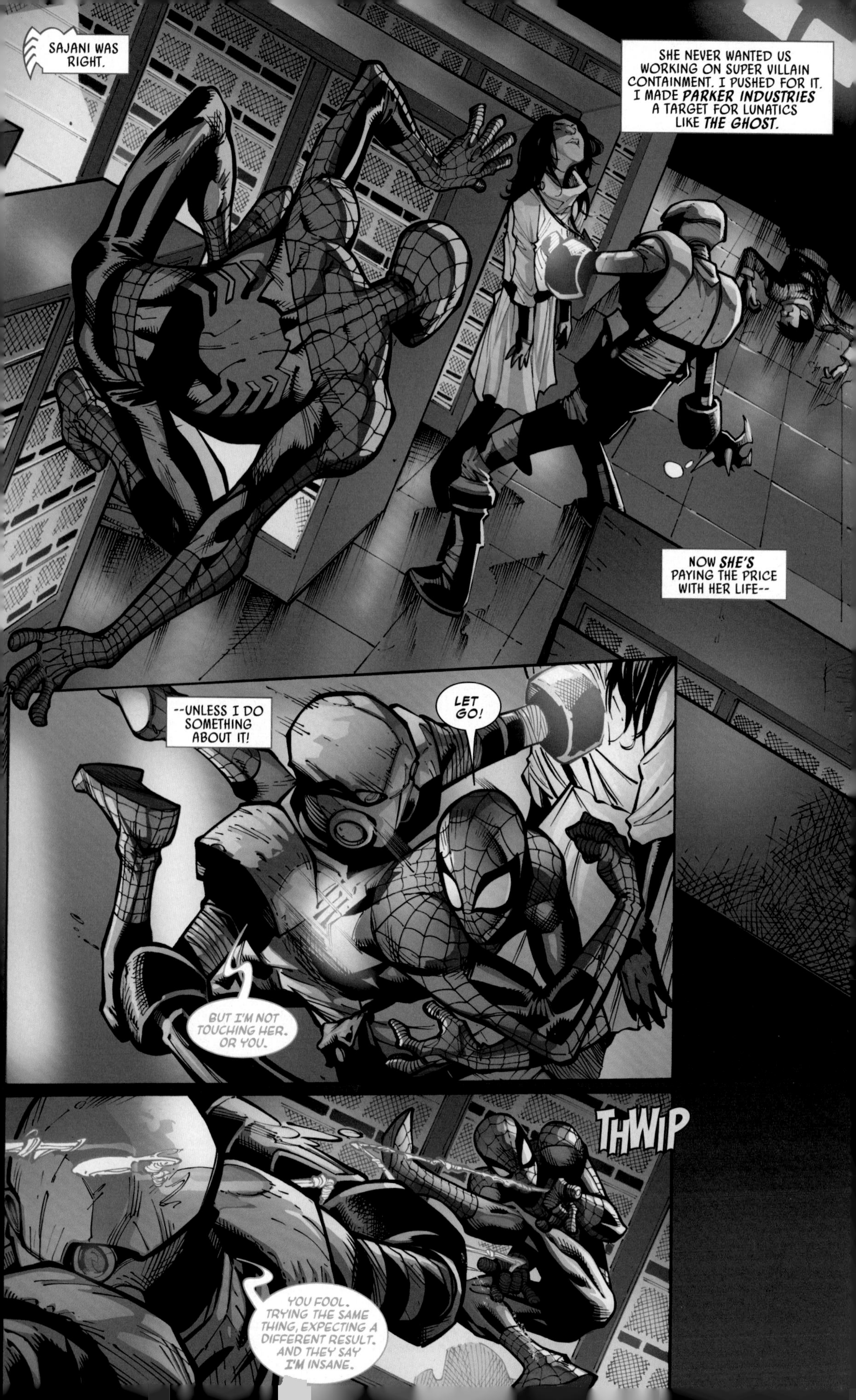
SAJANI WAS RIGHT.
SHE NEVER WANTED US WORKING ON SUPER VILLAIN CONTAINMENT. I PUSHED FOR IT. I MADE PARKER INDUSTRIES A TARGET FOR LUNATICS LIKE THE GHOST.
NOW SHE'S PAYING THE PRICE WITH HER LIFE--
--UNLESS I DO SOMETHING ABOUT IT!
LET GO!
BUT I'M NOT TOUCHING HER. OR YOU.
THWIP
YOU FOOL. TRYING THE SAME THING, EXPECTING A DIFFERENT RESULT. AND THEY SAY I'M INSANE.

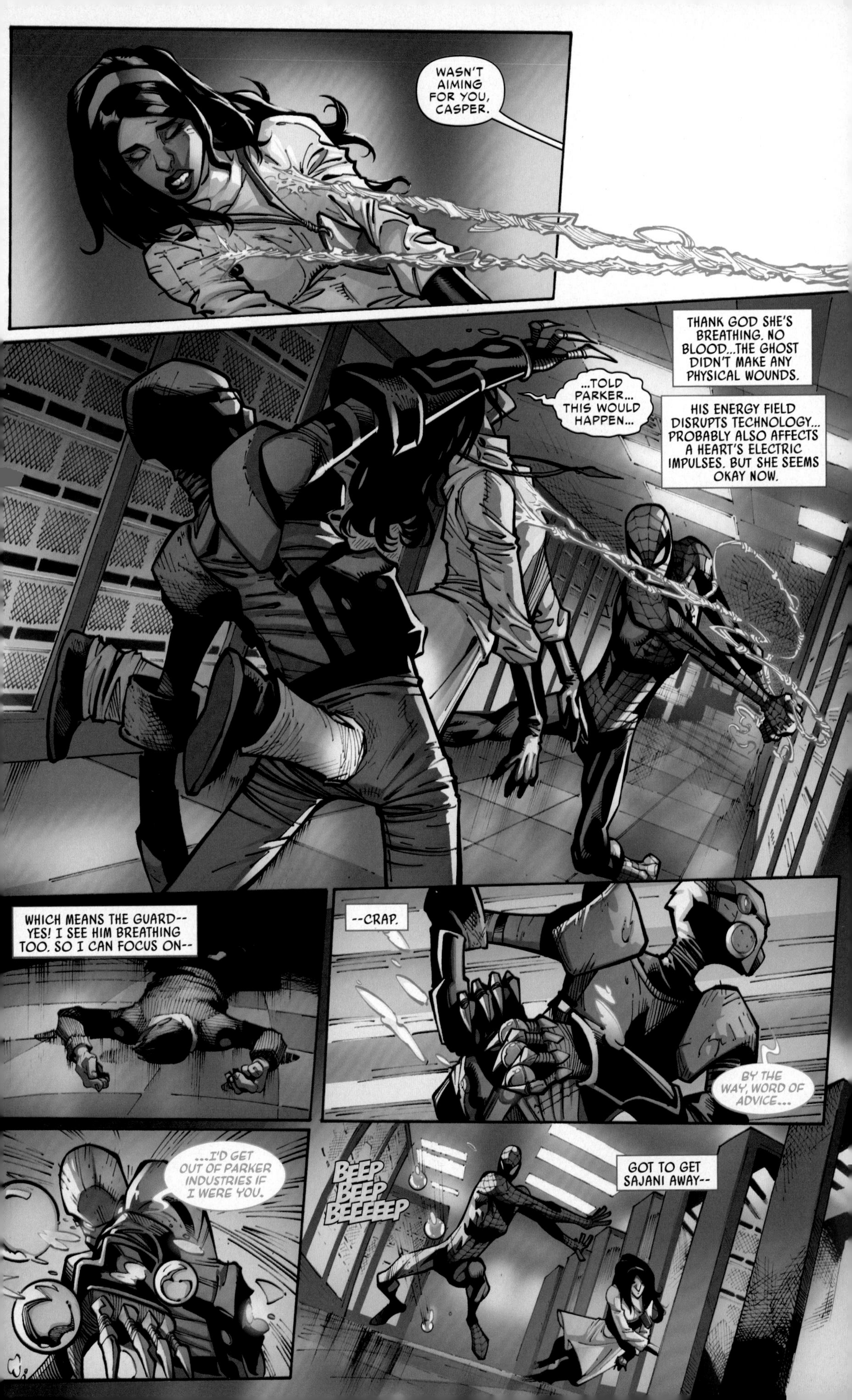
WASN'T AIMING FOR YOU, CASPER.
THANK GOD SHE'S BREATHING. NO BLOOD...THE GHOST DIDN'T MAKE ANY PHYSICAL WOUNDS.
...TOLD PARKER... THIS WOULD HAPPEN...
HIS ENERGY FIELD DISRUPTS TECHNOLOGY... PROBABLY ALSO AFFECTS A HEART'S ELECTRIC IMPULSES. BUT SHE SEEMS OKAY NOW.
WHICH MEANS THE GUARD-- YES! I SEE HIM BREATHING TOO. SO I CAN FOCUS ON--
--CRAP.
BY THE WAY, WORD OF ADVICE...
...I'D GET OUT OF PARKER INDUSTRIES IF I WERE YOU.
BEEP BEEP BEEEEEP
GOT TO GET SAJANI AWAY--

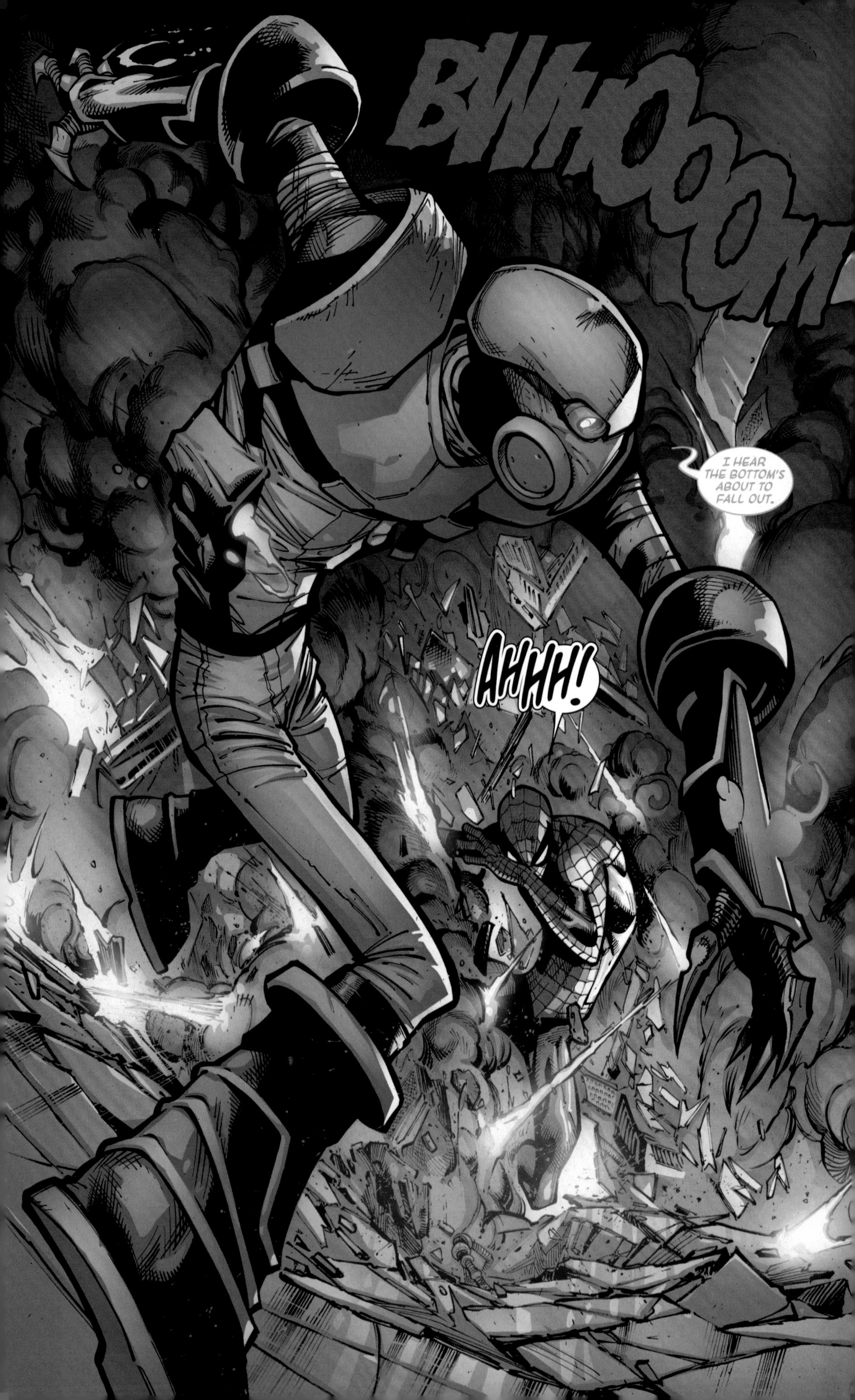
BWHOOOOM
I HEAR THE BOTTOM'S ABOUT TO FALL OUT.
AHHH!

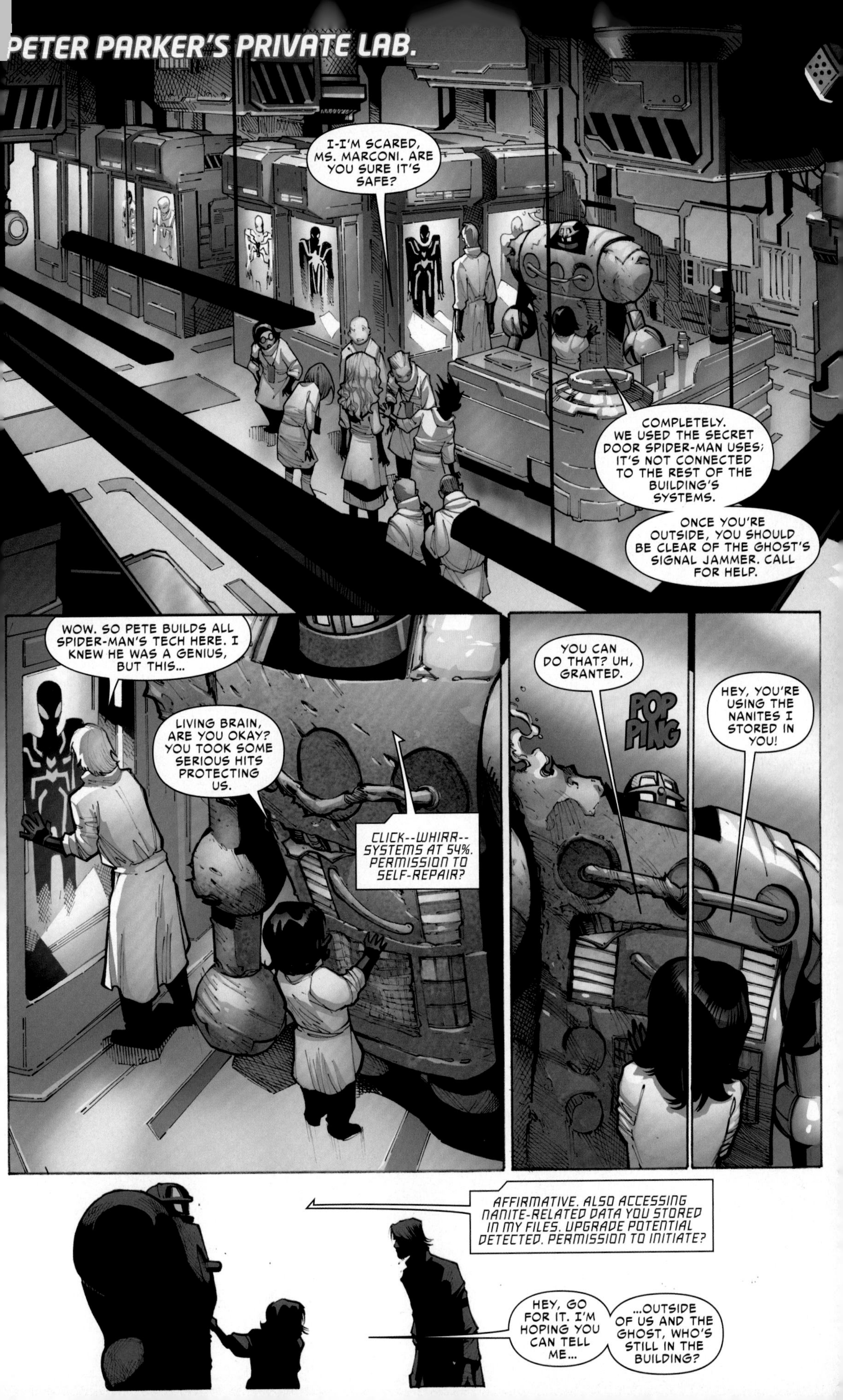
PETER PARKER'S PRIVATE LAB.
I-I'M SCARED, MS. MARCONI. ARE YOU SURE IT'S SAFE?
COMPLETELY. WE USED THE SECRET DOOR SPIDER-MAN USES; IT'S NOT CONNECTED TO THE REST OF THE BUILDING'S SYSTEMS.
ONCE YOU'RE OUTSIDE, YOU SHOULD BE CLEAR OF THE GHOST'S SIGNAL JAMMER. CALL FOR HELP.
WOW. SO PETE BUILDS ALL SPIDER-MAN'S TECH HERE. I KNEW HE WAS A GENIUS, BUT THIS...
LIVING BRAIN, ARE YOU OKAY? YOU TOOK SOME SERIOUS HITS PROTECTING US.
CLICK--WHIRR--SYSTEMS AT 54%. PERMISSION TO SELF-REPAIR?
YOU CAN DO THAT? UH, GRANTED.
POP
PING
HEY, YOU'RE USING THE NANITES I STORED IN YOU!
AFFIRMATIVE. ALSO ACCESSING NANITE-RELATED DATA YOU STORED IN MY FILES. UPGRADE POTENTIAL DETECTED. PERMISSION TO INITIATE?
HEY, GO FOR IT. I'M HOPING YOU CAN TELL ME...
...OUTSIDE OF US AND THE GHOST, WHO'S STILL IN THE BUILDING?

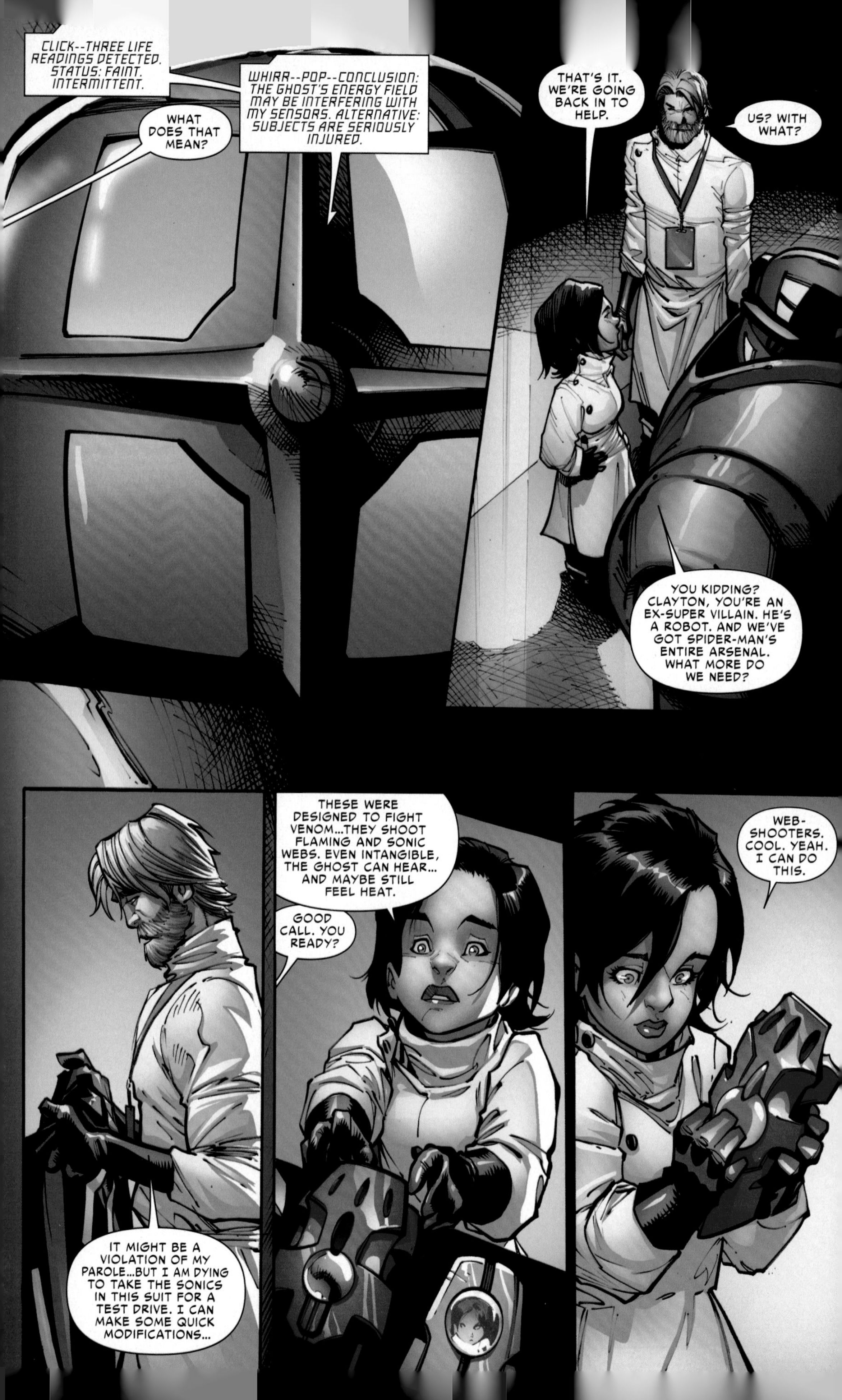
CLICK--THREE LIFE READINGS DETECTED. STATUS: FAINT. INTERMITTENT.
WHAT DOES THAT MEAN?
WHIRR--POP--CONCLUSION: THE GHOST'S ENERGY FIELD MAY BE INTERFERING WITH MY SENSORS. ALTERNATIVE: SUBJECTS ARE SERIOUSLY INJURED.
THAT'S IT. WE'RE GOING BACK IN TO HELP.
US? WITH WHAT?
YOU KIDDING? CLAYTON, YOU'RE AN EX-SUPER VILLAIN. HE'S A ROBOT. AND WE'VE GOT SPIDER-MAN'S ENTIRE ARSENAL. WHAT MORE DO WE NEED?
IT MIGHT BE A VIOLATION OF MY PAROLE...BUT I AM DYING TO TAKE THE SONICS IN THIS SUIT FOR A TEST DRIVE. I CAN MAKE SOME QUICK MODIFICATIONS...
THESE WERE DESIGNED TO FIGHT VENOM...THEY SHOOT FLAMING AND SONIC WEBS. EVEN INTANGIBLE, THE GHOST CAN HEAR... AND MAYBE STILL FEEL HEAT.
GOOD CALL. YOU READY?
WEB-SHOOTERS. COOL. YEAH. I CAN DO THIS.

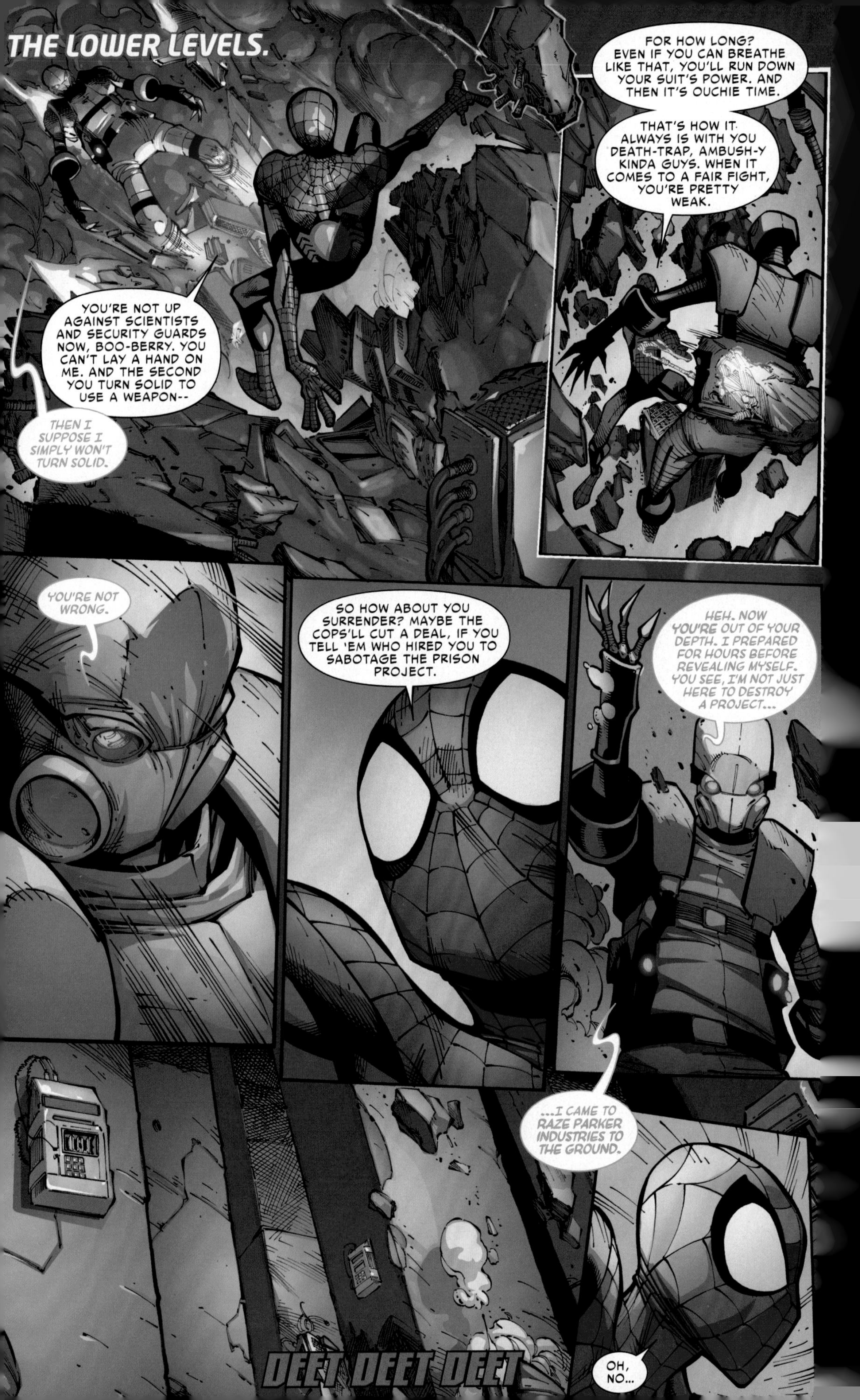
THE LOWER LEVELS.
FOR HOW LONG? EVEN IF YOU CAN BREATHE LIKE THAT, YOU'LL RUN DOWN YOUR SUIT'S POWER. AND THEN IT'S OUCHIE TIME.
THAT'S HOW IT ALWAYS IS WITH YOU DEATH-TRAP, AMBUSH-Y KINDA GUYS. WHEN IT COMES TO A FAIR FIGHT, YOU'RE PRETTY WEAK.
YOU'RE NOT UP AGAINST SCIENTISTS AND SECURITY GUARDS NOW, BOO-BERRY. YOU CAN'T LAY A HAND ON ME. AND THE SECOND YOU TURN SOLID TO USE A WEAPON--
THEN I SUPPOSE I SIMPLY WON'T TURN SOLID.
YOU'RE NOT WRONG.
SO HOW ABOUT YOU SURRENDER? MAYBE THE COPS'LL CUT A DEAL, IF YOU TELL 'EM WHO HIRED YOU TO SABOTAGE THE PRISON PROJECT.
HEH. NOW YOU'RE OUT OF YOUR DEPTH. I PREPARED FOR HOURS BEFORE REVEALING MYSELF. YOU SEE, I'M NOT JUST HERE TO DESTROY A PROJECT...
...I CAME TO RAZE PARKER INDUSTRIES TO THE GROUND.
DEET DEET DEET
OH, NO...

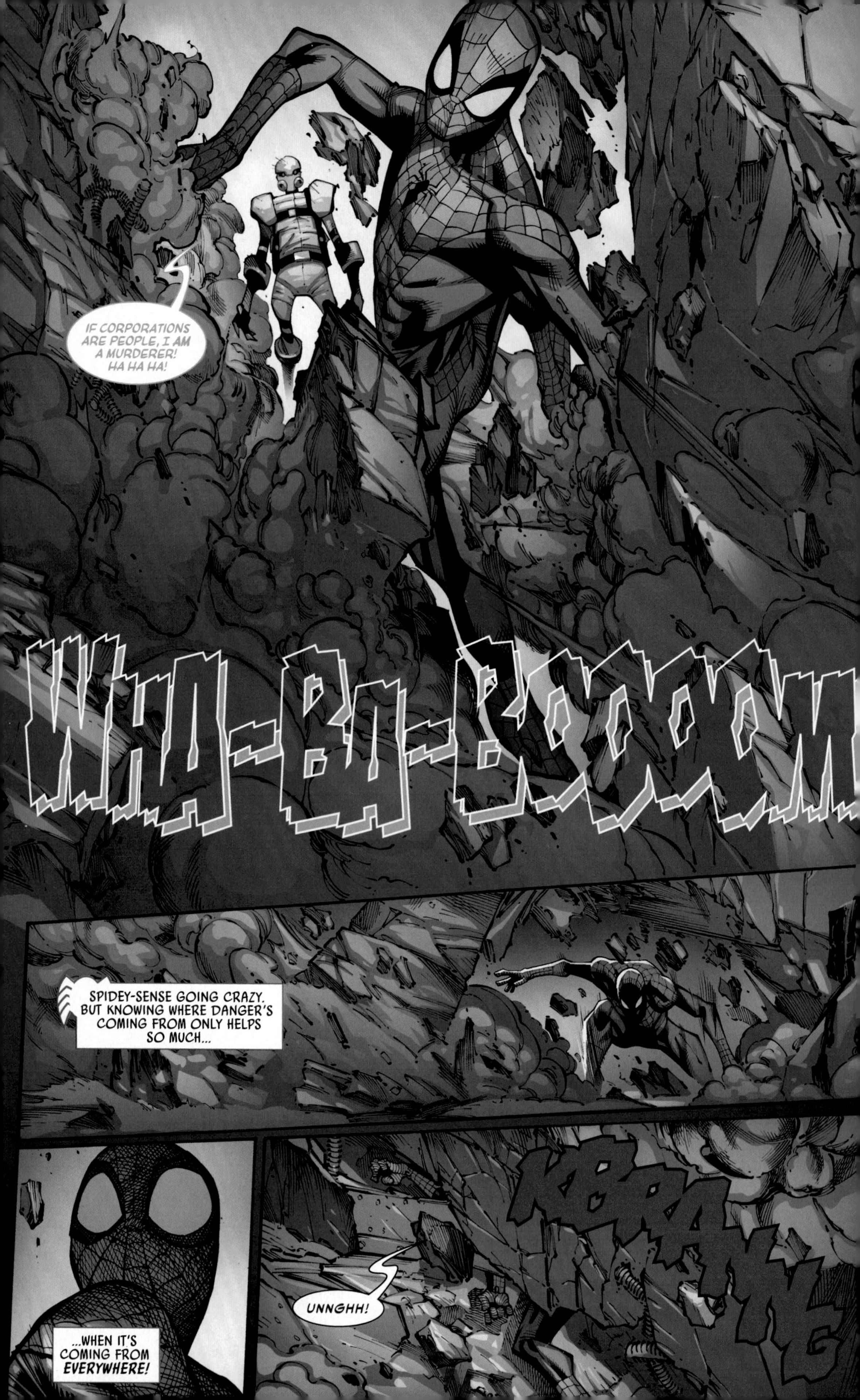
IF CORPORATIONS ARE PEOPLE, I AM A MURDERER! HA HA HA!
WHA-BA-BOOOOM
SPIDEY-SENSE GOING CRAZY. BUT KNOWING WHERE DANGER'S COMING FROM ONLY HELPS SO MUCH...
...WHEN IT'S COMING FROM *EVERYWHERE!*
UNNGHH!

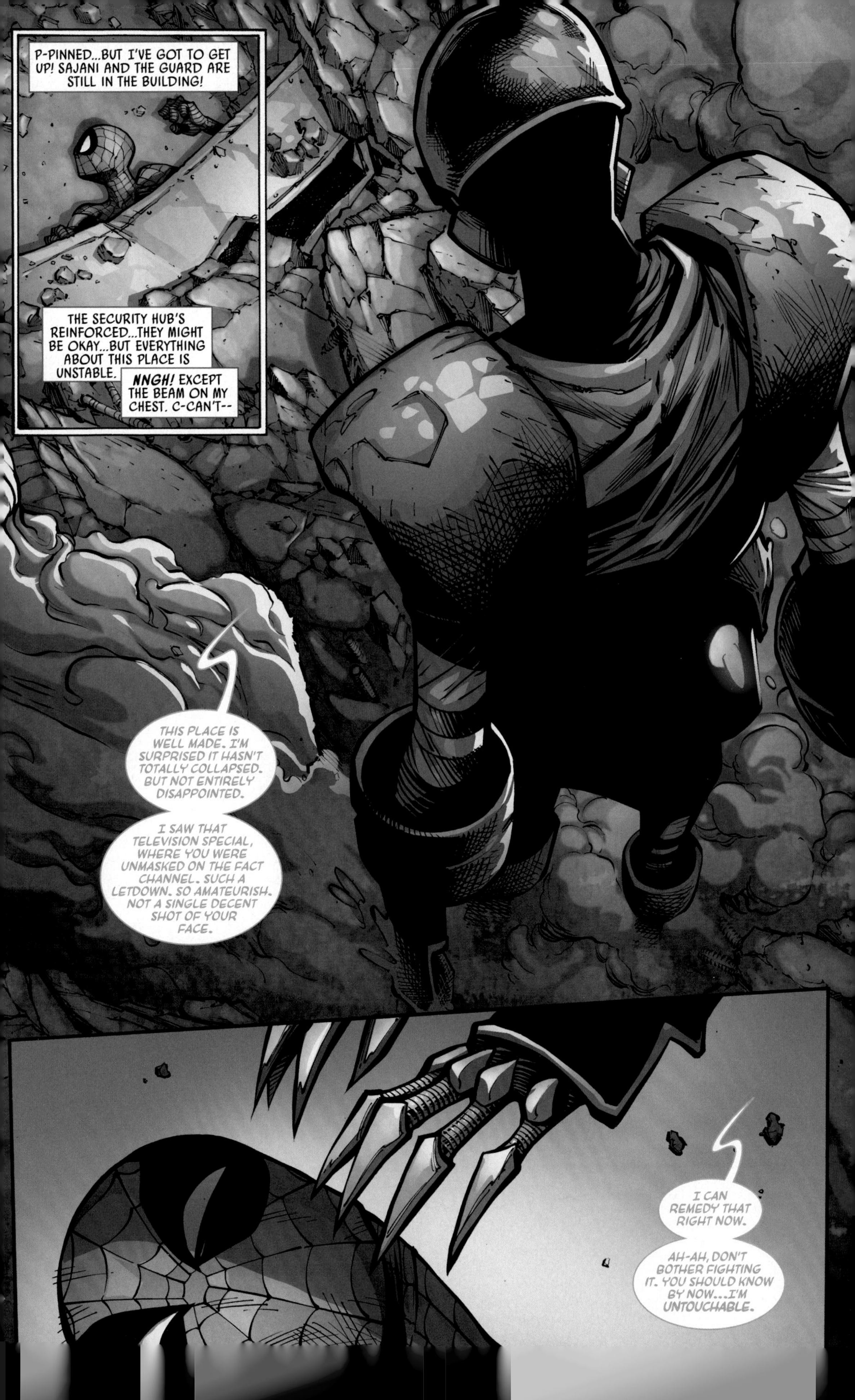
P-PINNED...BUT I'VE GOT TO GET UP! SAJANI AND THE GUARD ARE STILL IN THE BUILDING!
THE SECURITY HUB'S REINFORCED...THEY MIGHT BE OKAY...BUT EVERYTHING ABOUT THIS PLACE IS UNSTABLE.
NNGH! EXCEPT THE BEAM ON MY CHEST. C-CAN'T--
THIS PLACE IS WELL MADE. I'M SURPRISED IT HASN'T TOTALLY COLLAPSED. BUT NOT ENTIRELY DISAPPOINTED.
I SAW THAT TELEVISION SPECIAL, WHERE YOU WERE UNMASKED ON THE FACT CHANNEL. SUCH A LETDOWN. SO AMATEURISH. NOT A SINGLE DECENT SHOT OF YOUR FACE.
I CAN REMEDY THAT RIGHT NOW.
AH-AH, DON'T BOTHER FIGHTING IT. YOU SHOULD KNOW BY NOW...I'M UNTOUCHABLE.

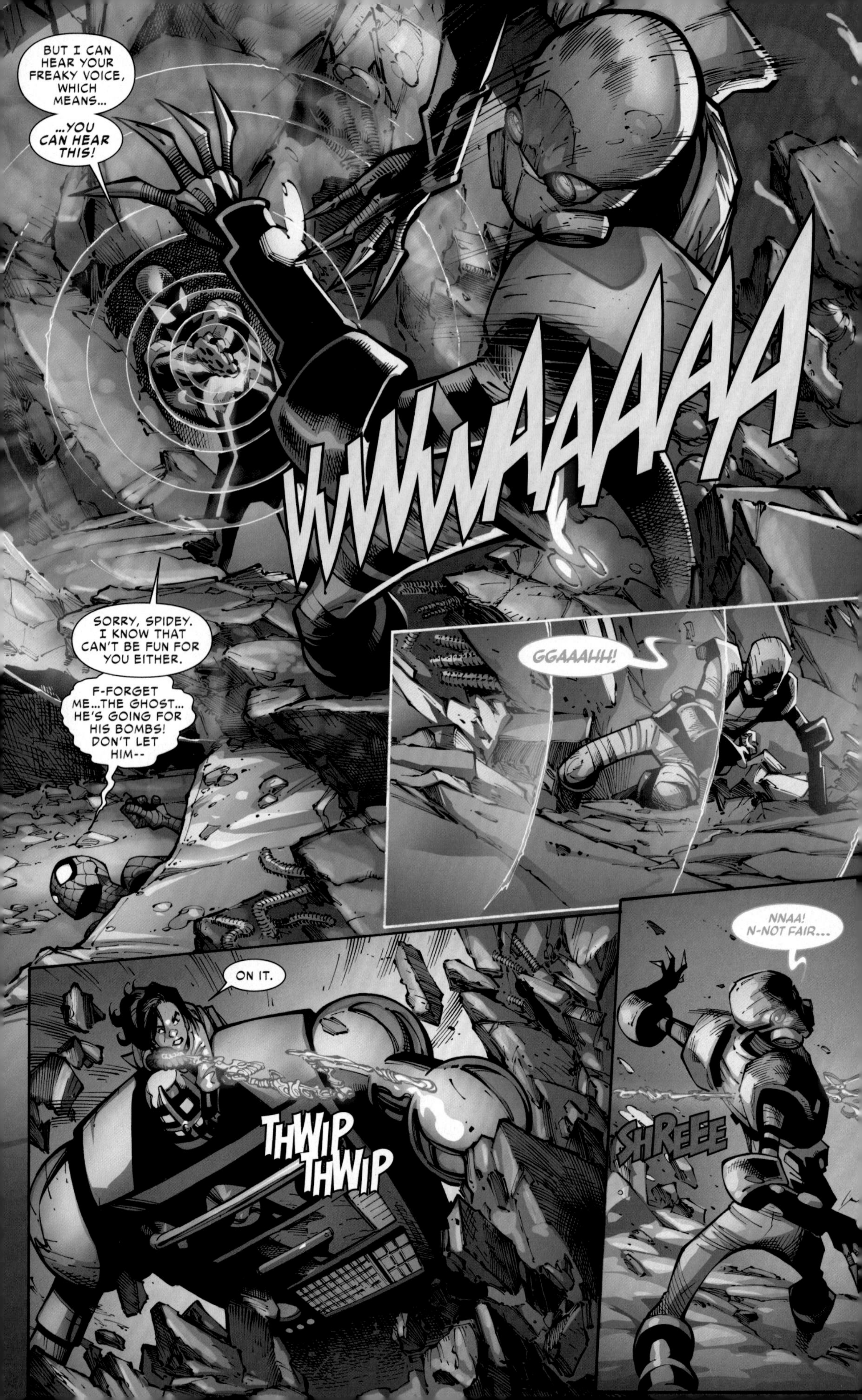
BUT I CAN HEAR YOUR FREAKY VOICE, WHICH MEANS...
...YOU CAN HEAR THIS!
VWWWAAAAAA
SORRY, SPIDEY. I KNOW THAT CAN'T BE FUN FOR YOU EITHER.
F-FORGET ME...THE GHOST... HE'S GOING FOR HIS BOMBS! DON'T LET HIM--
GGAAAHH!
ON IT.
THWIP THWIP
NNAA! N-NOT FAIR...
SHREEE

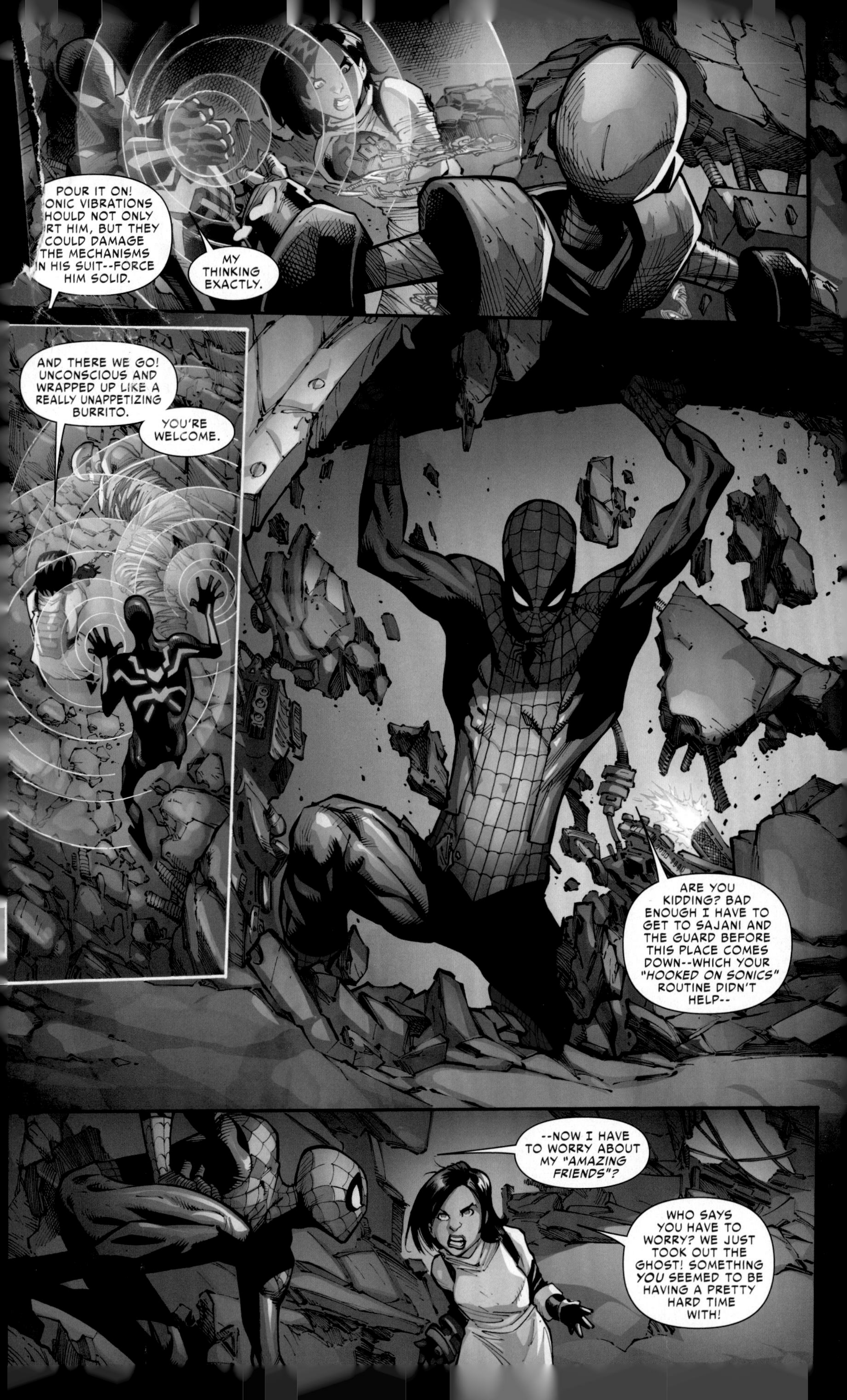

POUR IT ON! ONIC VIBRATIONS HOULD NOT ONLY URT HIM, BUT THEY COULD DAMAGE THE MECHANISMS N HIS SUIT--FORCE HIM SOLID.
MY THINKING EXACTLY.
AND THERE WE GO! UNCONSCIOUS AND WRAPPED UP LIKE A REALLY UNAPPETIZING BURRITO.
YOU'RE WELCOME.
ARE YOU KIDDING? BAD ENOUGH I HAVE TO GET TO SAJANI AND THE GUARD BEFORE THIS PLACE COMES DOWN--WHICH YOUR "HOOKED ON SONICS" ROUTINE DIDN'T HELP--
--NOW I HAVE TO WORRY ABOUT MY "AMAZING FRIENDS"?
WHO SAYS YOU HAVE TO WORRY? WE JUST TOOK OUT THE GHOST! SOMETHING YOU SEEMED TO BE HAVING A PRETTY HARD TIME WITH!

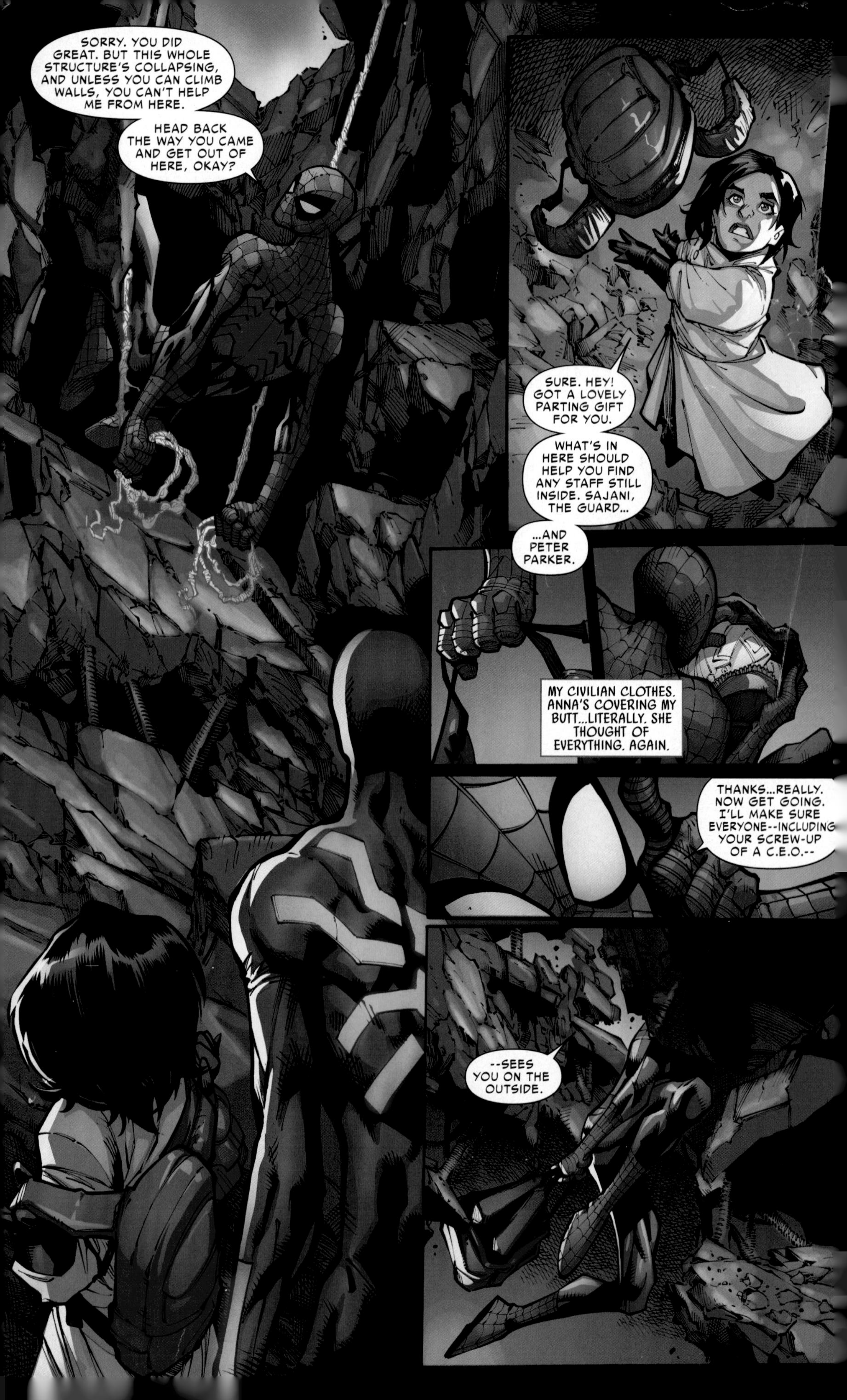
SORRY. YOU DID GREAT. BUT THIS WHOLE STRUCTURE'S COLLAPSING, AND UNLESS YOU CAN CLIMB WALLS, YOU CAN'T HELP ME FROM HERE.
HEAD BACK THE WAY YOU CAME AND GET OUT OF HERE, OKAY?
SURE. HEY! GOT A LOVELY PARTING GIFT FOR YOU.
WHAT'S IN HERE SHOULD HELP YOU FIND ANY STAFF STILL INSIDE. SAJANI, THE GUARD...
...AND PETER PARKER.
MY CIVILIAN CLOTHES. ANNA'S COVERING MY BUTT...LITERALLY. SHE THOUGHT OF EVERYTHING. AGAIN.
THANKS...REALLY. NOW GET GOING. I'LL MAKE SURE EVERYONE--INCLUDING YOUR SCREW-UP OF A C.E.O.--
--SEES YOU ON THE OUTSIDE.

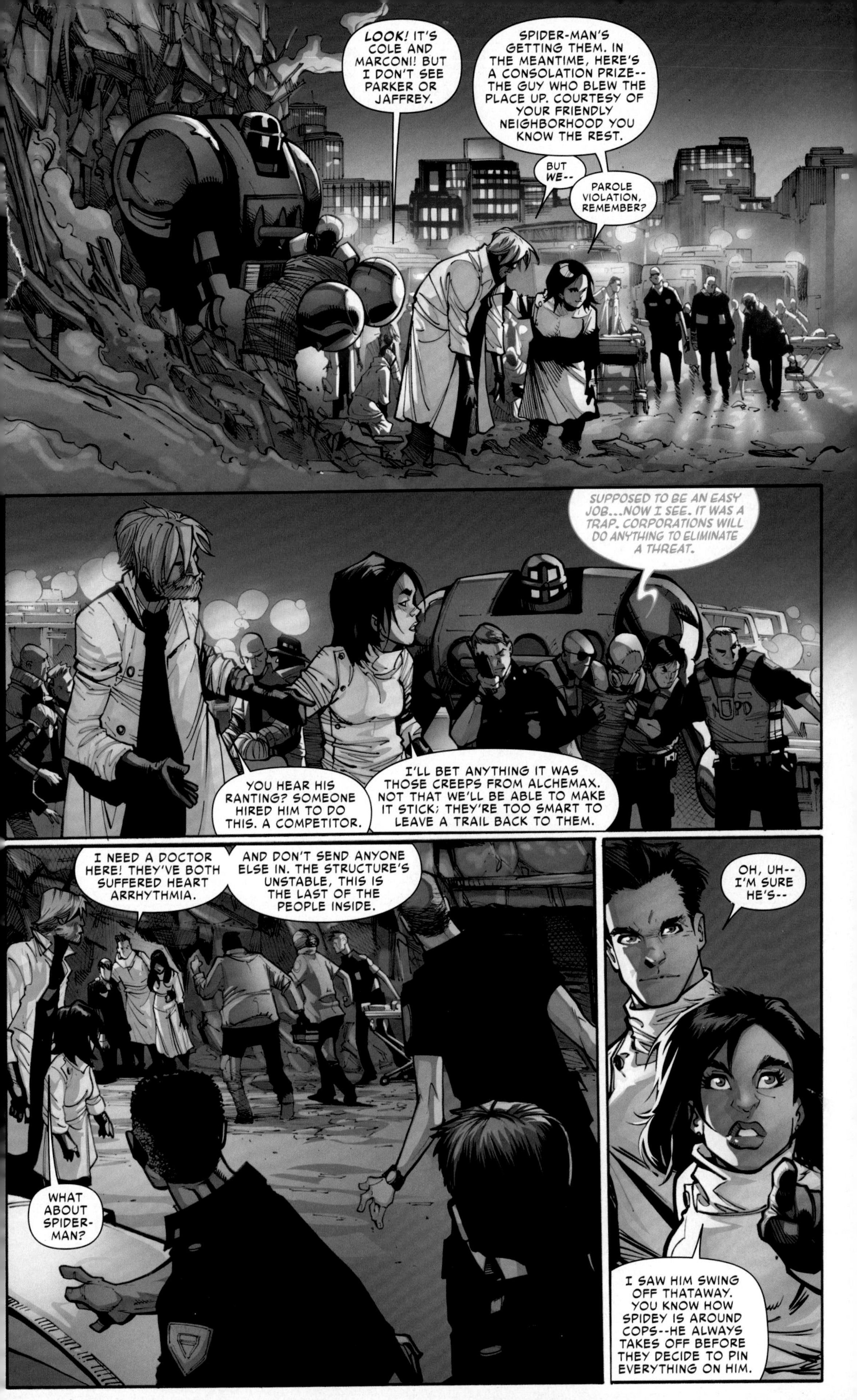
LOOK! IT'S COLE AND MARCONI! BUT I DON'T SEE PARKER OR JAFFREY.
SPIDER-MAN'S GETTING THEM. IN THE MEANTIME, HERE'S A CONSOLATION PRIZE-- THE GUY WHO BLEW THE PLACE UP. COURTESY OF YOUR FRIENDLY NEIGHBORHOOD YOU KNOW THE REST.
BUT WE--
PAROLE VIOLATION, REMEMBER?
SUPPOSED TO BE AN EASY JOB...NOW I SEE. IT WAS A TRAP. CORPORATIONS WILL DO ANYTHING TO ELIMINATE A THREAT.
YOU HEAR HIS RANTING? SOMEONE HIRED HIM TO DO THIS. A COMPETITOR.
I'LL BET ANYTHING IT WAS THOSE CREEPS FROM ALCHEMAX. NOT THAT WE'LL BE ABLE TO MAKE IT STICK; THEY'RE TOO SMART TO LEAVE A TRAIL BACK TO THEM.
I NEED A DOCTOR HERE! THEY'VE BOTH SUFFERED HEART ARRHYTHMIA.
AND DON'T SEND ANYONE ELSE IN. THE STRUCTURE'S UNSTABLE, THIS IS THE LAST OF THE PEOPLE INSIDE.
WHAT ABOUT SPIDER-MAN?
OH, UH-- I'M SURE HE'S--
I SAW HIM SWING OFF THATAWAY. YOU KNOW HOW SPIDEY IS AROUND COPS--HE ALWAYS TAKES OFF BEFORE THEY DECIDE TO PIN EVERYTHING ON HIM.

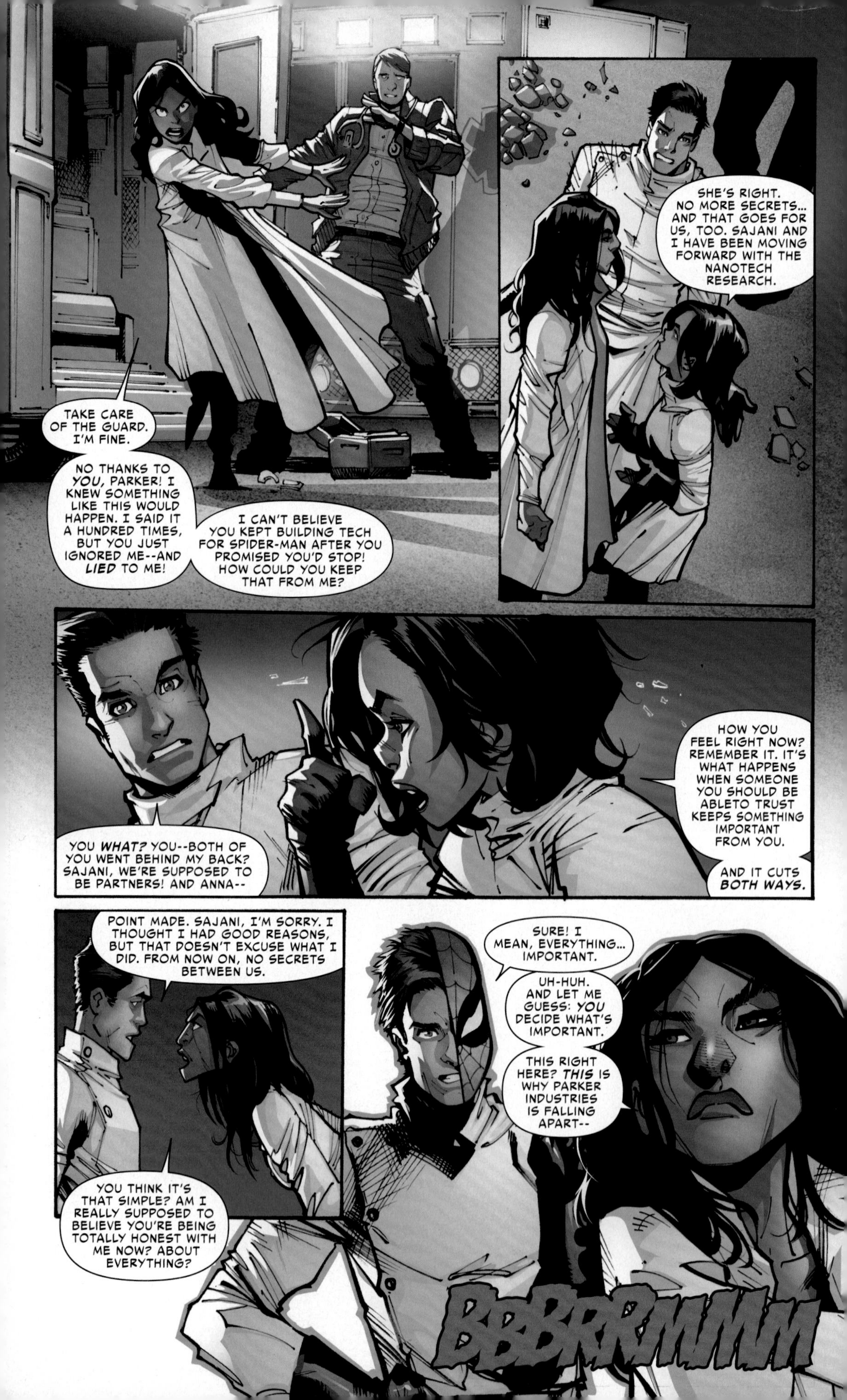
TAKE CARE OF THE GUARD. I'M FINE.
NO THANKS TO *YOU*, PARKER! I KNEW SOMETHING LIKE THIS WOULD HAPPEN. I SAID IT A HUNDRED TIMES, BUT YOU JUST IGNORED ME--AND *LIED* TO ME!
I CAN'T BELIEVE YOU KEPT BUILDING TECH FOR SPIDER-MAN AFTER YOU PROMISED YOU'D STOP! HOW COULD YOU KEEP THAT FROM ME?
SHE'S RIGHT. NO MORE SECRETS... AND THAT GOES FOR US, TOO. SAJANI AND I HAVE BEEN MOVING FORWARD WITH THE NANOTECH RESEARCH.
YOU *WHAT?* YOU--BOTH OF YOU WENT BEHIND MY BACK? SAJANI, WE'RE SUPPOSED TO BE PARTNERS! AND ANNA--
HOW YOU FEEL RIGHT NOW? REMEMBER IT. IT'S WHAT HAPPENS WHEN SOMEONE YOU SHOULD BE ABLETO TRUST KEEPS SOMETHING IMPORTANT FROM YOU.
AND IT CUTS *BOTH WAYS.*
POINT MADE. SAJANI, I'M SORRY. I THOUGHT I HAD GOOD REASONS, BUT THAT DOESN'T EXCUSE WHAT I DID. FROM NOW ON, NO SECRETS BETWEEN US.
YOU THINK IT'S THAT SIMPLE? AM I REALLY SUPPOSED TO BELIEVE YOU'RE BEING TOTALLY HONEST WITH ME NOW? ABOUT EVERYTHING?
SURE! I MEAN, EVERYTHING... IMPORTANT.
UH-HUH. AND LET ME GUESS: *YOU* DECIDE WHAT'S IMPORTANT.
THIS RIGHT HERE? *THIS* IS WHY PARKER INDUSTRIES IS FALLING APART--
BBBRRMMMM

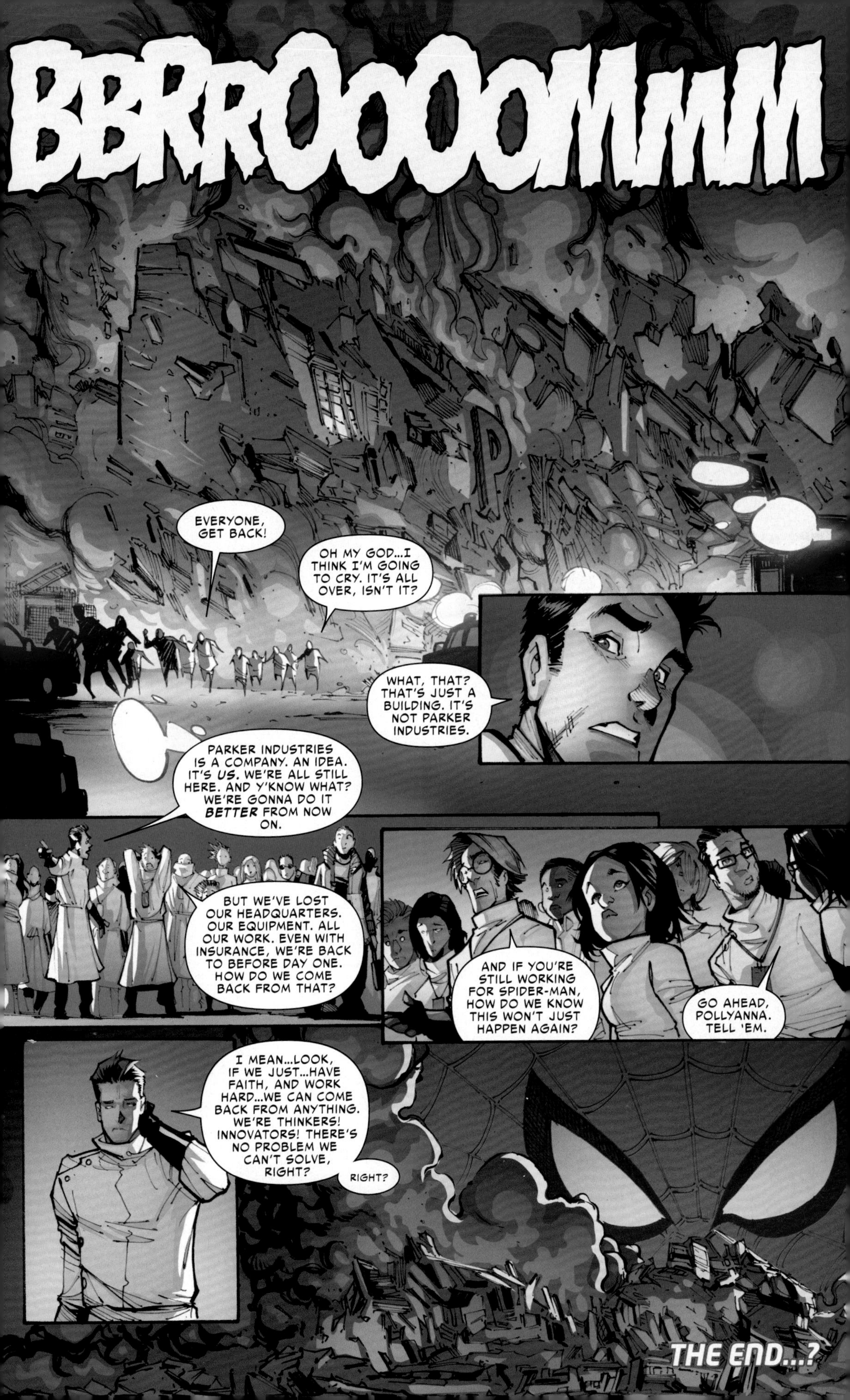
BBRROOOOMMM
EVERYONE, GET BACK!
OH MY GOD...I THINK I'M GOING TO CRY. IT'S ALL OVER, ISN'T IT?
WHAT, THAT? THAT'S JUST A BUILDING. IT'S NOT PARKER INDUSTRIES.
PARKER INDUSTRIES IS A COMPANY. AN IDEA. IT'S US. WE'RE ALL STILL HERE. AND Y'KNOW WHAT? WE'RE GONNA DO IT BETTER FROM NOW ON.
BUT WE'VE LOST OUR HEADQUARTERS. OUR EQUIPMENT. ALL OUR WORK. EVEN WITH INSURANCE, WE'RE BACK TO BEFORE DAY ONE. HOW DO WE COME BACK FROM THAT?
AND IF YOU'RE STILL WORKING FOR SPIDER-MAN, HOW DO WE KNOW THIS WON'T JUST HAPPEN AGAIN?
GO AHEAD, POLLYANNA. TELL 'EM.
I MEAN...LOOK, IF WE JUST...HAVE FAITH, AND WORK HARD...WE CAN COME BACK FROM ANYTHING. WE'RE THINKERS! INNOVATORS! THERE'S NO PROBLEM WE CAN'T SOLVE, RIGHT?
RIGHT?
THE END...?

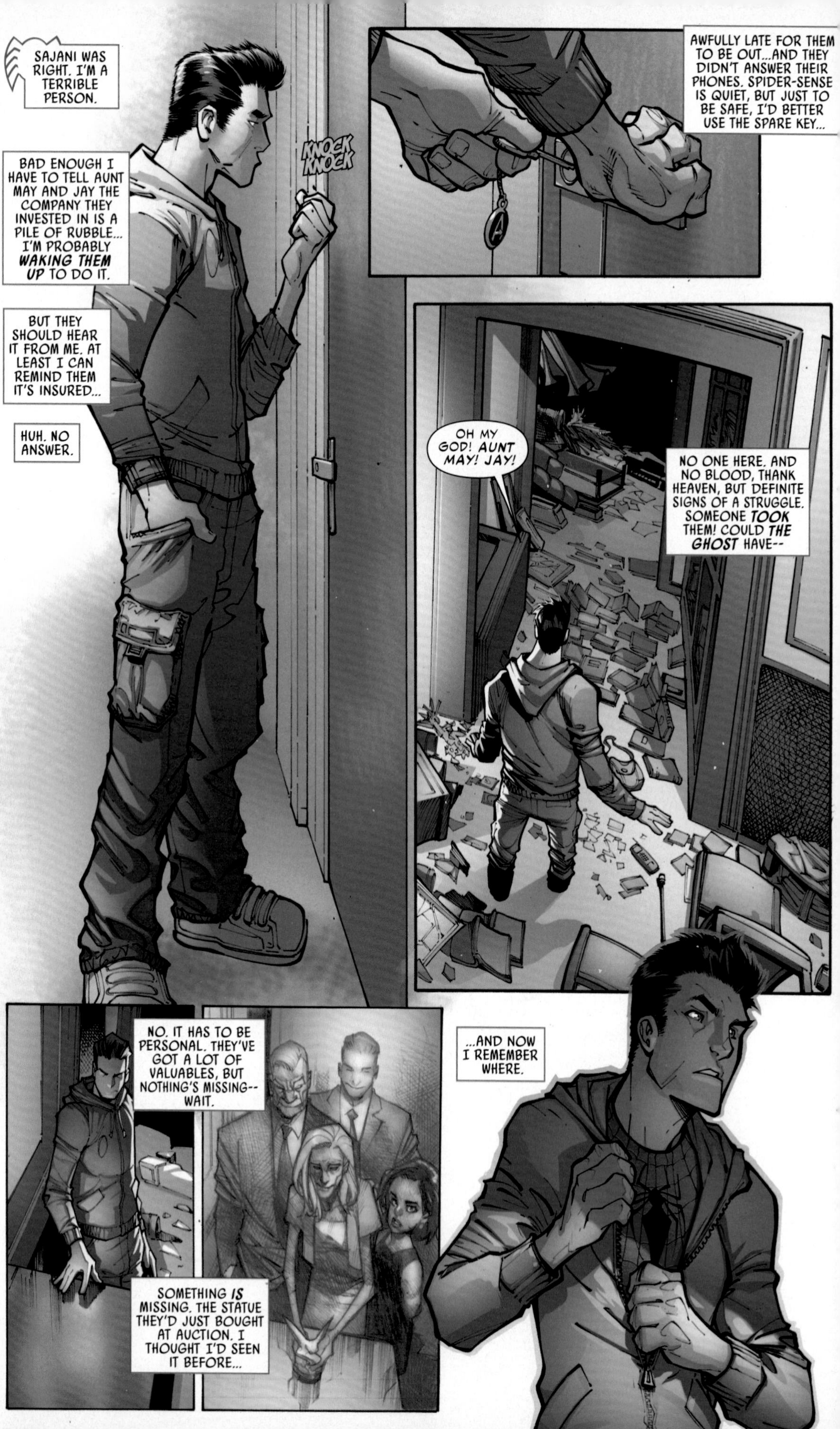
SAJANI WAS RIGHT. I'M A TERRIBLE PERSON.
BAD ENOUGH I HAVE TO TELL AUNT MAY AND JAY THE COMPANY THEY INVESTED IN IS A PILE OF RUBBLE... I'M PROBABLY WAKING THEM UP TO DO IT.
KNOCK KNOCK
BUT THEY SHOULD HEAR IT FROM ME. AT LEAST I CAN REMIND THEM IT'S INSURED...
HUH. NO ANSWER.
AWFULLY LATE FOR THEM TO BE OUT...AND THEY DIDN'T ANSWER THEIR PHONES. SPIDER-SENSE IS QUIET, BUT JUST TO BE SAFE, I'D BETTER USE THE SPARE KEY...
OH MY GOD! AUNT MAY! JAY!
NO ONE HERE. AND NO BLOOD, THANK HEAVEN, BUT DEFINITE SIGNS OF A STRUGGLE. SOMEONE TOOK THEM! COULD THE GHOST HAVE--
NO. IT HAS TO BE PERSONAL. THEY'VE GOT A LOT OF VALUABLES, BUT NOTHING'S MISSING--WAIT.
SOMETHING IS MISSING. THE STATUE THEY'D JUST BOUGHT AT AUCTION. I THOUGHT I'D SEEN IT BEFORE...
...AND NOW I REMEMBER WHERE.

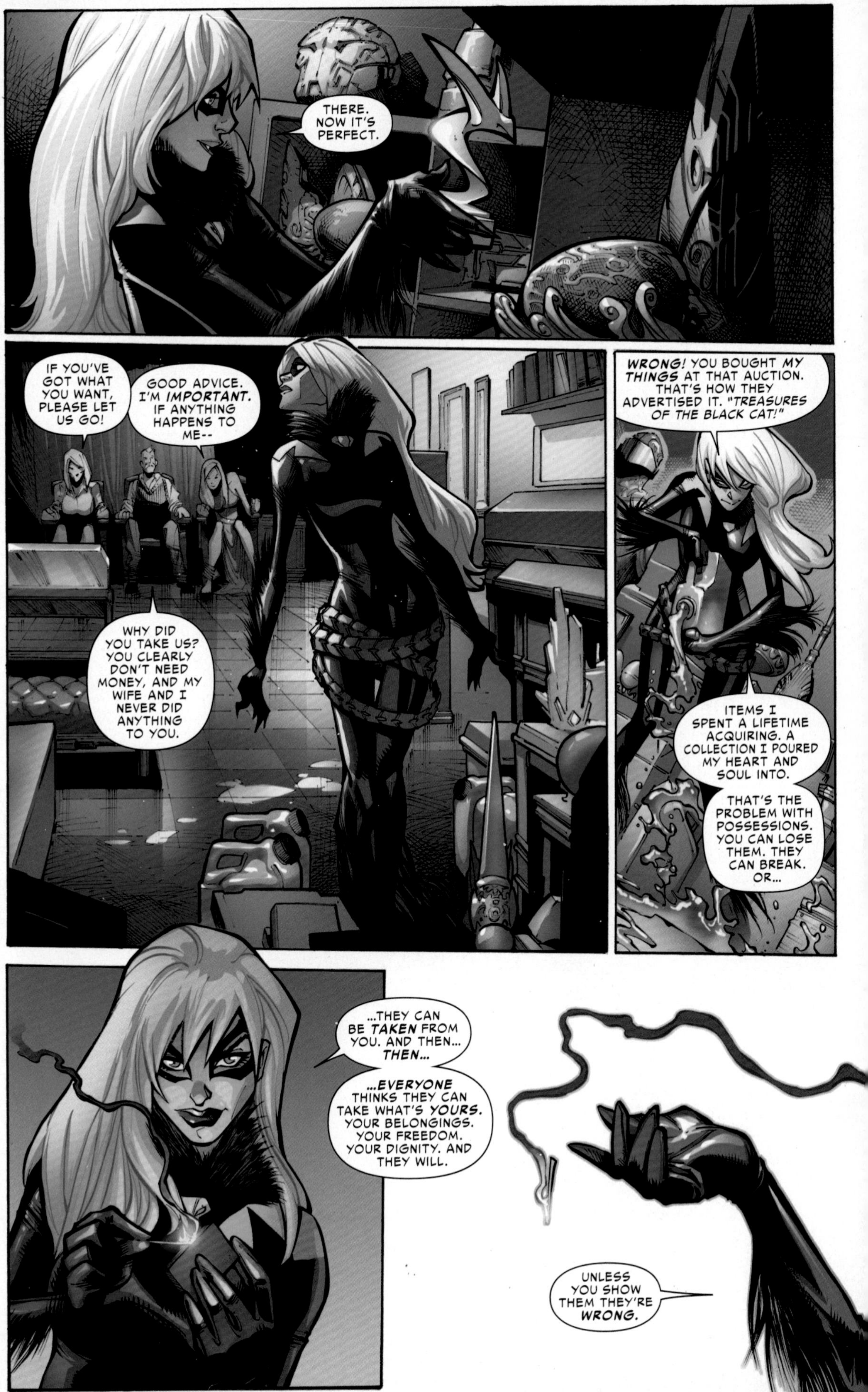
THERE. NOW IT'S PERFECT.
IF YOU'VE GOT WHAT YOU WANT, PLEASE LET US GO!
GOOD ADVICE. I'M *IMPORTANT.* IF ANYTHING HAPPENS TO ME--
WHY DID YOU TAKE US? YOU CLEARLY DON'T NEED MONEY, AND MY WIFE AND I NEVER DID ANYTHING TO YOU.
WRONG! YOU BOUGHT *MY THINGS* AT THAT AUCTION. THAT'S HOW THEY ADVERTISED IT. *"TREASURES OF THE BLACK CAT!"*
ITEMS I SPENT A LIFETIME ACQUIRING. A COLLECTION I POURED MY HEART AND SOUL INTO.
THAT'S THE PROBLEM WITH POSSESSIONS. YOU CAN LOSE THEM. THEY CAN BREAK. OR...
...THEY CAN BE *TAKEN* FROM YOU. AND THEN... *THEN...*
...EVERYONE THINKS THEY CAN TAKE WHAT'S *YOURS.* YOUR BELONGINGS. YOUR FREEDOM. YOUR DIGNITY. AND THEY WILL.
UNLESS YOU SHOW THEM THEY'RE *WRONG.*

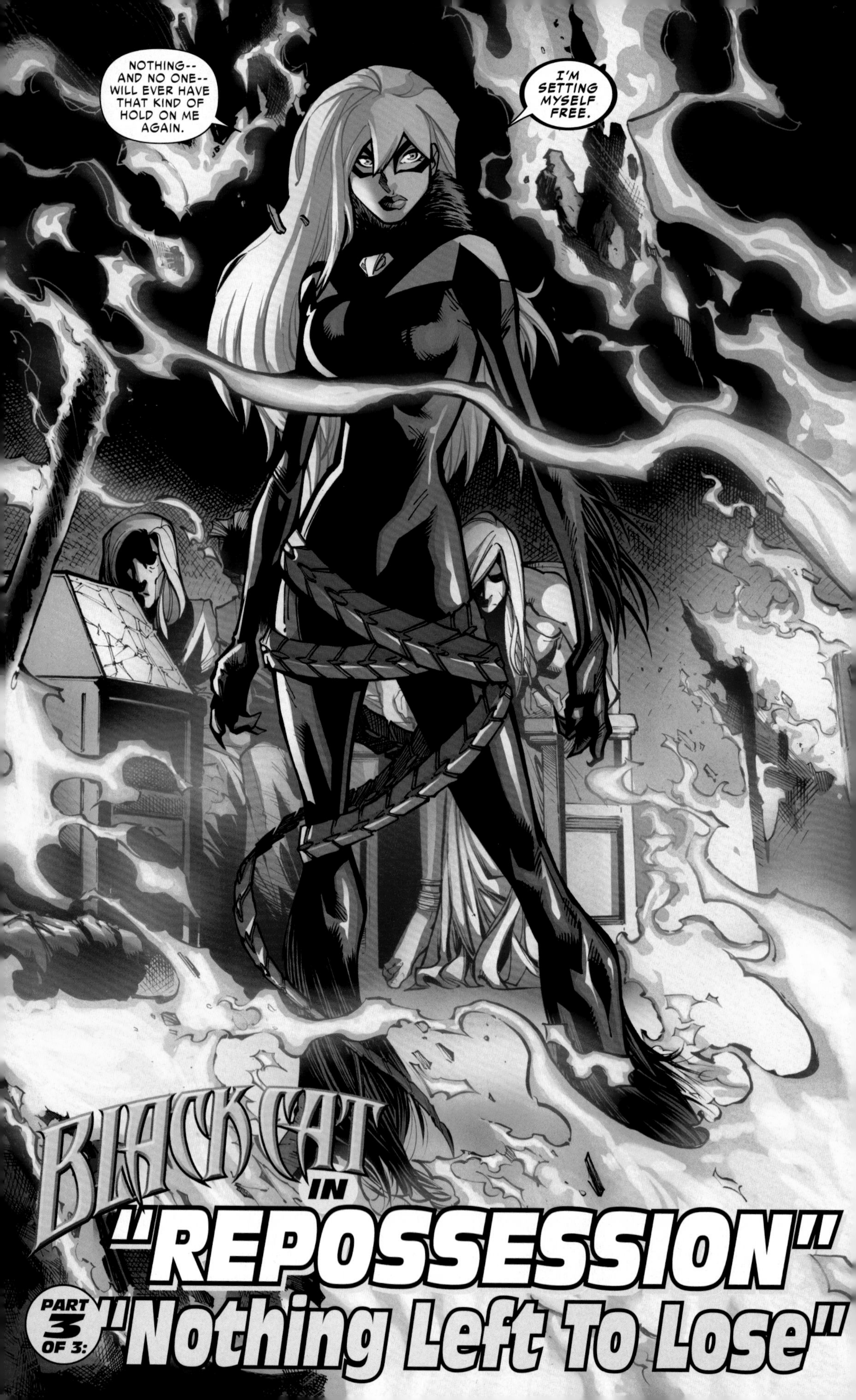
NOTHING-- AND NO ONE-- WILL EVER HAVE THAT KIND OF HOLD ON ME AGAIN.
I'M SETTING MYSELF FREE.
BLACK CAT
IN
"REPOSSESSION"
PART 3 OF 3: "Nothing Left To Lose"

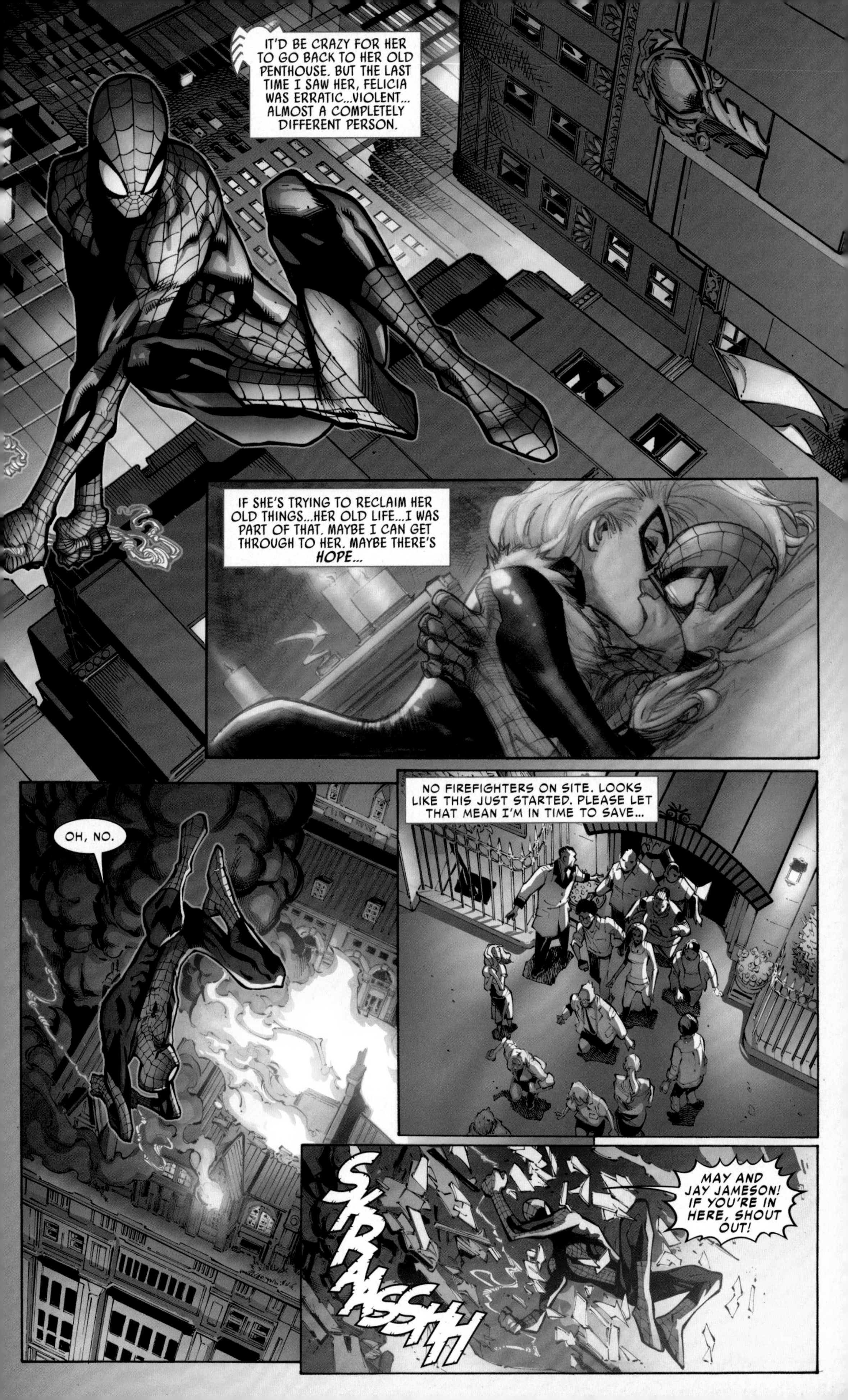
IT'D BE CRAZY FOR HER TO GO BACK TO HER OLD PENTHOUSE. BUT THE LAST TIME I SAW HER, FELICIA WAS ERRATIC...VIOLENT... ALMOST A COMPLETELY DIFFERENT PERSON.
IF SHE'S TRYING TO RECLAIM HER OLD THINGS...HER OLD LIFE...I WAS PART OF THAT. MAYBE I CAN GET THROUGH TO HER. MAYBE THERE'S *HOPE*...
OH, NO.
NO FIREFIGHTERS ON SITE. LOOKS LIKE THIS JUST STARTED. PLEASE LET THAT MEAN I'M IN TIME TO SAVE...
SKRASSHH
MAY AND JAY JAMESON! IF YOU'RE IN HERE, SHOUT OUT!

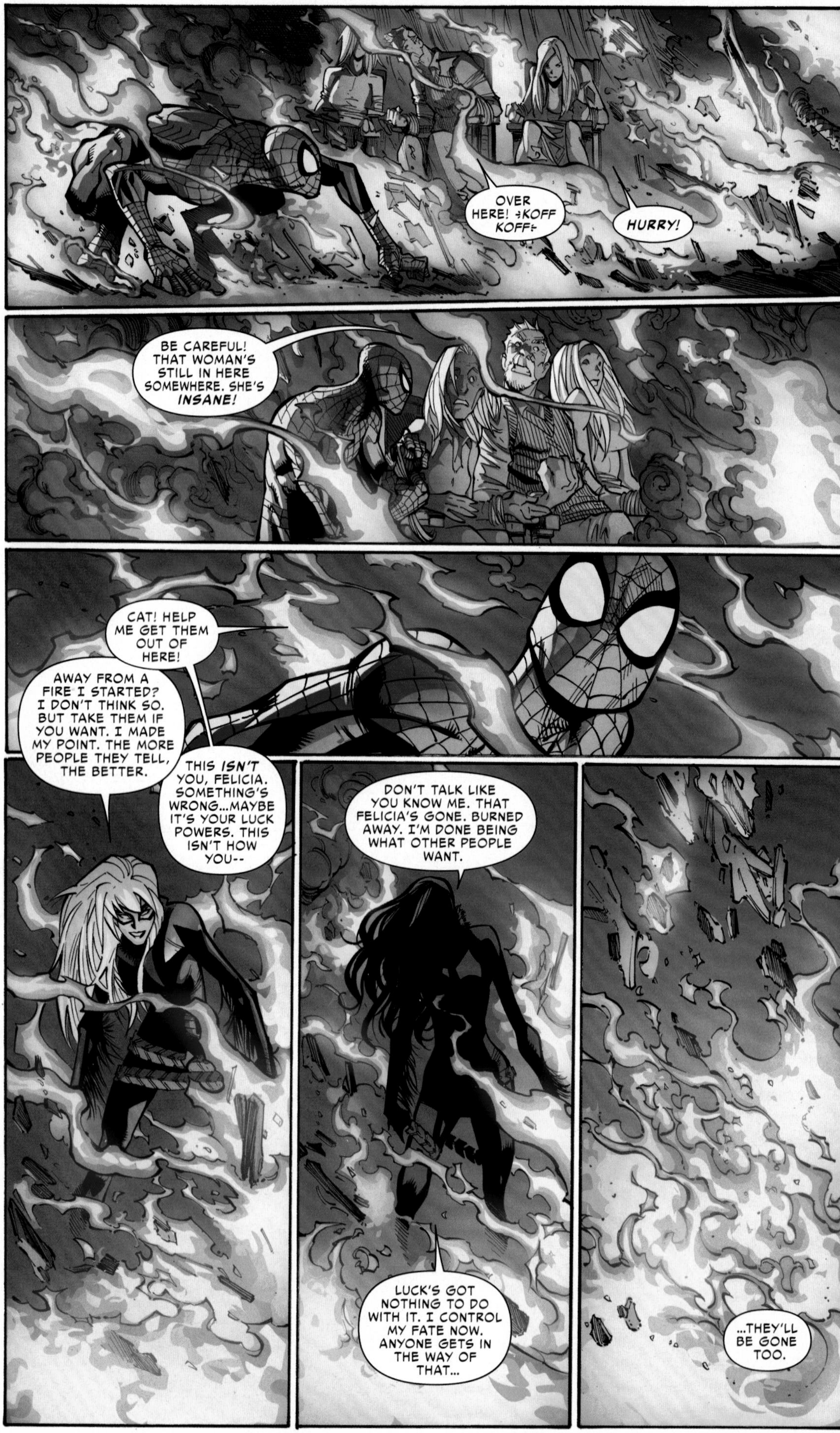

OVER HERE! ⊰KOFF KOFF⊱
HURRY!
BE CAREFUL! THAT WOMAN'S STILL IN HERE SOMEWHERE. SHE'S INSANE!
CAT! HELP ME GET THEM OUT OF HERE!
AWAY FROM A FIRE I STARTED? I DON'T THINK SO. BUT TAKE THEM IF YOU WANT. I MADE MY POINT. THE MORE PEOPLE THEY TELL, THE BETTER.
THIS ISN'T YOU, FELICIA. SOMETHING'S WRONG...MAYBE IT'S YOUR LUCK POWERS. THIS ISN'T HOW YOU--
DON'T TALK LIKE YOU KNOW ME. THAT FELICIA'S GONE. BURNED AWAY. I'M DONE BEING WHAT OTHER PEOPLE WANT.
LUCK'S GOT NOTHING TO DO WITH IT. I CONTROL MY FATE NOW. ANYONE GETS IN THE WAY OF THAT...
...THEY'LL BE GONE TOO.

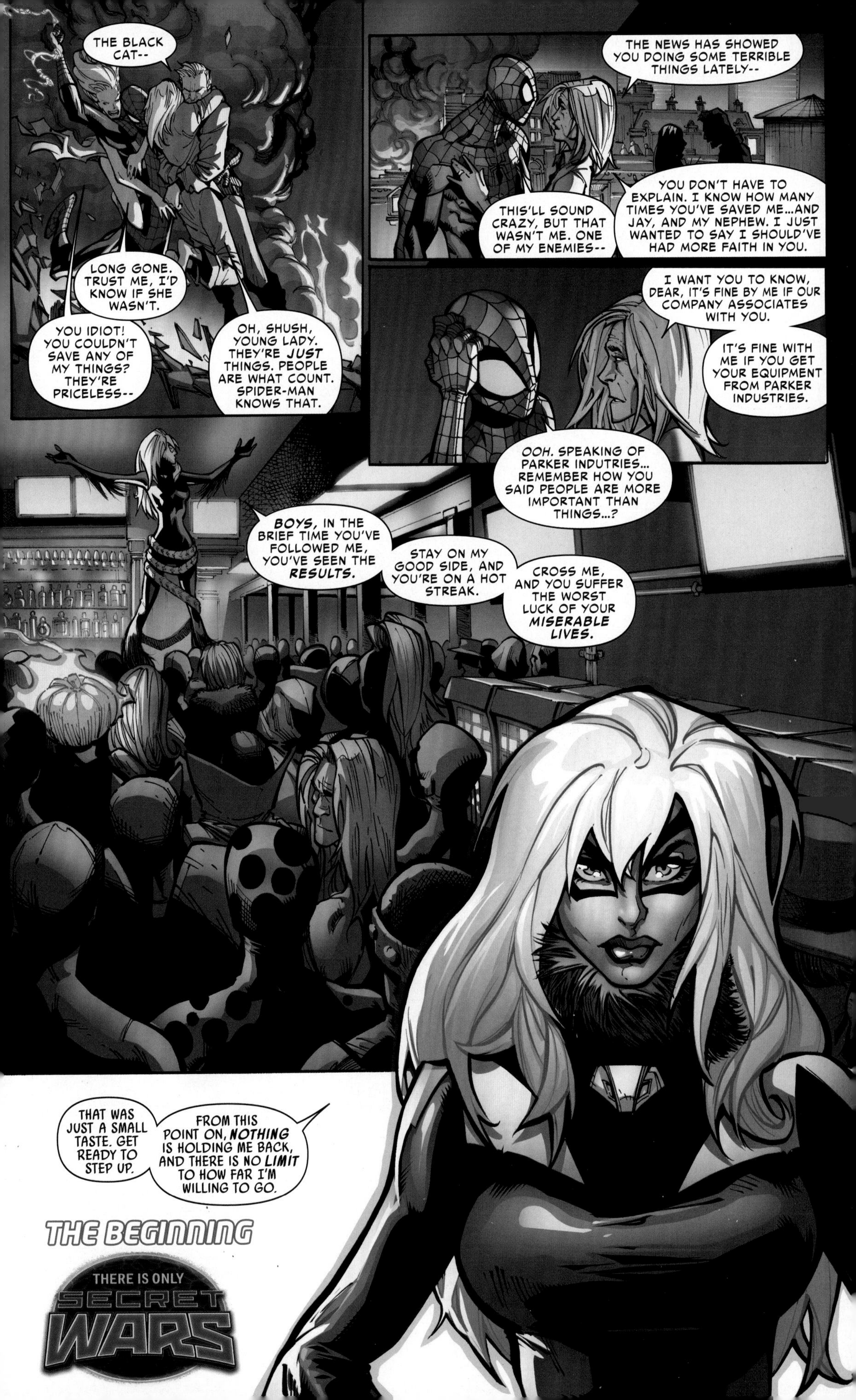

THE BLACK CAT--
LONG GONE. TRUST ME, I'D KNOW IF SHE WASN'T.
YOU IDIOT! YOU COULDN'T SAVE ANY OF MY THINGS? THEY'RE PRICELESS--
OH, SHUSH, YOUNG LADY. THEY'RE JUST THINGS. PEOPLE ARE WHAT COUNT. SPIDER-MAN KNOWS THAT.
THE NEWS HAS SHOWED YOU DOING SOME TERRIBLE THINGS LATELY--
THIS'LL SOUND CRAZY, BUT THAT WASN'T ME. ONE OF MY ENEMIES--
YOU DON'T HAVE TO EXPLAIN. I KNOW HOW MANY TIMES YOU'VE SAVED ME...AND JAY, AND MY NEPHEW. I JUST WANTED TO SAY I SHOULD'VE HAD MORE FAITH IN YOU.
I WANT YOU TO KNOW, DEAR, IT'S FINE BY ME IF OUR COMPANY ASSOCIATES WITH YOU.
IT'S FINE WITH ME IF YOU GET YOUR EQUIPMENT FROM PARKER INDUSTRIES.
OOH. SPEAKING OF PARKER INDUTRIES... REMEMBER HOW YOU SAID PEOPLE ARE MORE IMPORTANT THAN THINGS...?
BOYS, IN THE BRIEF TIME YOU'VE FOLLOWED ME, YOU'VE SEEN THE RESULTS.
STAY ON MY GOOD SIDE, AND YOU'RE ON A HOT STREAK.
CROSS ME, AND YOU SUFFER THE WORST LUCK OF YOUR MISERABLE LIVES.
THAT WAS JUST A SMALL TASTE. GET READY TO STEP UP.
FROM THIS POINT ON, NOTHING IS HOLDING ME BACK, AND THERE IS NO LIMIT TO HOW FAR I'M WILLING TO GO.
THE BEGINNING
THERE IS ONLY
SECRET WARS

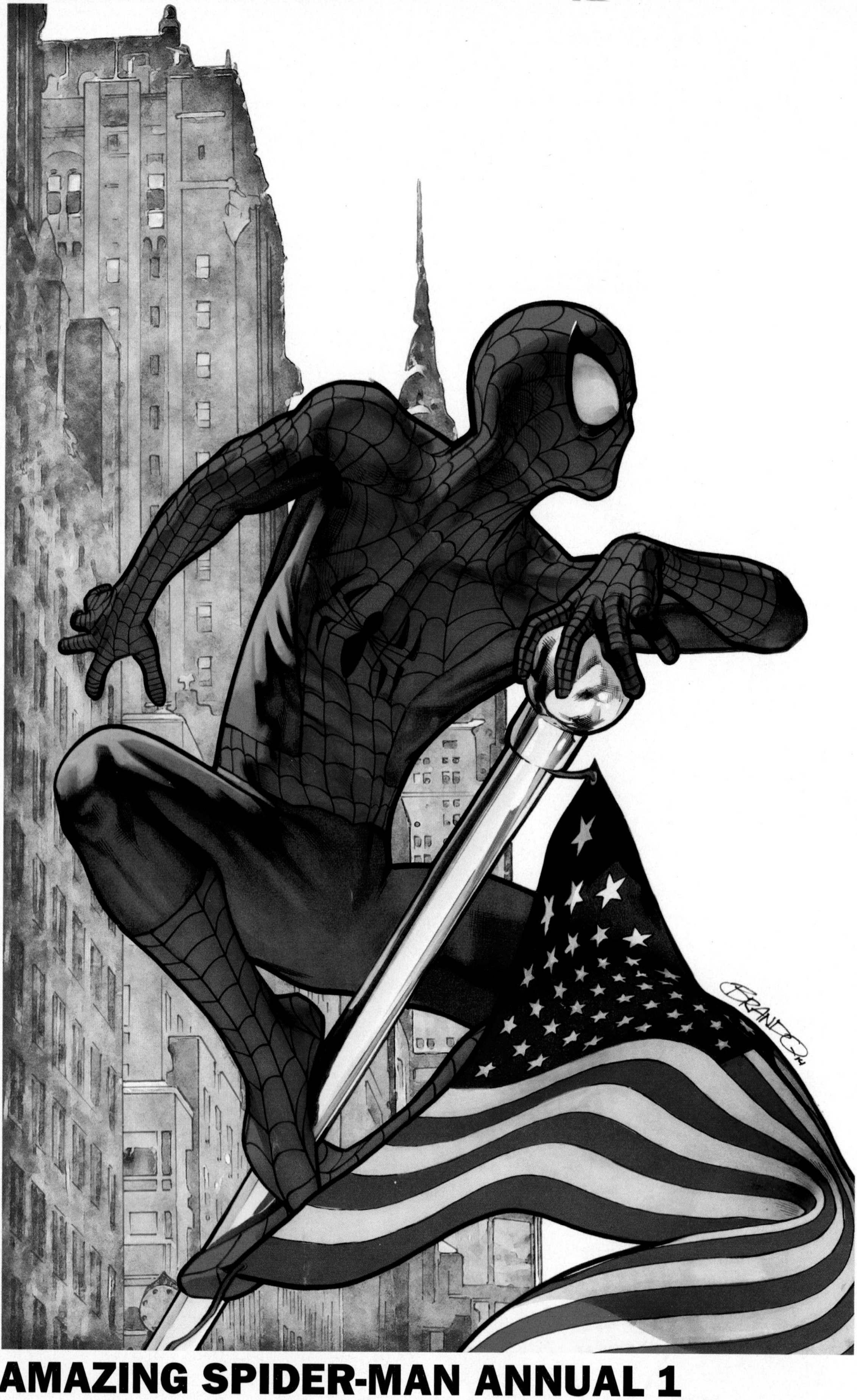
BRANDO

AMAZING SPIDER-MAN ANNUAL 1

PETER?! PETER?!

HEY, SAJANI, WHAT'S GOING ON?

WHERE YOU GOING?

IT'S QUITTING TIME. I'M BEAT, HEADING HOME.

DID YOU GET A CHANCE TO READ THAT REPORT ABOUT THE UTILIZATION OF MICROSCOPIC ELECTRODES IN THE THREE-DIMENSIONAL PRINTING OF LITHIUM ION BATTERIES?

YES?

PETER, PLEASE GIVE IT A READ? I'LL E-MAIL IT TO YOU AGAIN.

WE NEED TO GET YOUR TWO CENTS TOMORROW MORNING SO THE TEAM CAN FINALLY MOVE FORWARD.

OF COURSE, FOR SURE. I'M GOING STRAIGHT HOME.

I'LL BE PUTTING ON MY SILK JAMMYS, POPPING OPEN A PINT OF ROCKY ROAD AND THEN I'LL CURL RIGHT UP AND READ THAT FANTASTIC REPORT.

JUST READ IT, OKAY?

WILL DO. GOOD NIGHT.

GO STRAIGHT HOME. READ THE REPORT.

GO STRAIGHT HOME. READ THE REPORT.

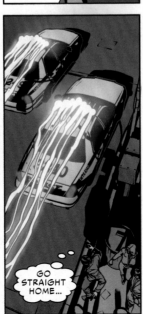

GO STRAIGHT HOME...

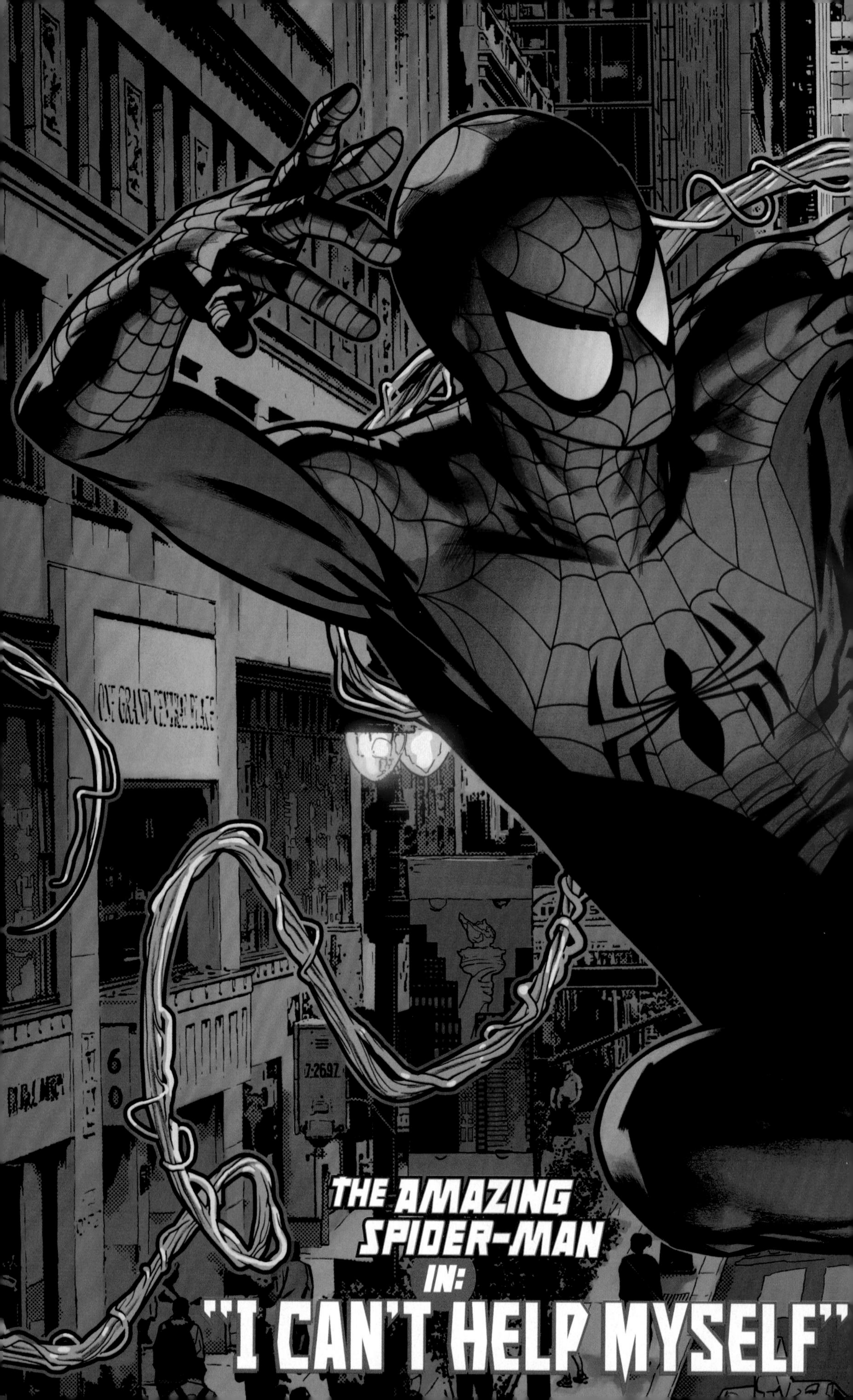
ONE GRAND CENTRAL PLACE
THE AMAZING SPIDER-MAN IN:
"I CAN'T HELP MYSELF"

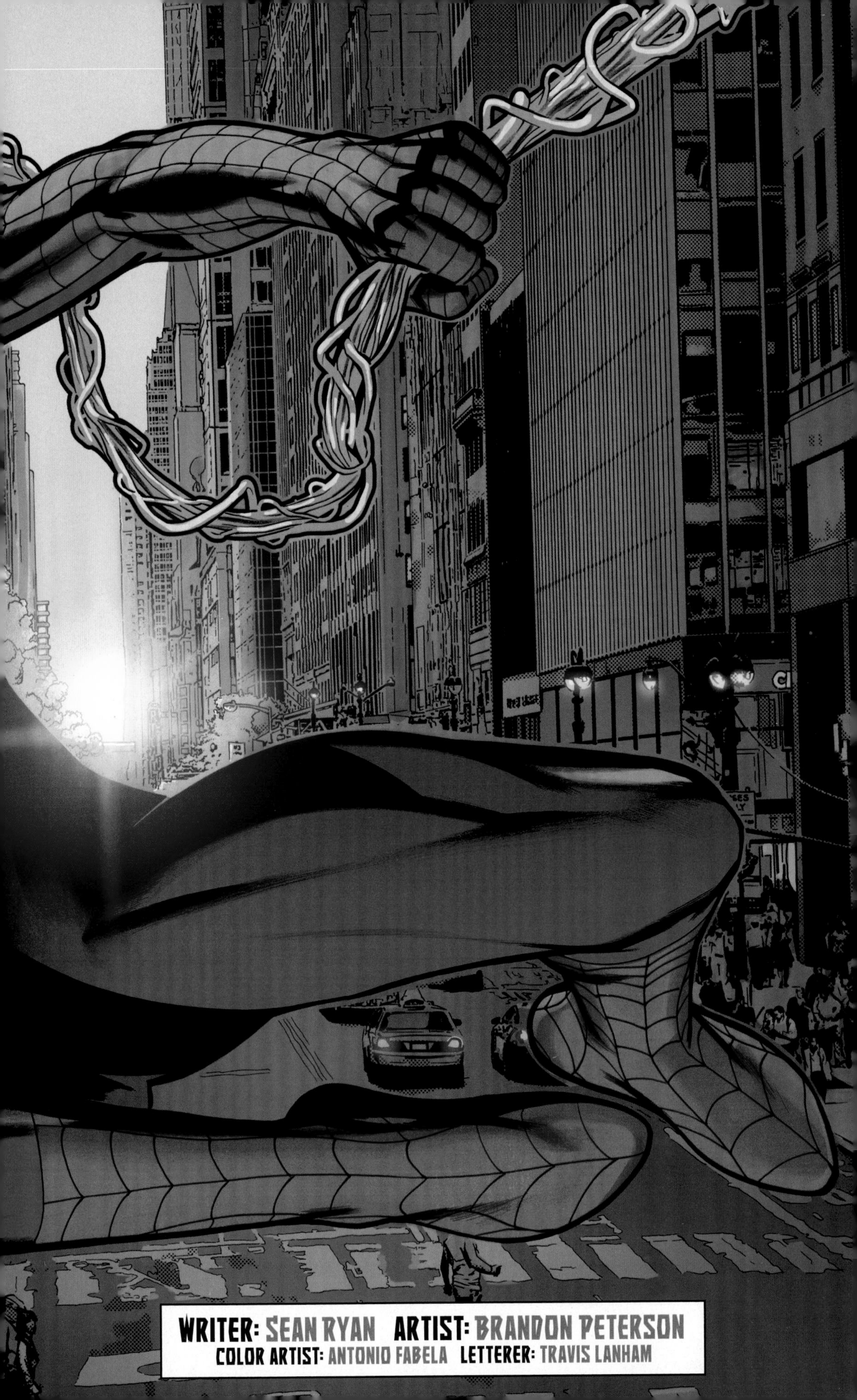
WRITER: SEAN RYAN ARTIST: BRANDON PETERSON
COLOR ARTIST: ANTONIO FABELA LETTERER: TRAVIS LANHAM

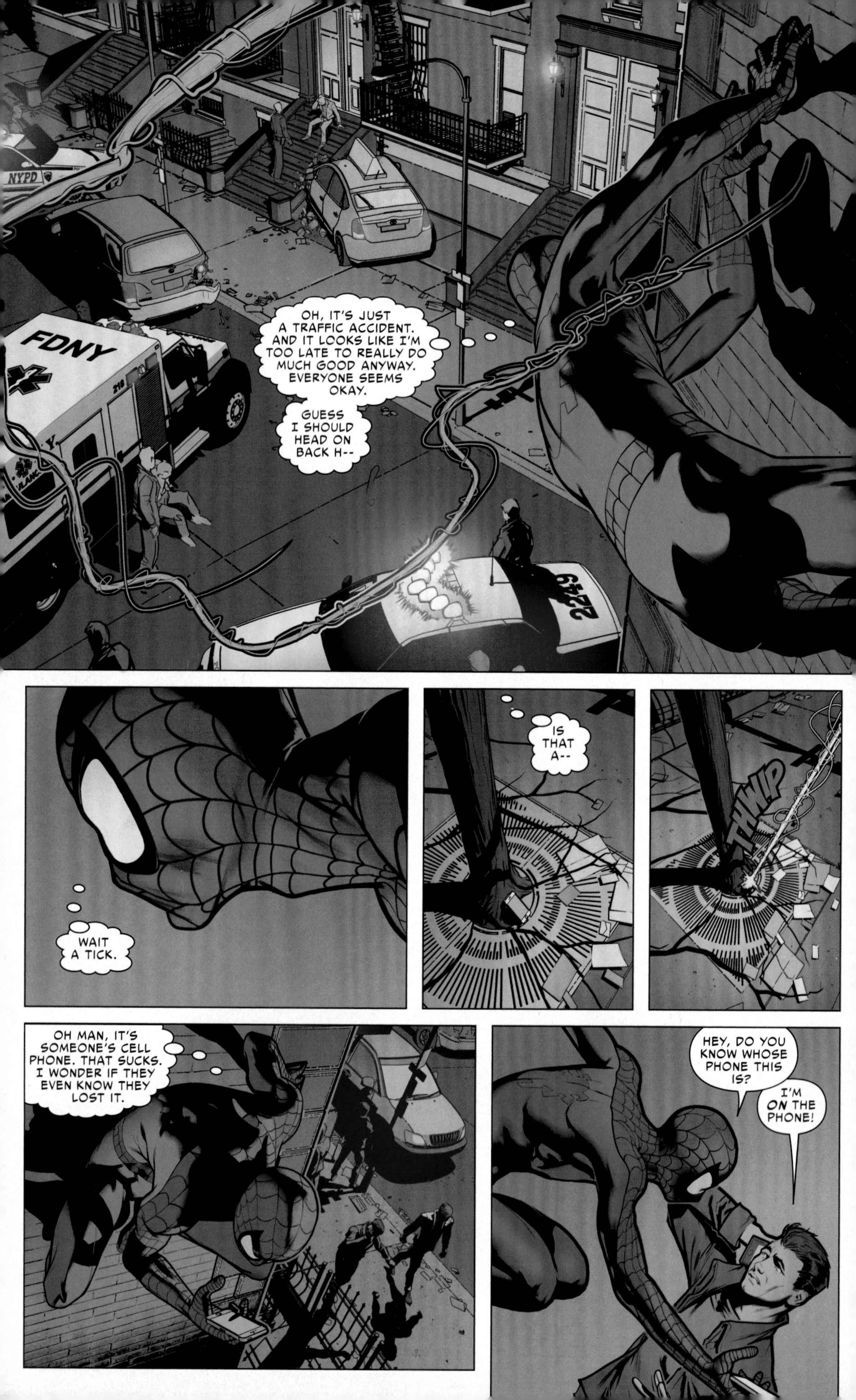
OH, IT'S JUST A TRAFFIC ACCIDENT. AND IT LOOKS LIKE I'M TOO LATE TO REALLY DO MUCH GOOD ANYWAY. EVERYONE SEEMS OKAY.
GUESS I SHOULD HEAD ON BACK H--
WAIT A TICK.
IS THAT A--
THWIP
OH MAN, IT'S SOMEONE'S CELL PHONE. THAT SUCKS. I WONDER IF THEY EVEN KNOW THEY LOST IT.
HEY, DO YOU KNOW WHOSE PHONE THIS IS?
I'M *ON* THE PHONE!

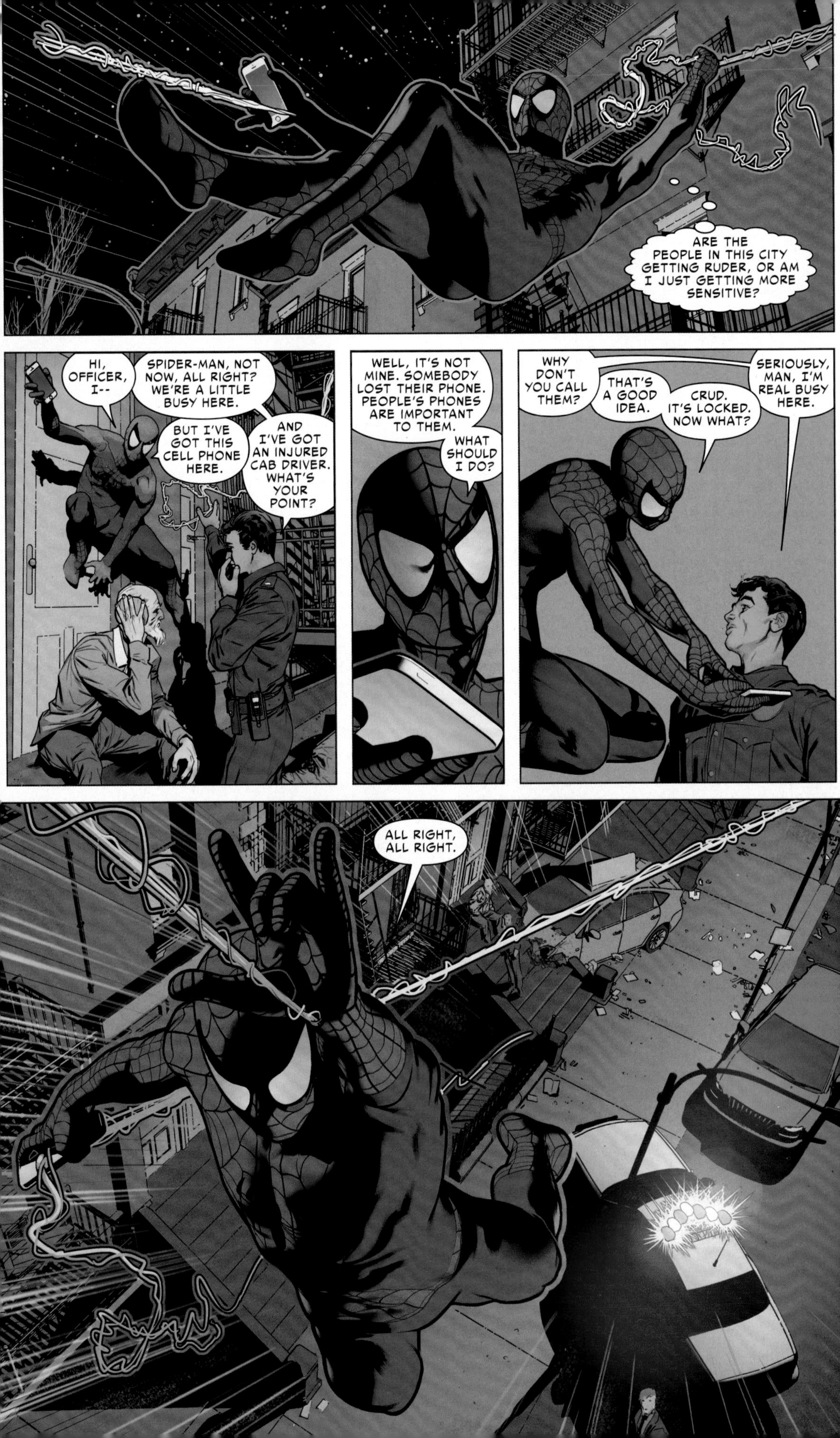
ARE THE PEOPLE IN THIS CITY GETTING RUDER, OR AM I JUST GETTING MORE SENSITIVE?
HI, OFFICER, I--
SPIDER-MAN, NOT NOW, ALL RIGHT? WE'RE A LITTLE BUSY HERE.
BUT I'VE GOT THIS CELL PHONE HERE.
AND I'VE GOT AN INJURED CAB DRIVER. WHAT'S YOUR POINT?
WELL, IT'S NOT MINE. SOMEBODY LOST THEIR PHONE. PEOPLE'S PHONES ARE IMPORTANT TO THEM.
WHAT SHOULD I DO?
WHY DON'T YOU CALL THEM?
THAT'S A GOOD IDEA.
CRUD. IT'S LOCKED. NOW WHAT?
SERIOUSLY, MAN, I'M REAL BUSY HERE.
ALL RIGHT, ALL RIGHT.

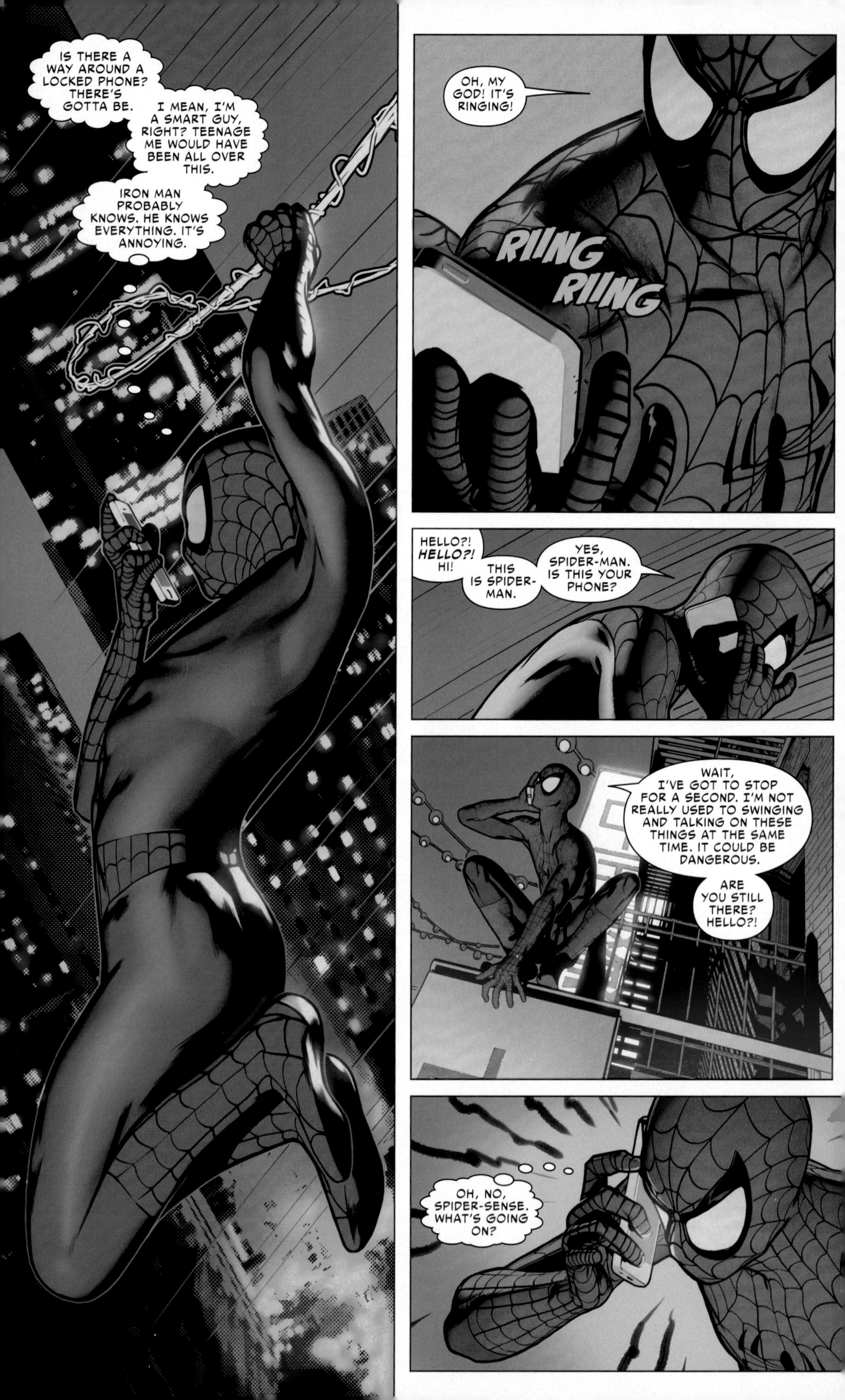
IS THERE A WAY AROUND A LOCKED PHONE? THERE'S GOTTA BE.
I MEAN, I'M A SMART GUY, RIGHT? TEENAGE ME WOULD HAVE BEEN ALL OVER THIS.
IRON MAN PROBABLY KNOWS. HE KNOWS EVERYTHING. IT'S ANNOYING.
OH, MY GOD! IT'S RINGING!
RIING RIING
HELLO?! HELLO?! HI!
THIS IS SPIDER-MAN.
YES, SPIDER-MAN. IS THIS YOUR PHONE?
WAIT, I'VE GOT TO STOP FOR A SECOND. I'M NOT REALLY USED TO SWINGING AND TALKING ON THESE THINGS AT THE SAME TIME. IT COULD BE DANGEROUS.
ARE YOU STILL THERE? HELLO?!
OH, NO, SPIDER-SENSE. WHAT'S GOING ON?

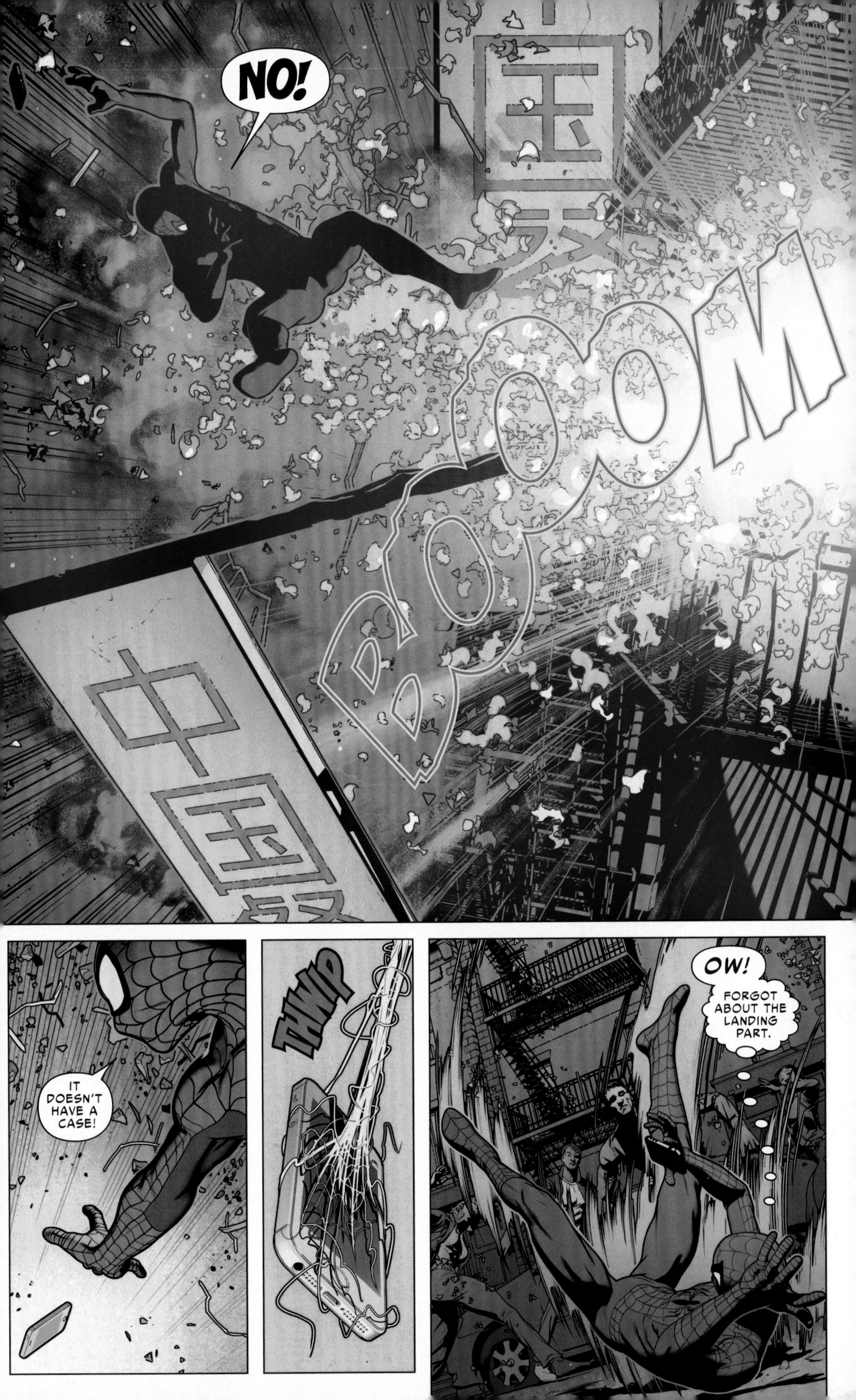
NO!
BOOOM
中国
IT DOESN'T HAVE A CASE!
THWIP
OW!
FORGOT ABOUT THE LANDING PART.

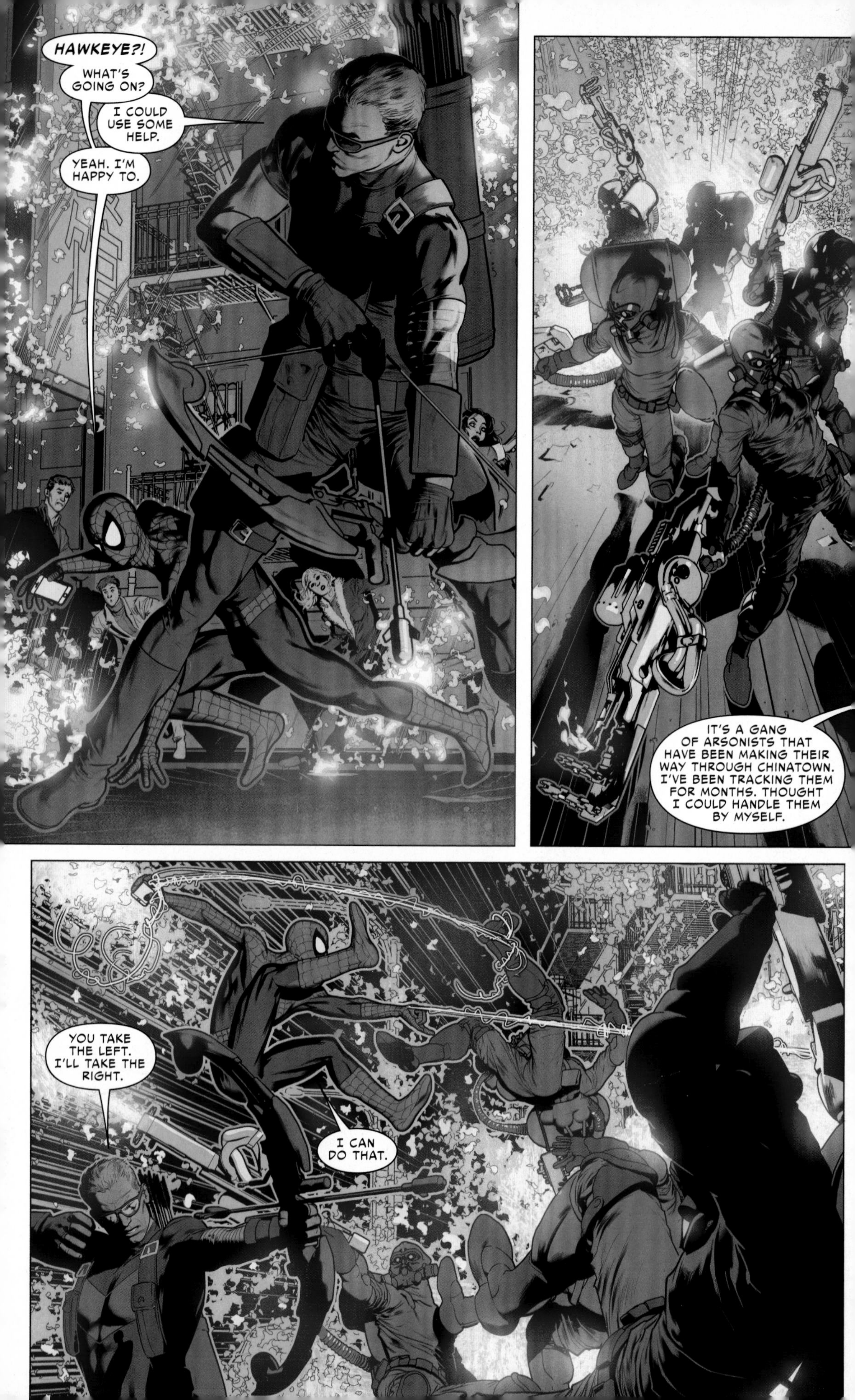
HAWKEYE?!
WHAT'S GOING ON?
I COULD USE SOME HELP.
YEAH. I'M HAPPY TO.
IT'S A GANG OF ARSONISTS THAT HAVE BEEN MAKING THEIR WAY THROUGH CHINATOWN. I'VE BEEN TRACKING THEM FOR MONTHS. THOUGHT I COULD HANDLE THEM BY MYSELF.
YOU TAKE THE LEFT. I'LL TAKE THE RIGHT.
I CAN DO THAT.

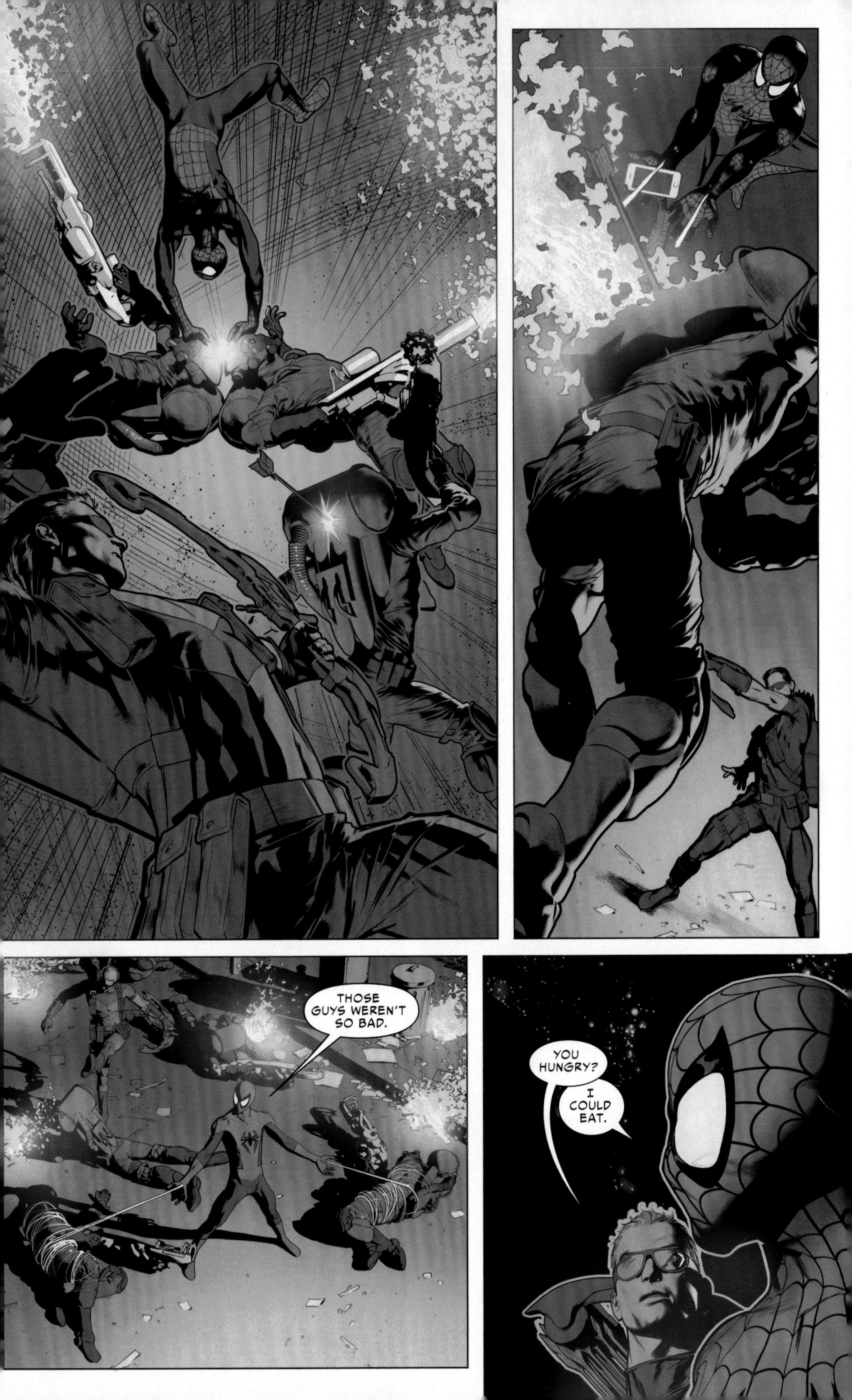
THOSE GUYS WEREN'T SO BAD.
YOU HUNGRY?
I COULD EAT.

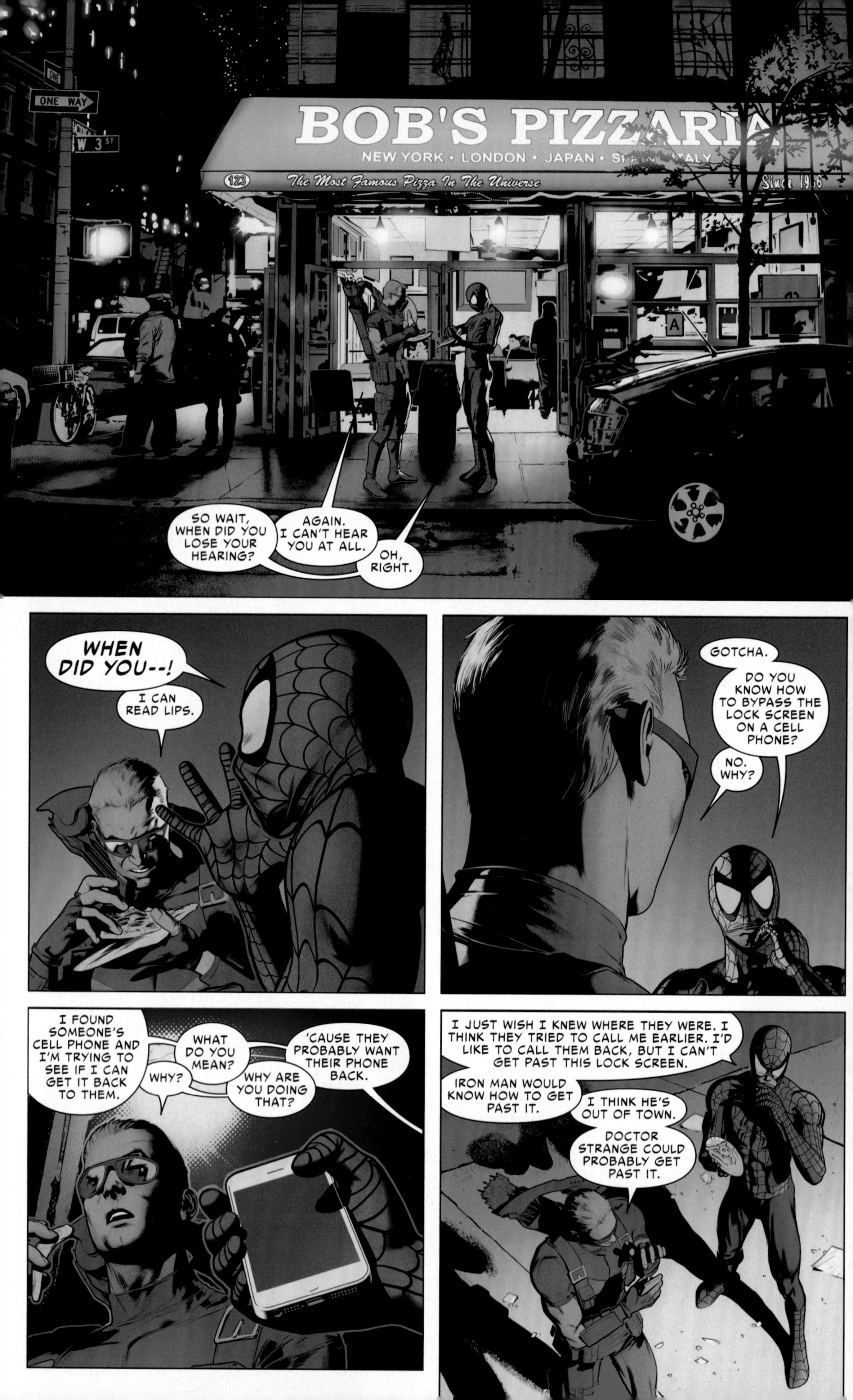
ONE WAY
W 3 ST
BOB'S PIZZARIA
The Most Famous Pizza In The Universe
SO WAIT, WHEN DID YOU LOSE YOUR HEARING?
AGAIN. I CAN'T HEAR YOU AT ALL.
OH, RIGHT.
WHEN DID YOU--!
I CAN READ LIPS.
GOTCHA.
DO YOU KNOW HOW TO BYPASS THE LOCK SCREEN ON A CELL PHONE?
NO. WHY?
I FOUND SOMEONE'S CELL PHONE AND I'M TRYING TO SEE IF I CAN GET IT BACK TO THEM.
WHY?
WHAT DO YOU MEAN?
WHY ARE YOU DOING THAT?
'CAUSE THEY PROBABLY WANT THEIR PHONE BACK.
I JUST WISH I KNEW WHERE THEY WERE. I THINK THEY TRIED TO CALL ME EARLIER. I'D LIKE TO CALL THEM BACK, BUT I CAN'T GET PAST THIS LOCK SCREEN.
IRON MAN WOULD KNOW HOW TO GET PAST IT.
I THINK HE'S OUT OF TOWN.
DOCTOR STRANGE COULD PROBABLY GET PAST IT.

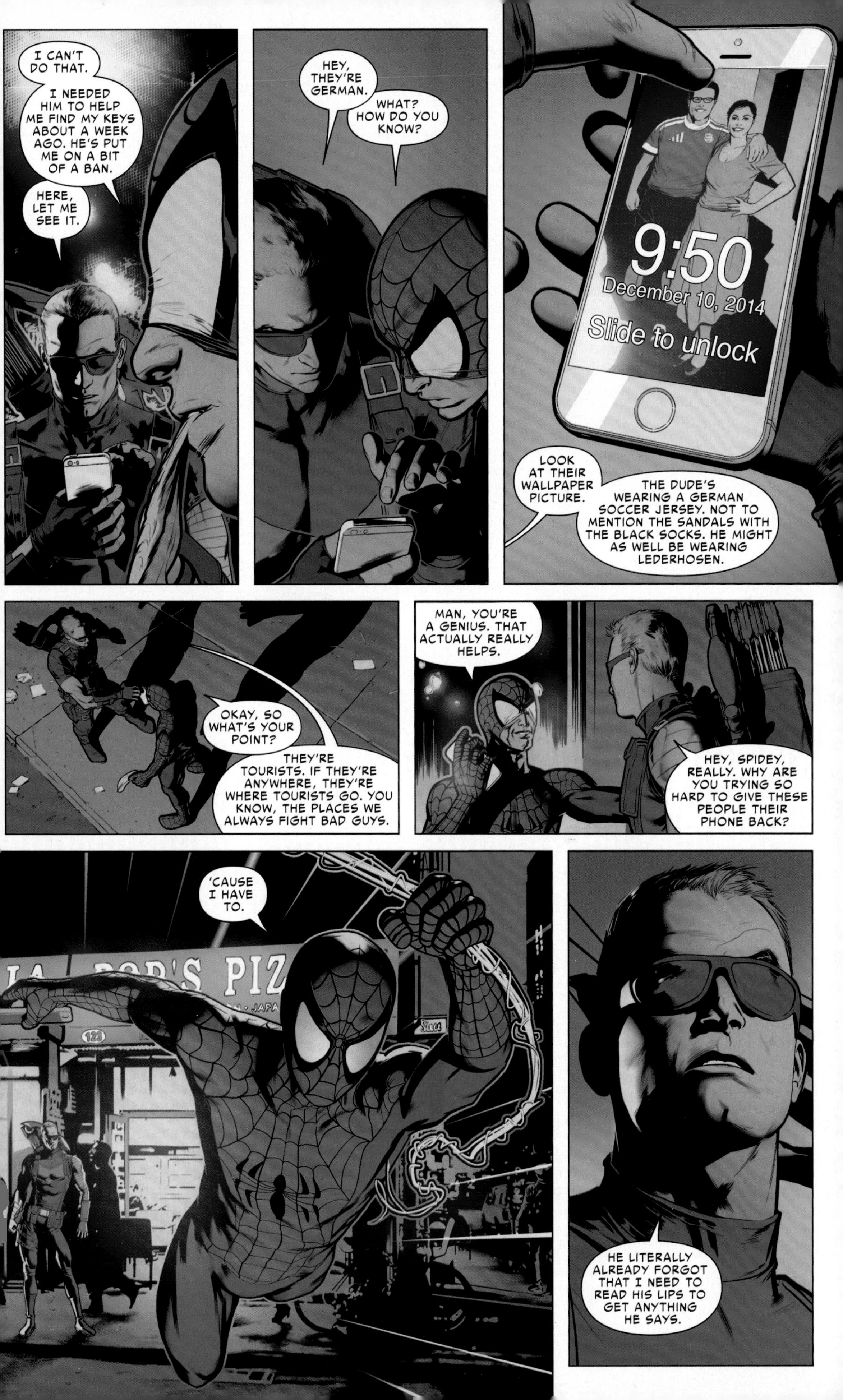
I CAN'T DO THAT.
I NEEDED HIM TO HELP ME FIND MY KEYS ABOUT A WEEK AGO. HE'S PUT ME ON A BIT OF A BAN.
HERE, LET ME SEE IT.
HEY, THEY'RE GERMAN.
WHAT? HOW DO YOU KNOW?
9:50
December 10, 2014
Slide to unlock
LOOK AT THEIR WALLPAPER PICTURE.
THE DUDE'S WEARING A GERMAN SOCCER JERSEY. NOT TO MENTION THE SANDALS WITH THE BLACK SOCKS. HE MIGHT AS WELL BE WEARING LEDERHOSEN.
OKAY, SO WHAT'S YOUR POINT?
THEY'RE TOURISTS. IF THEY'RE ANYWHERE, THEY'RE WHERE TOURISTS GO. YOU KNOW, THE PLACES WE ALWAYS FIGHT BAD GUYS.
MAN, YOU'RE A GENIUS. THAT ACTUALLY REALLY HELPS.
HEY, SPIDEY, REALLY. WHY ARE YOU TRYING SO HARD TO GIVE THESE PEOPLE THEIR PHONE BACK?
'CAUSE I HAVE TO.
HE LITERALLY ALREADY FORGOT THAT I NEED TO READ HIS LIPS TO GET ANYTHING HE SAYS.

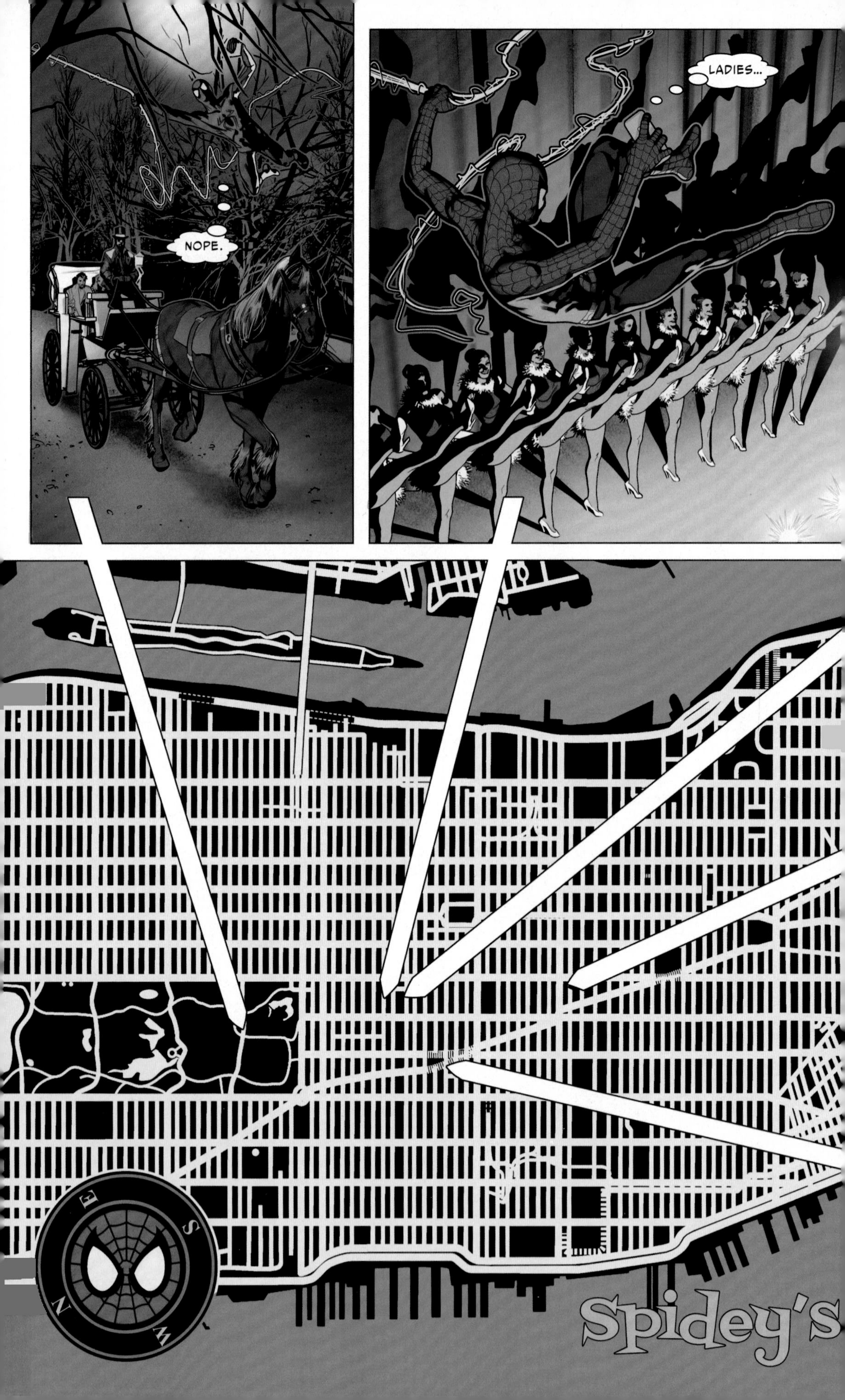

NOPE.
LADIES...
Spidey's

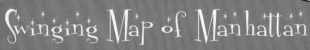

Swinging Map of Manhattan

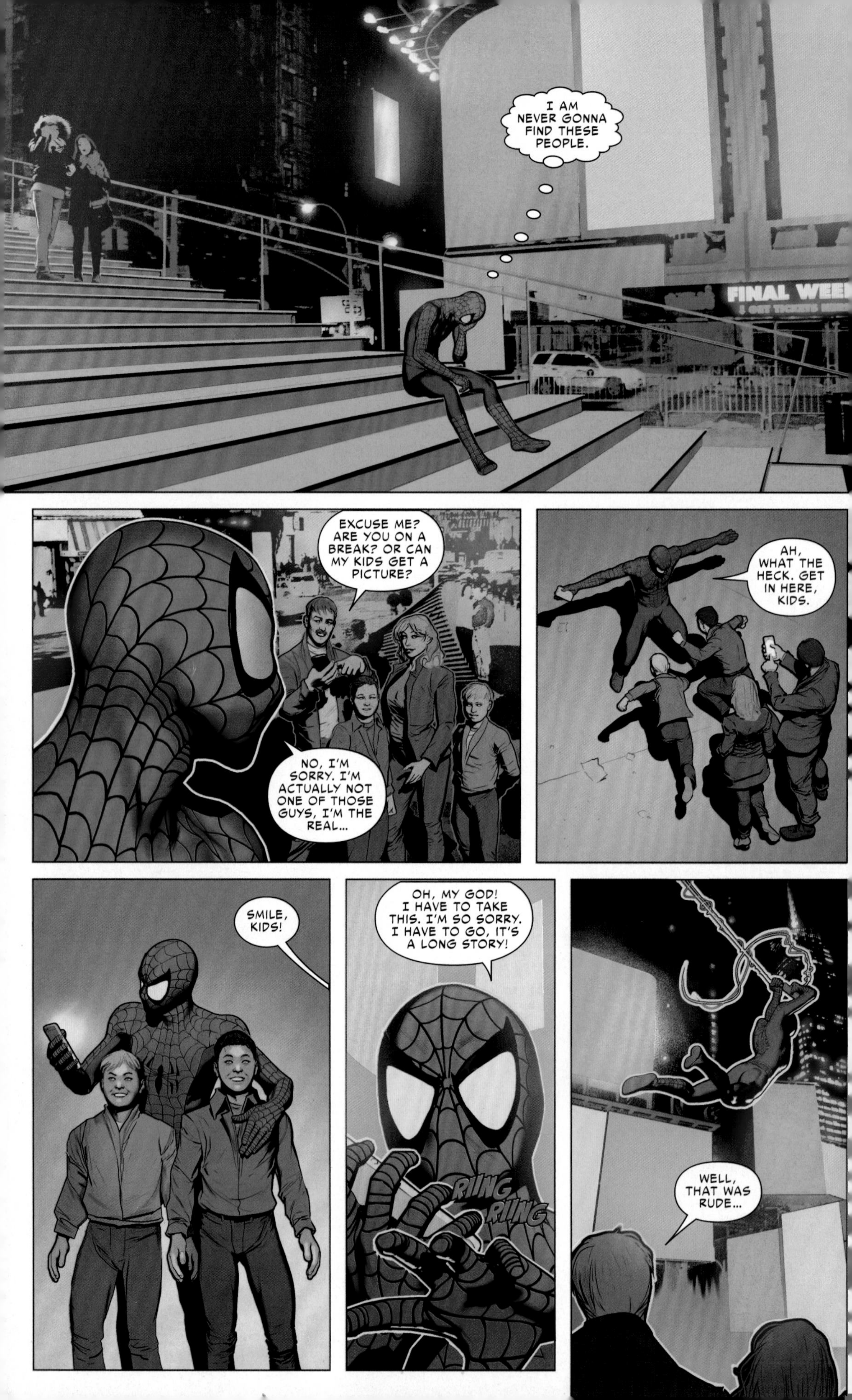
I AM NEVER GONNA FIND THESE PEOPLE.
FINAL WEE
EXCUSE ME? ARE YOU ON A BREAK? OR CAN MY KIDS GET A PICTURE?
NO, I'M SORRY. I'M ACTUALLY NOT ONE OF THOSE GUYS, I'M THE REAL...
AH, WHAT THE HECK. GET IN HERE, KIDS.
SMILE, KIDS!
OH, MY GOD! I HAVE TO TAKE THIS. I'M SO SORRY. I HAVE TO GO, IT'S A LONG STORY!
RIING RIING
WELL, THAT WAS RUDE...

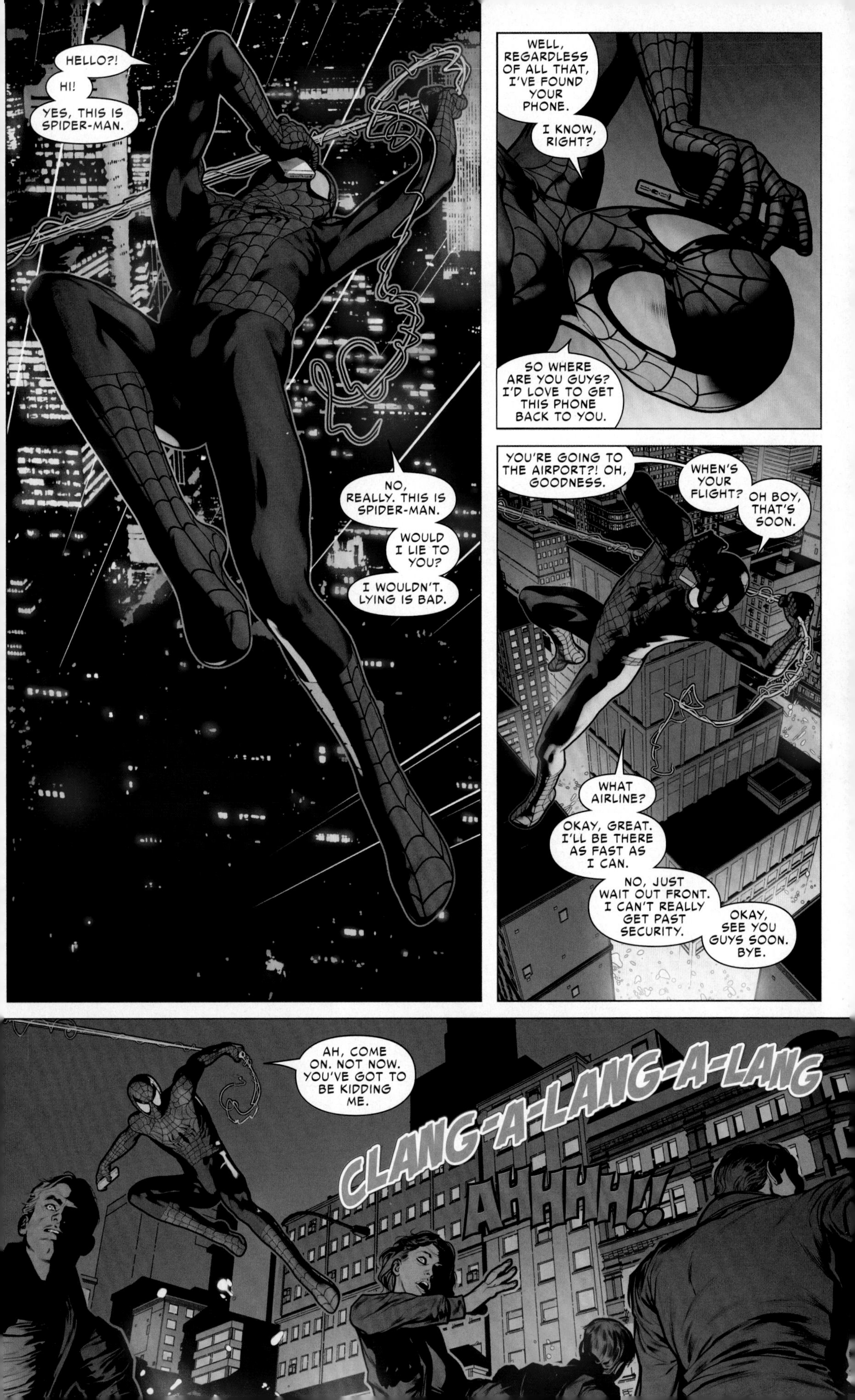
HELLO?!
HI!
YES, THIS IS SPIDER-MAN.
NO, REALLY. THIS IS SPIDER-MAN.
WOULD I LIE TO YOU?
I WOULDN'T. LYING IS BAD.
WELL, REGARDLESS OF ALL THAT, I'VE FOUND YOUR PHONE.
I KNOW, RIGHT?
SO WHERE ARE YOU GUYS? I'D LOVE TO GET THIS PHONE BACK TO YOU.
YOU'RE GOING TO THE AIRPORT?! OH, GOODNESS.
WHEN'S YOUR FLIGHT?
OH BOY, THAT'S SOON.
WHAT AIRLINE?
OKAY, GREAT. I'LL BE THERE AS FAST AS I CAN.
NO, JUST WAIT OUT FRONT. I CAN'T REALLY GET PAST SECURITY.
OKAY, SEE YOU GUYS SOON. BYE.
AH, COME ON. NOT NOW. YOU'VE GOT TO BE KIDDING ME.
CLANG-A-LANG-A-LANG
AHHHH!!

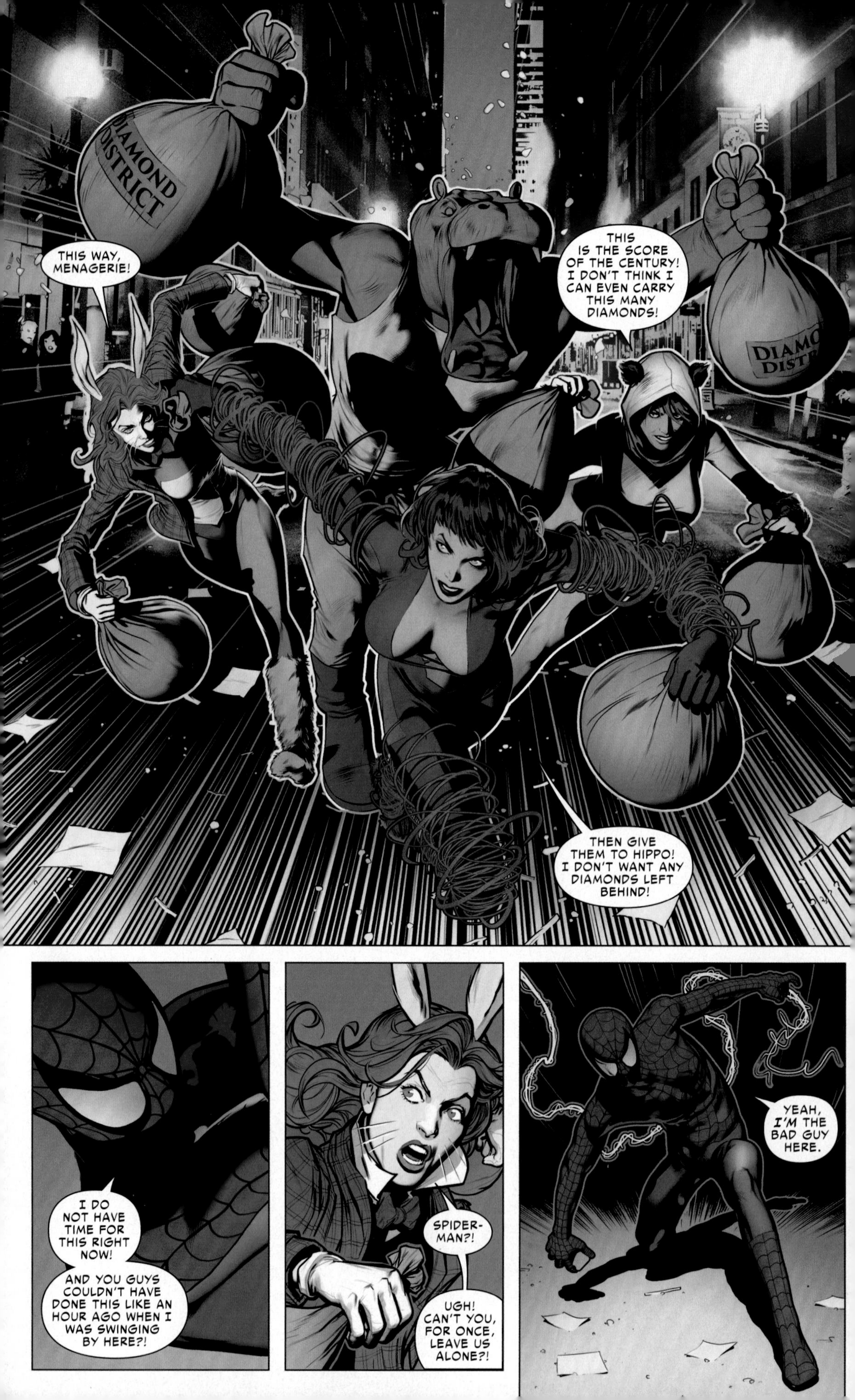
DIAMOND DISTRICT
THIS WAY, MENAGERIE!
THIS IS THE SCORE OF THE CENTURY! I DON'T THINK I CAN EVEN CARRY THIS MANY DIAMONDS!
THEN GIVE THEM TO HIPPO! I DON'T WANT ANY DIAMONDS LEFT BEHIND!
I DO NOT HAVE TIME FOR THIS RIGHT NOW!
AND YOU GUYS COULDN'T HAVE DONE THIS LIKE AN HOUR AGO WHEN I WAS SWINGING BY HERE?!
SPIDER-MAN?!
UGH! CAN'T YOU, FOR ONCE, LEAVE US ALONE?!
YEAH, I'M THE BAD GUY HERE.

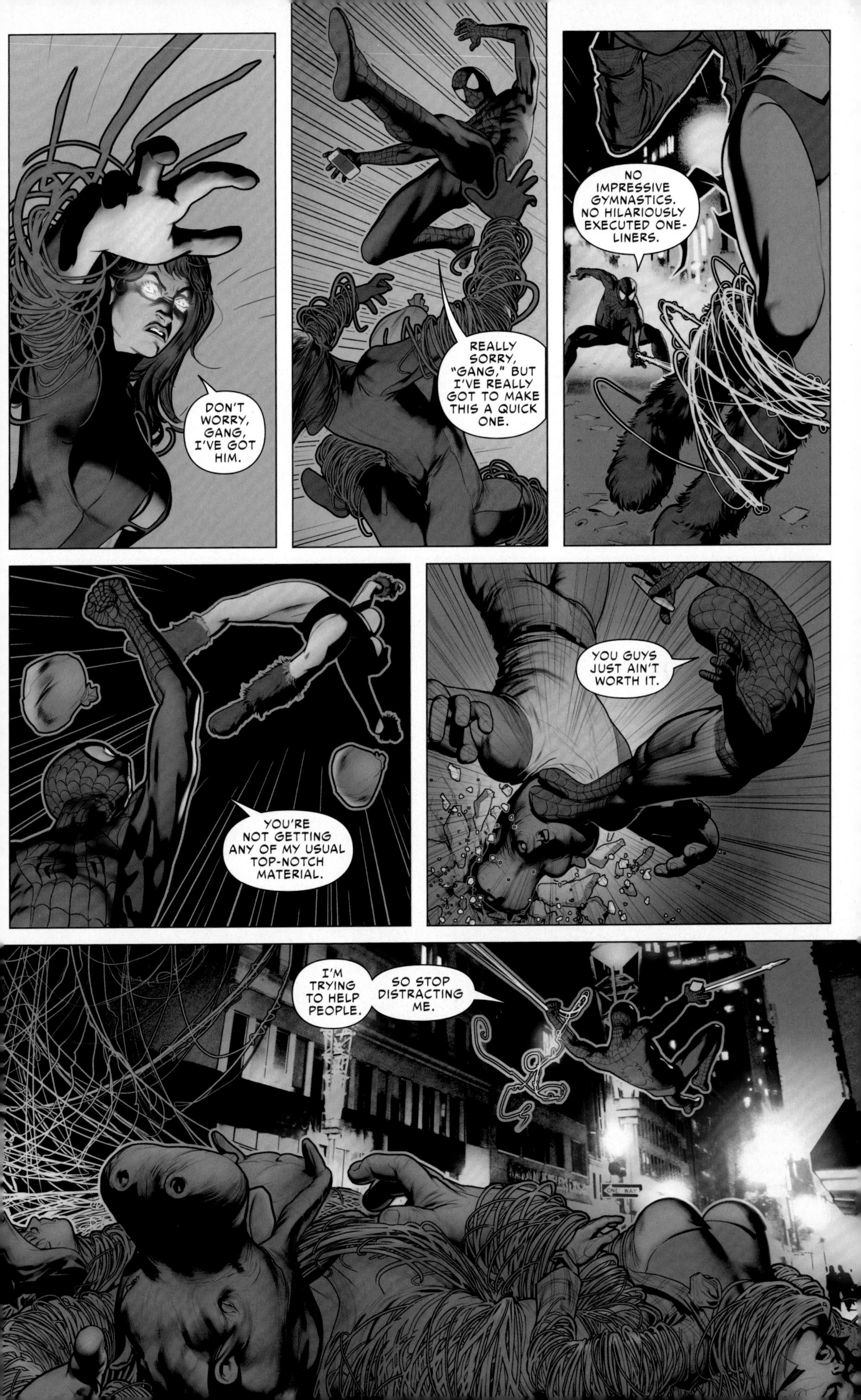
DON'T WORRY, GANG, I'VE GOT HIM.
REALLY SORRY, "GANG," BUT I'VE REALLY GOT TO MAKE THIS A QUICK ONE.
NO IMPRESSIVE GYMNASTICS. NO HILARIOUSLY EXECUTED ONE-LINERS.
YOU'RE NOT GETTING ANY OF MY USUAL TOP-NOTCH MATERIAL.
YOU GUYS JUST AIN'T WORTH IT.
I'M TRYING TO HELP PEOPLE.
SO STOP DISTRACTING ME.
ONE WAY

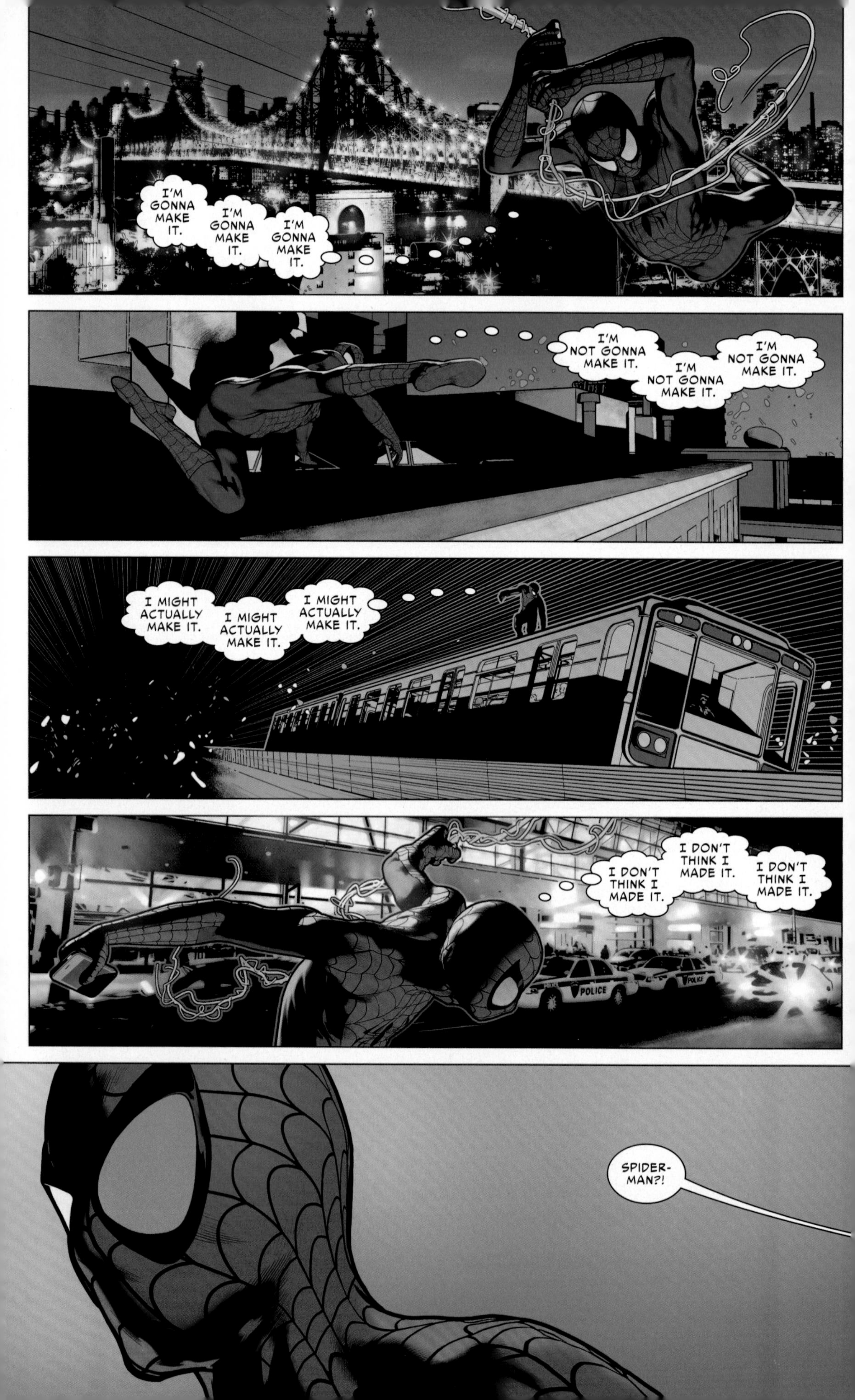
I'M GONNA MAKE IT.
I'M GONNA MAKE IT.
I'M GONNA MAKE IT.
I'M NOT GONNA MAKE IT.
I'M NOT GONNA MAKE IT.
I'M NOT GONNA MAKE IT.
I MIGHT ACTUALLY MAKE IT.
I MIGHT ACTUALLY MAKE IT.
I MIGHT ACTUALLY MAKE IT.
I DON'T THINK I MADE IT.
I DON'T THINK I MADE IT.
I DON'T THINK I MADE IT.
SPIDER-MAN?!

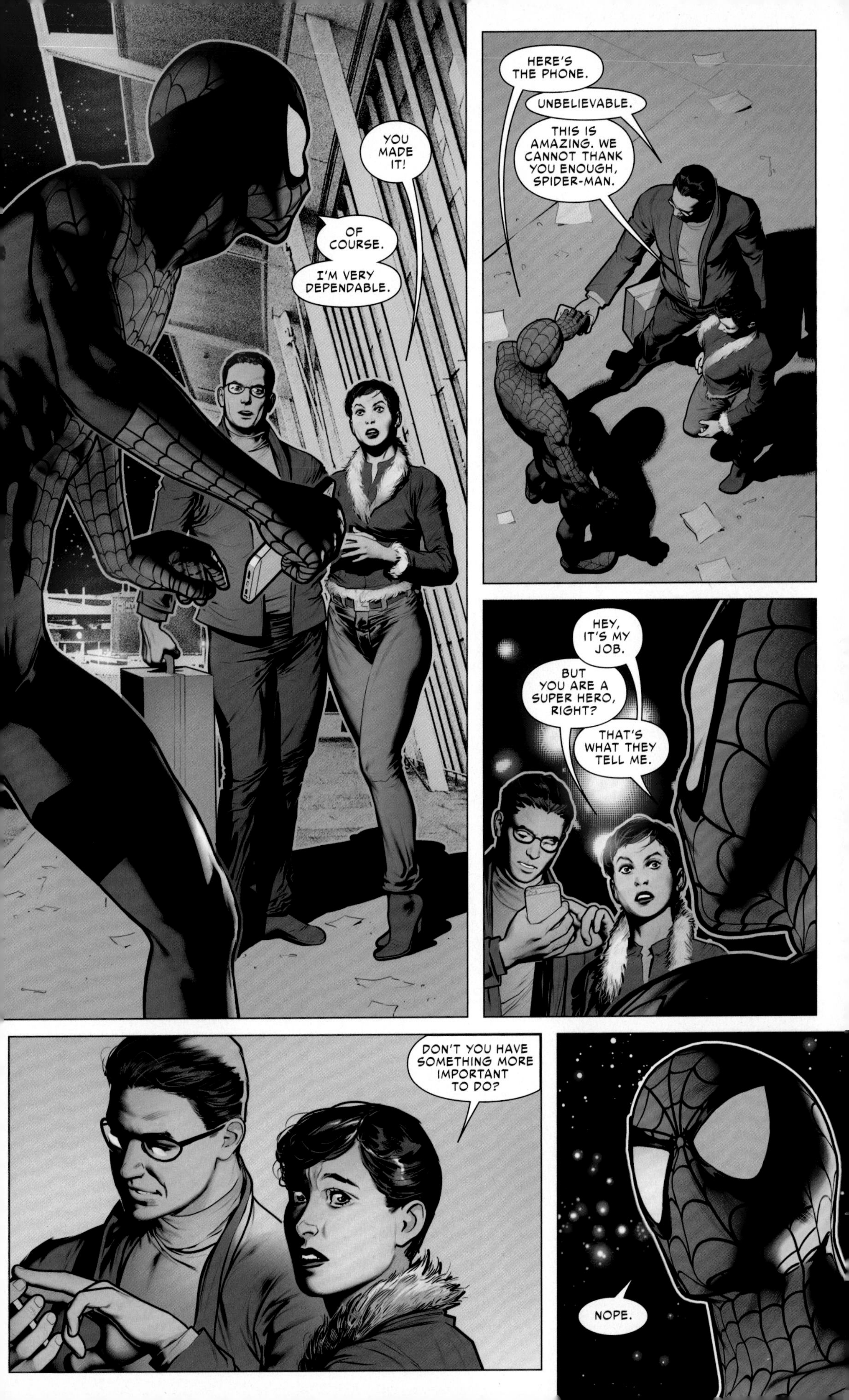
YOU MADE IT!
OF COURSE.
I'M VERY DEPENDABLE.
HERE'S THE PHONE.
UNBELIEVABLE.
THIS IS AMAZING. WE CANNOT THANK YOU ENOUGH, SPIDER-MAN.
HEY, IT'S MY JOB.
BUT YOU ARE A SUPER HERO, RIGHT?
THAT'S WHAT THEY TELL ME.
DON'T YOU HAVE SOMETHING MORE IMPORTANT TO DO?
NOPE.

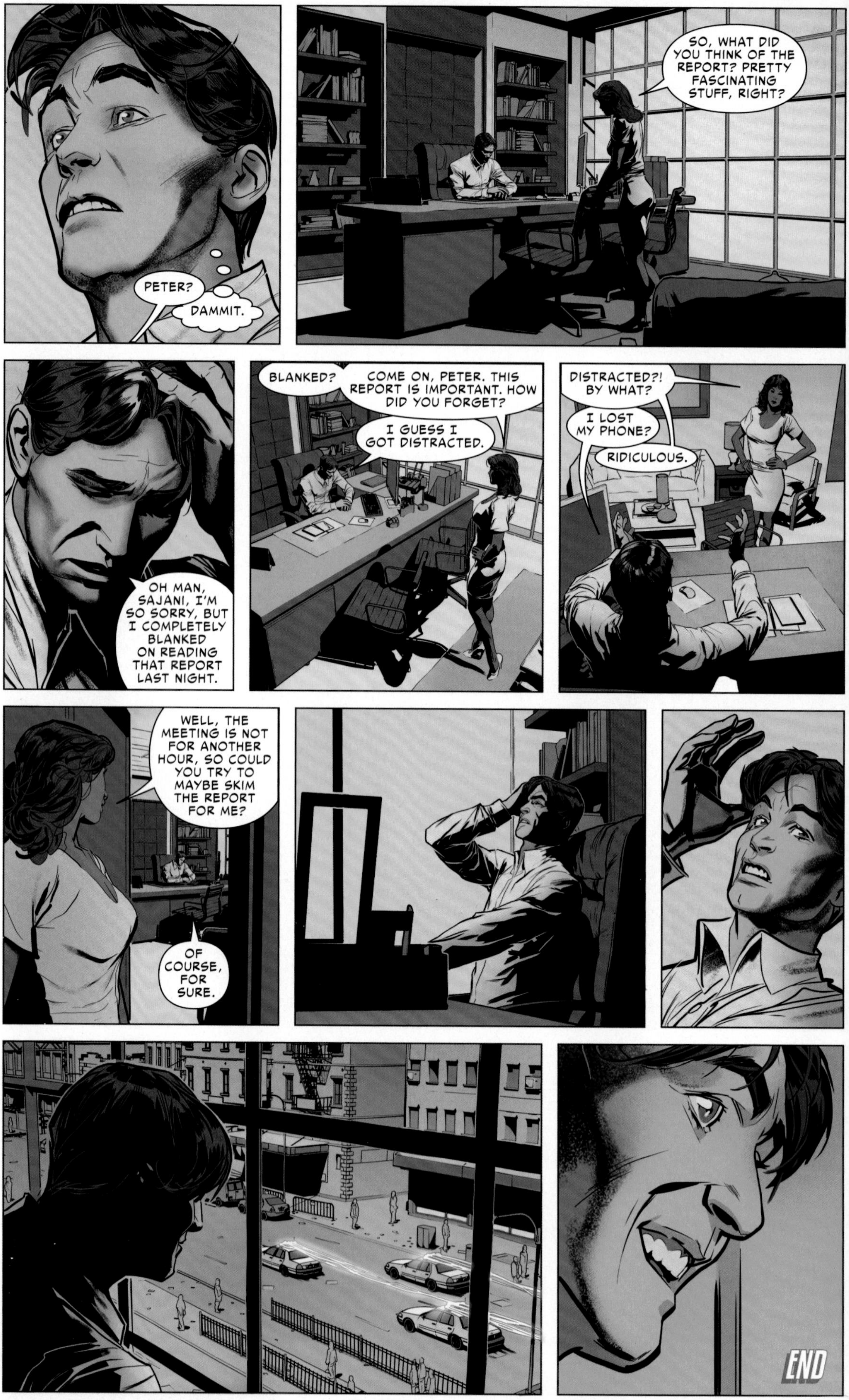
PETER?
DAMMIT.
SO, WHAT DID YOU THINK OF THE REPORT? PRETTY FASCINATING STUFF, RIGHT?
OH MAN, SAJANI, I'M SO SORRY, BUT I COMPLETELY BLANKED ON READING THAT REPORT LAST NIGHT.
BLANKED?
COME ON, PETER. THIS REPORT IS IMPORTANT. HOW DID YOU FORGET?
I GUESS I GOT DISTRACTED.
DISTRACTED?! BY WHAT?
I LOST MY PHONE?
RIDICULOUS.
WELL, THE MEETING IS NOT FOR ANOTHER HOUR, SO COULD YOU TRY TO MAYBE SKIM THE REPORT FOR ME?
OF COURSE, FOR SURE.
END

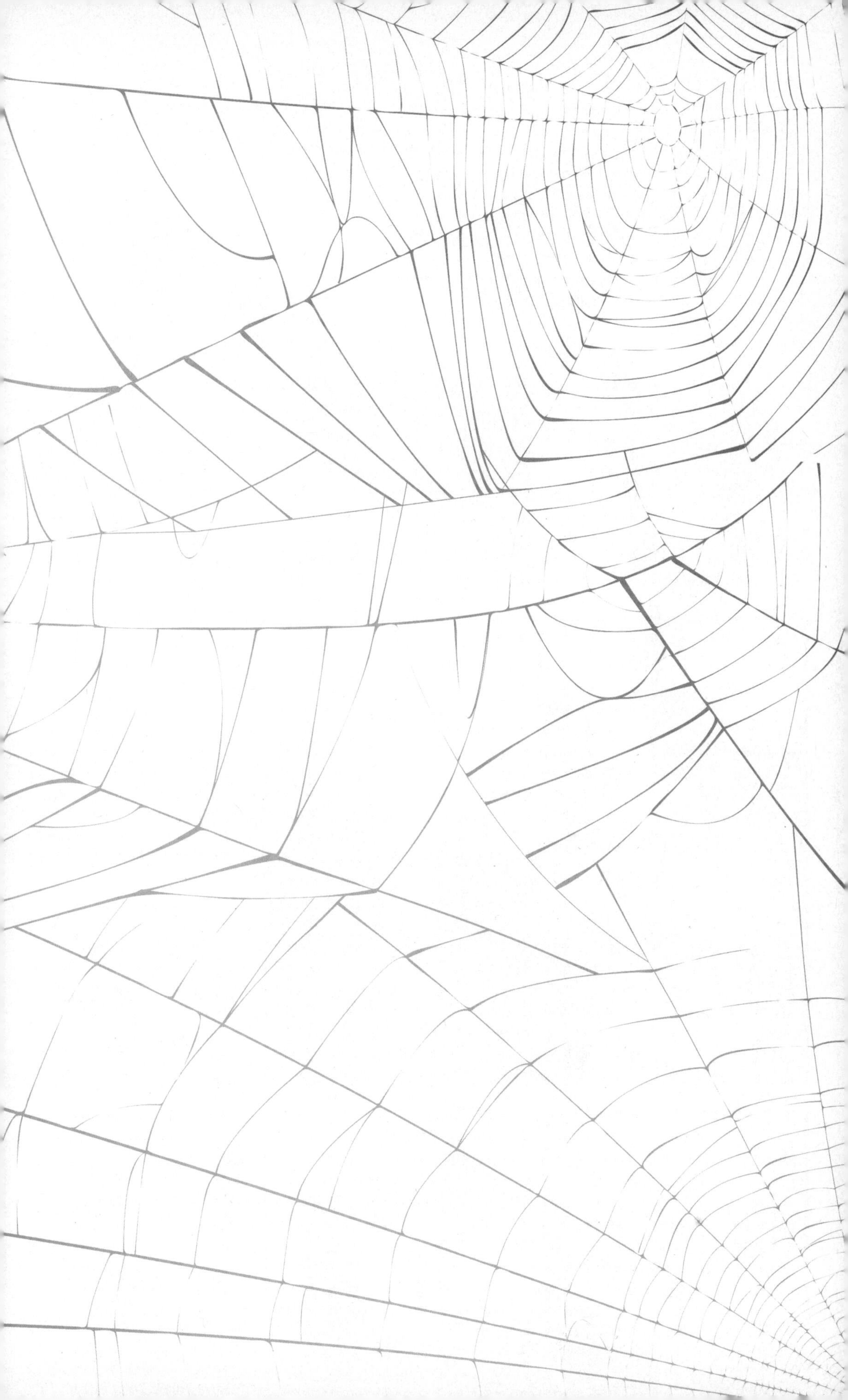

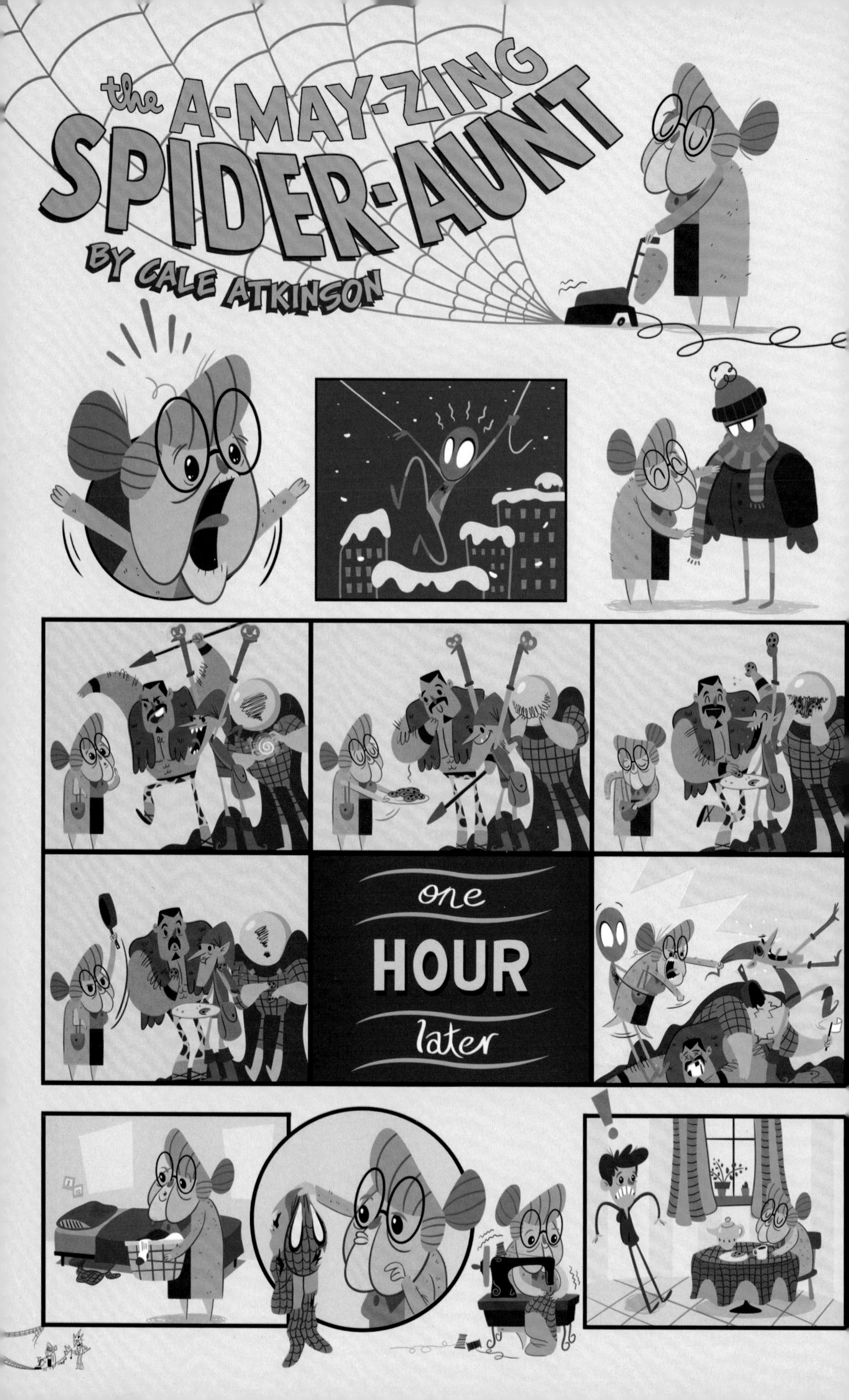
the A-MAY-ZING SPIDER-AUNT
BY CALE ATKINSON
one HOUR later

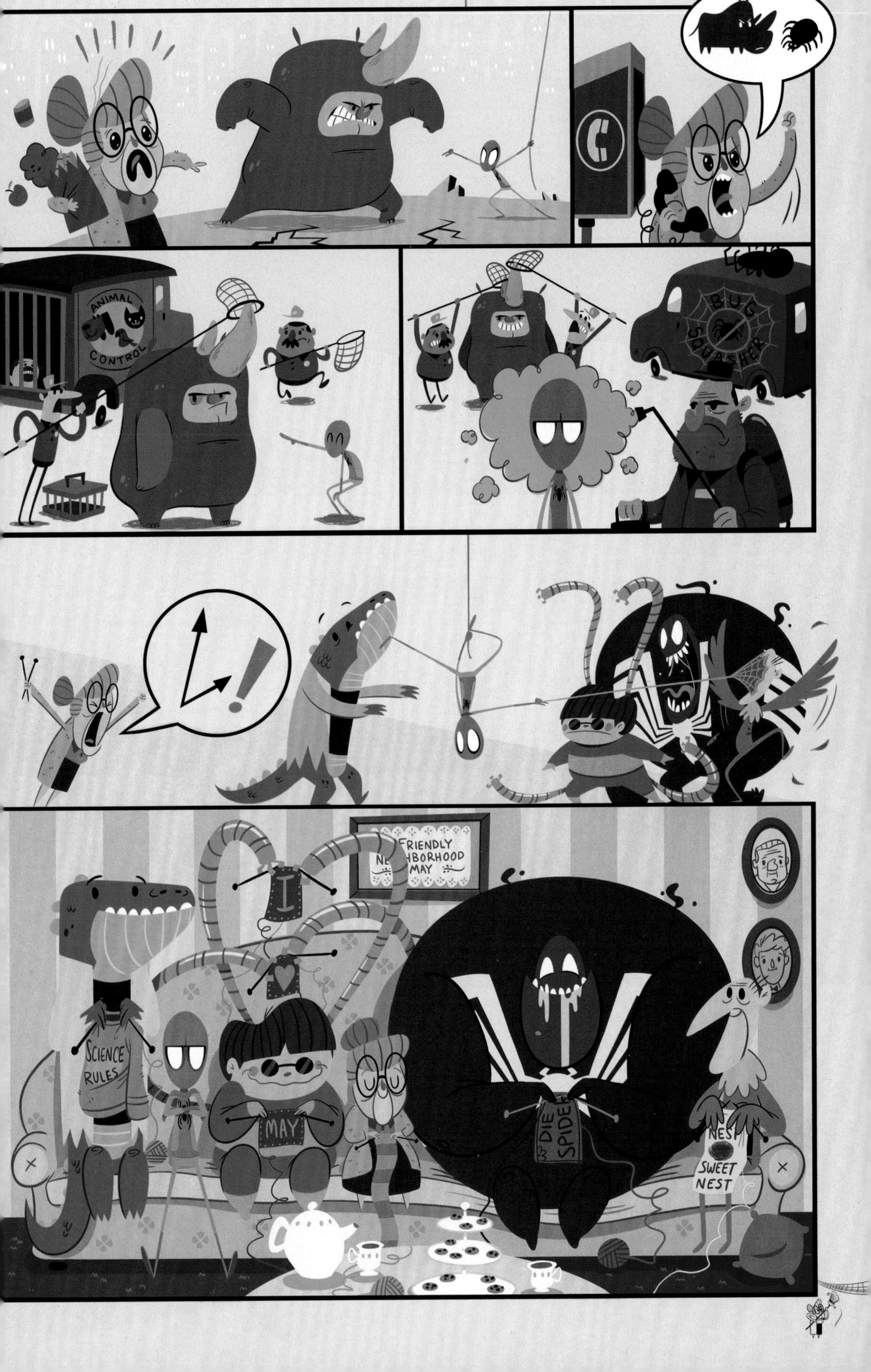
ANIMAL CONTROL
BUG SQUASHER
FRIENDLY
NE HBORHOOD
MAY
SCIENCE RULES
MAY
DIE SPIDE
NEST
SWEET NEST

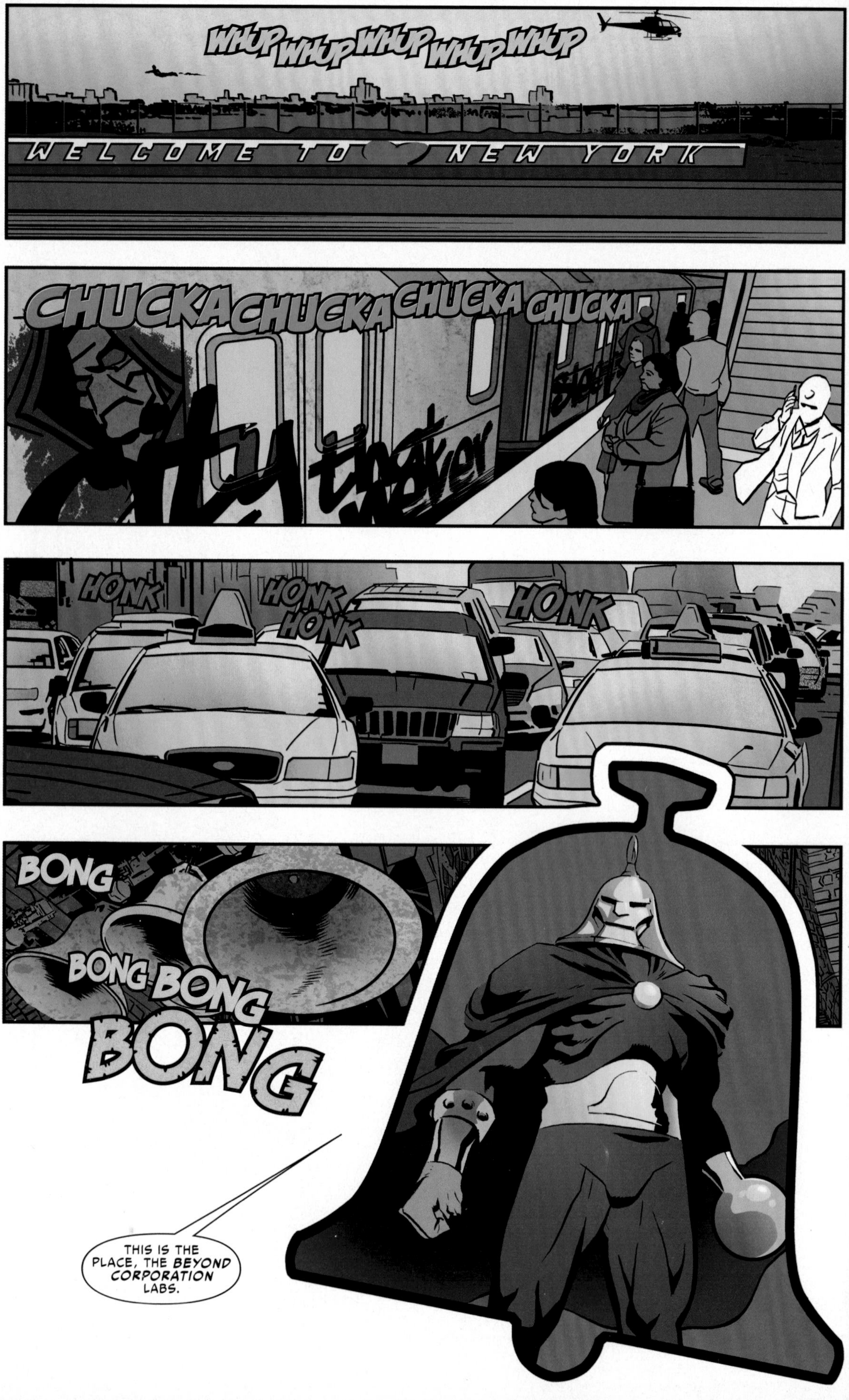
WHUP WHUP WHUP WHUP WHUP
WELCOME TO NEW YORK
CHUCKA CHUCKA CHUCKA CHUCKA
HONK
HONK HONK
HONK
BONG
BONG BONG
BONG
THIS IS THE PLACE, THE *BEYOND CORPORATION* LABS.

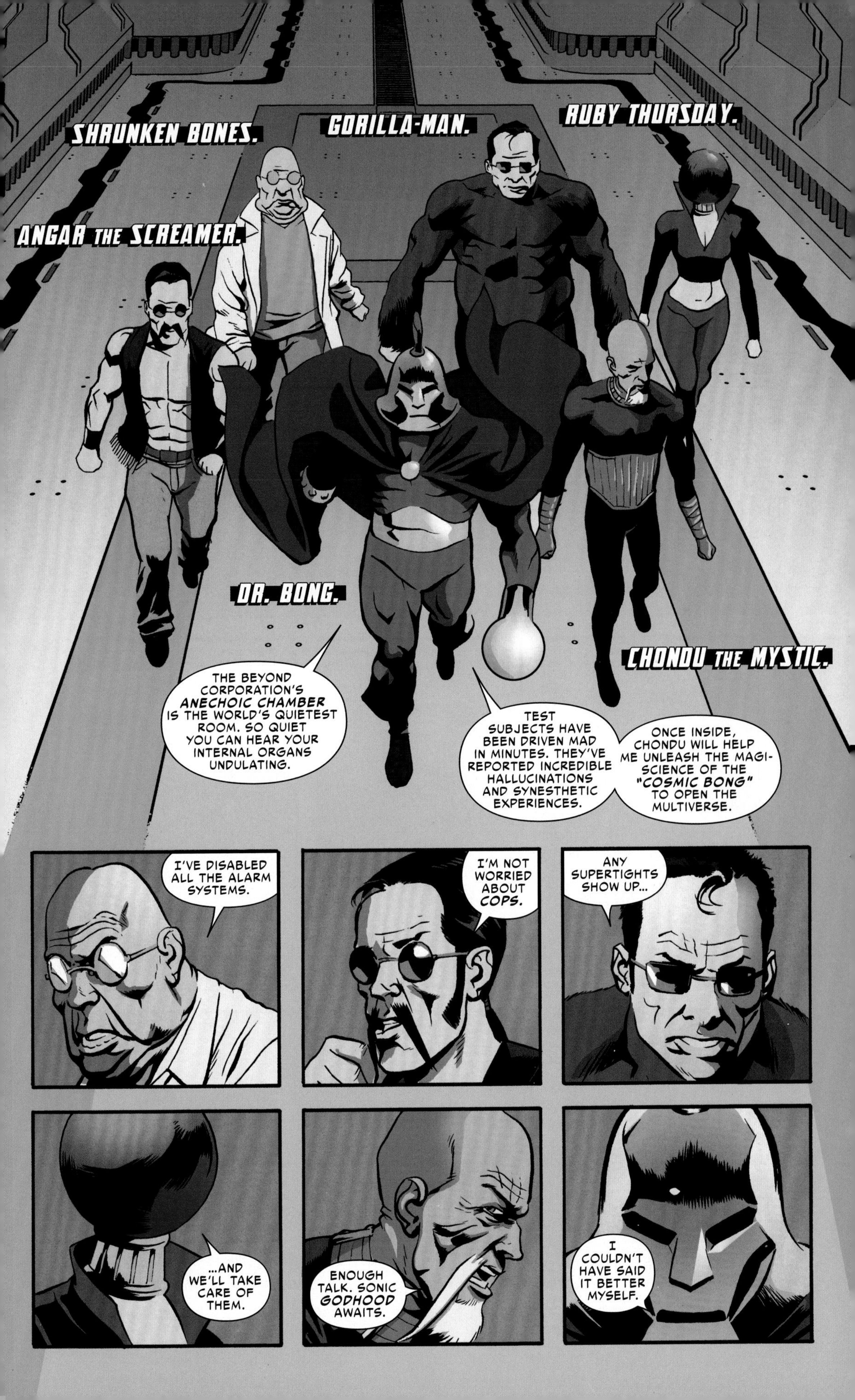
SHRUNKEN BONES.
GORILLA-MAN.
RUBY THURSDAY.
ANGAR THE SCREAMER.
DR. BONG.
CHONDU THE MYSTIC.
THE BEYOND CORPORATION'S ANECHOIC CHAMBER IS THE WORLD'S QUIETEST ROOM. SO QUIET YOU CAN HEAR YOUR INTERNAL ORGANS UNDULATING.
TEST SUBJECTS HAVE BEEN DRIVEN MAD IN MINUTES. THEY'VE REPORTED INCREDIBLE HALLUCINATIONS AND SYNESTHETIC EXPERIENCES.
ONCE INSIDE, CHONDU WILL HELP ME UNLEASH THE MAGI-SCIENCE OF THE "COSMIC BONG" TO OPEN THE MULTIVERSE.
I'VE DISABLED ALL THE ALARM SYSTEMS.
I'M NOT WORRIED ABOUT COPS.
ANY SUPERTIGHTS SHOW UP...
...AND WE'LL TAKE CARE OF THEM.
ENOUGH TALK. SONIC GODHOOD AWAITS.
I COULDN'T HAVE SAID IT BETTER MYSELF.

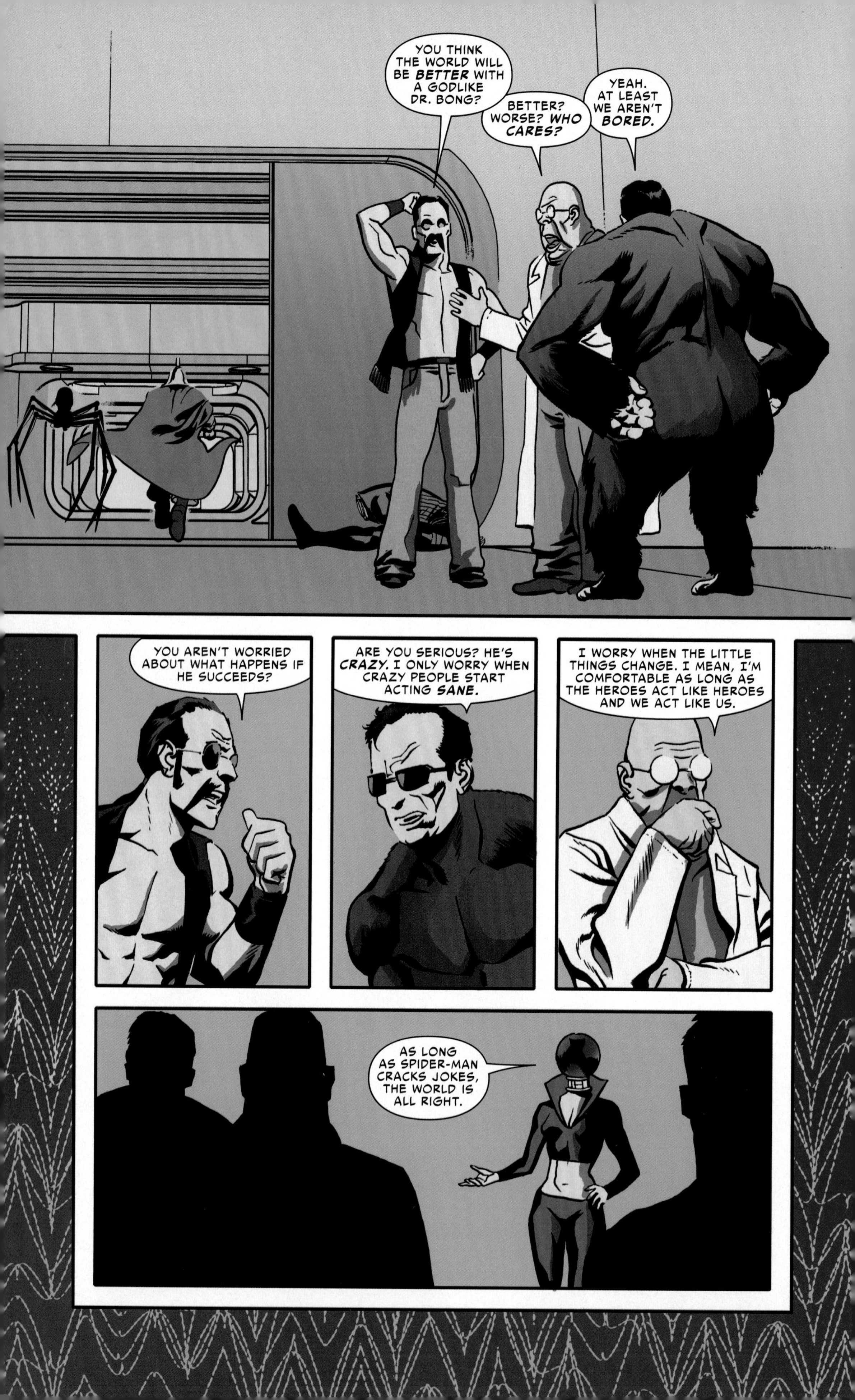
YOU THINK THE WORLD WILL BE BETTER WITH A GODLIKE DR. BONG?
BETTER? WORSE? WHO CARES?
YEAH. AT LEAST WE AREN'T BORED.
YOU AREN'T WORRIED ABOUT WHAT HAPPENS IF HE SUCCEEDS?
ARE YOU SERIOUS? HE'S CRAZY. I ONLY WORRY WHEN CRAZY PEOPLE START ACTING SANE.
I WORRY WHEN THE LITTLE THINGS CHANGE. I MEAN, I'M COMFORTABLE AS LONG AS THE HEROES ACT LIKE HEROES AND WE ACT LIKE US.
AS LONG AS SPIDER-MAN CRACKS JOKES, THE WORLD IS ALL RIGHT.

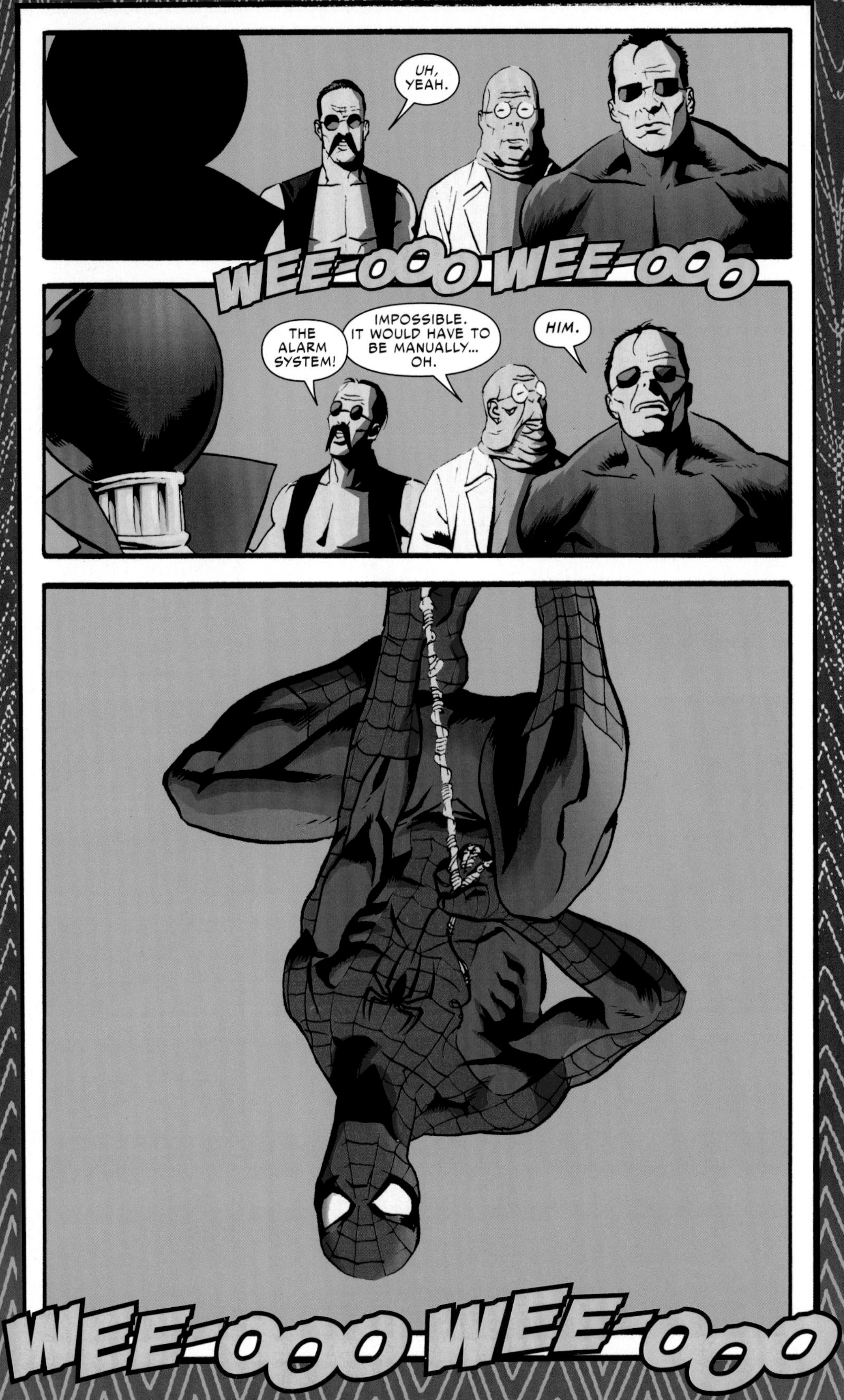
UH, YEAH.
WEE-OOO WEE-OOO
THE ALARM SYSTEM!
IMPOSSIBLE. IT WOULD HAVE TO BE MANUALLY... OH.
HIM.
WEE-OOO WEE-OOO

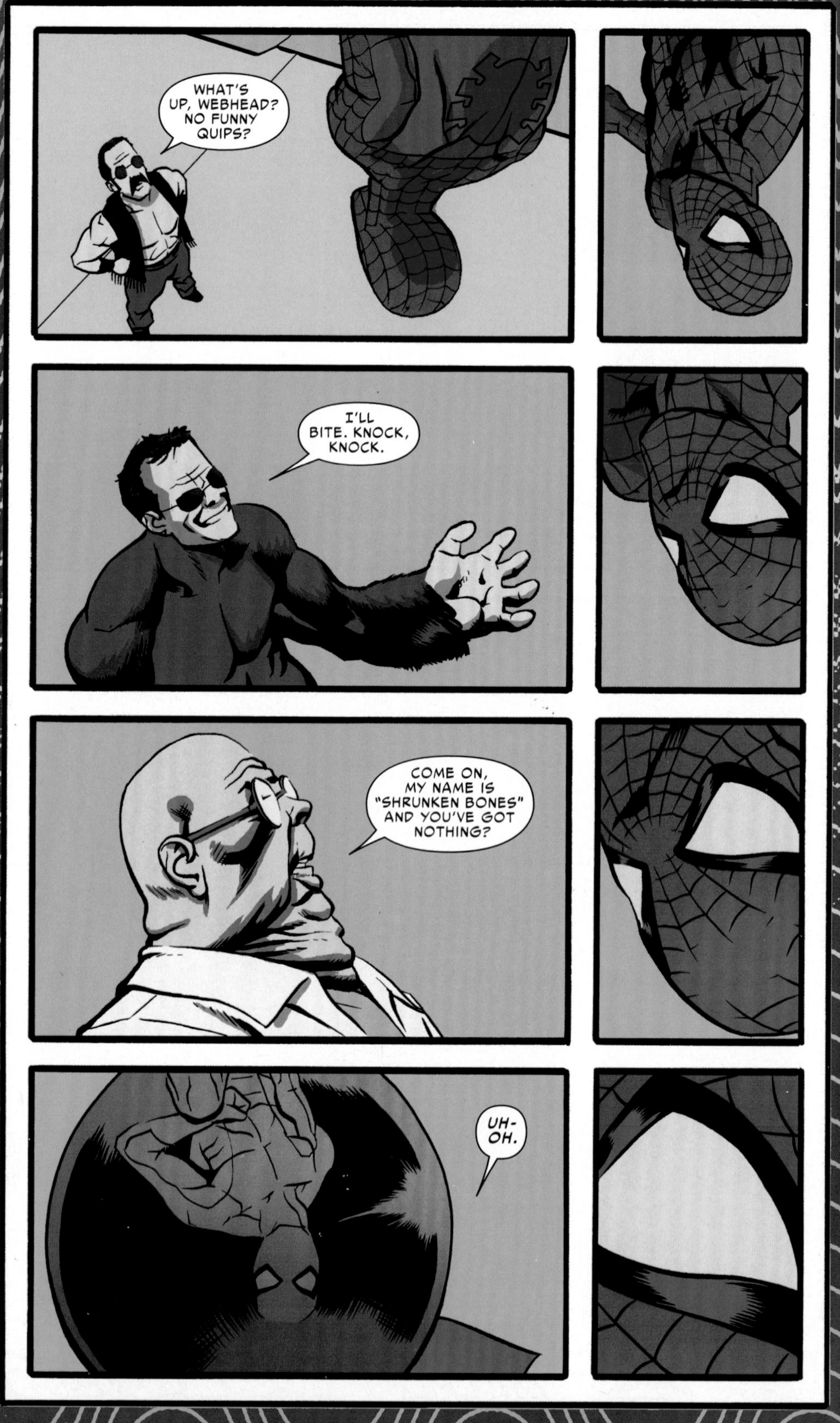
WHAT'S UP, WEBHEAD? NO FUNNY QUIPS?
I'LL BITE. KNOCK, KNOCK.
COME ON, MY NAME IS "SHRUNKEN BONES" AND YOU'VE GOT NOTHING?
UH-OH.

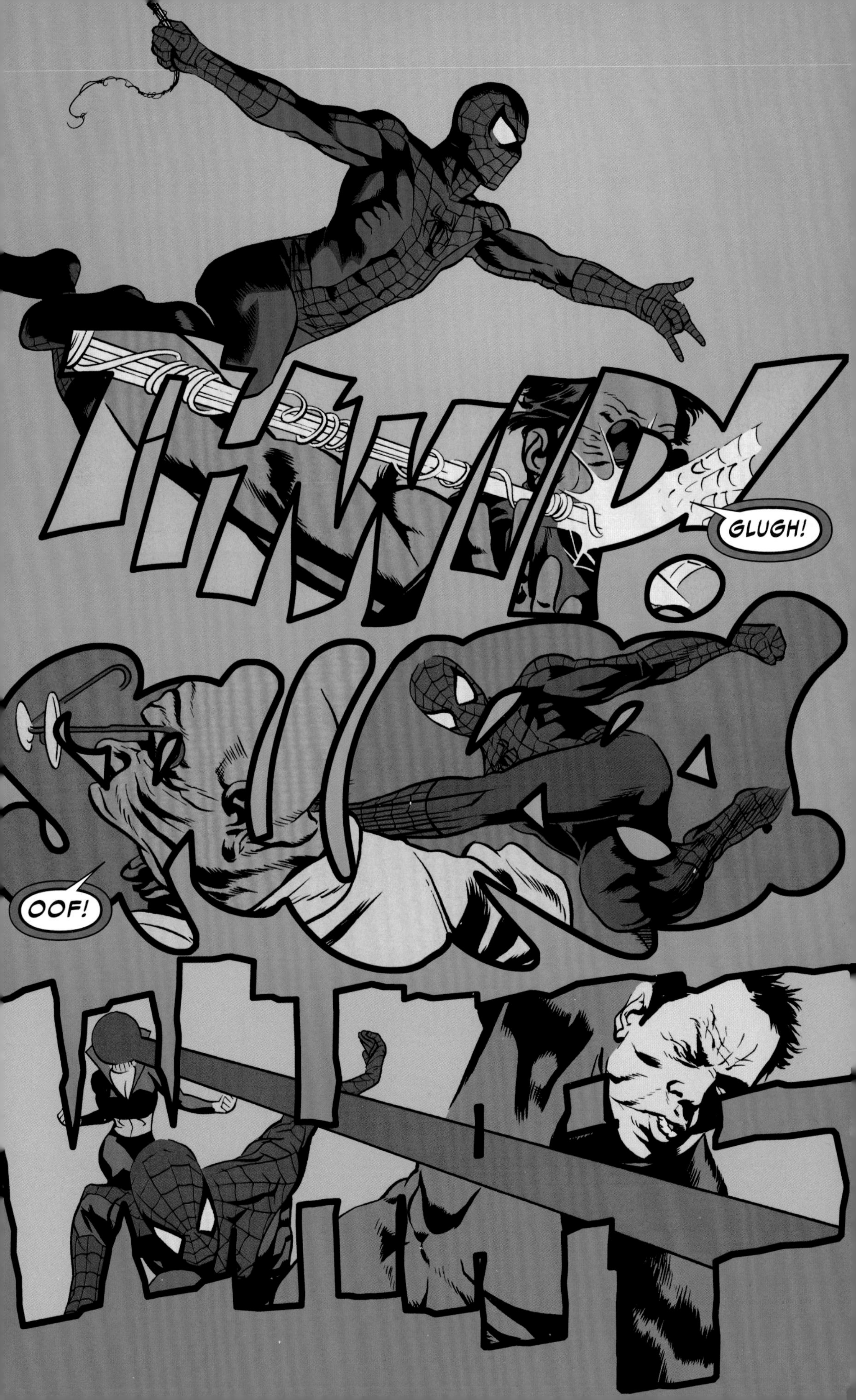
GLUGH!
OOF!

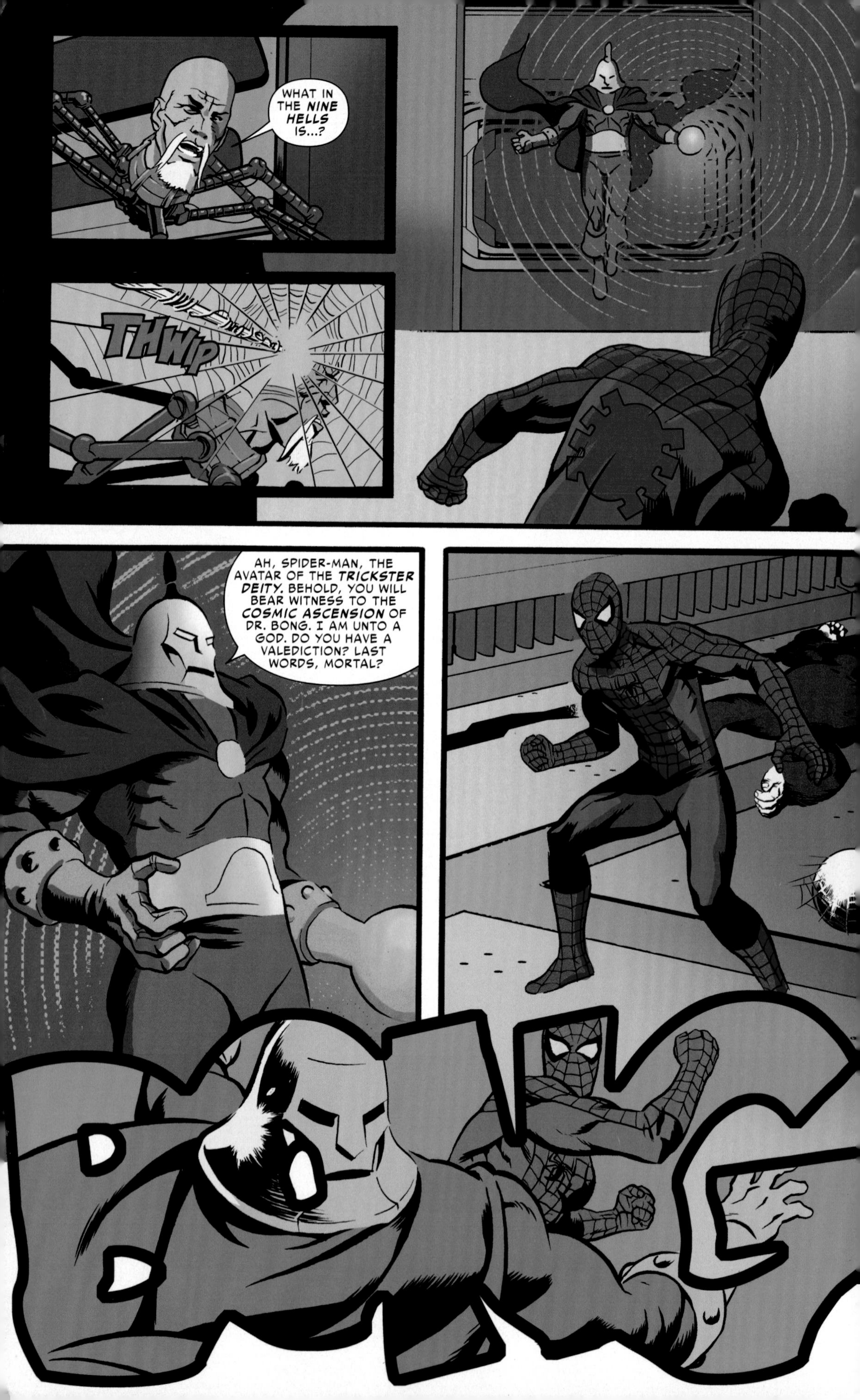
WHAT IN THE NINE HELLS IS...?
THWIP
AH, SPIDER-MAN, THE AVATAR OF THE TRICKSTER DEITY. BEHOLD, YOU WILL BEAR WITNESS TO THE COSMIC ASCENSION OF DR. BONG. I AM UNTO A GOD. DO YOU HAVE A VALEDICTION? LAST WORDS, MORTAL?

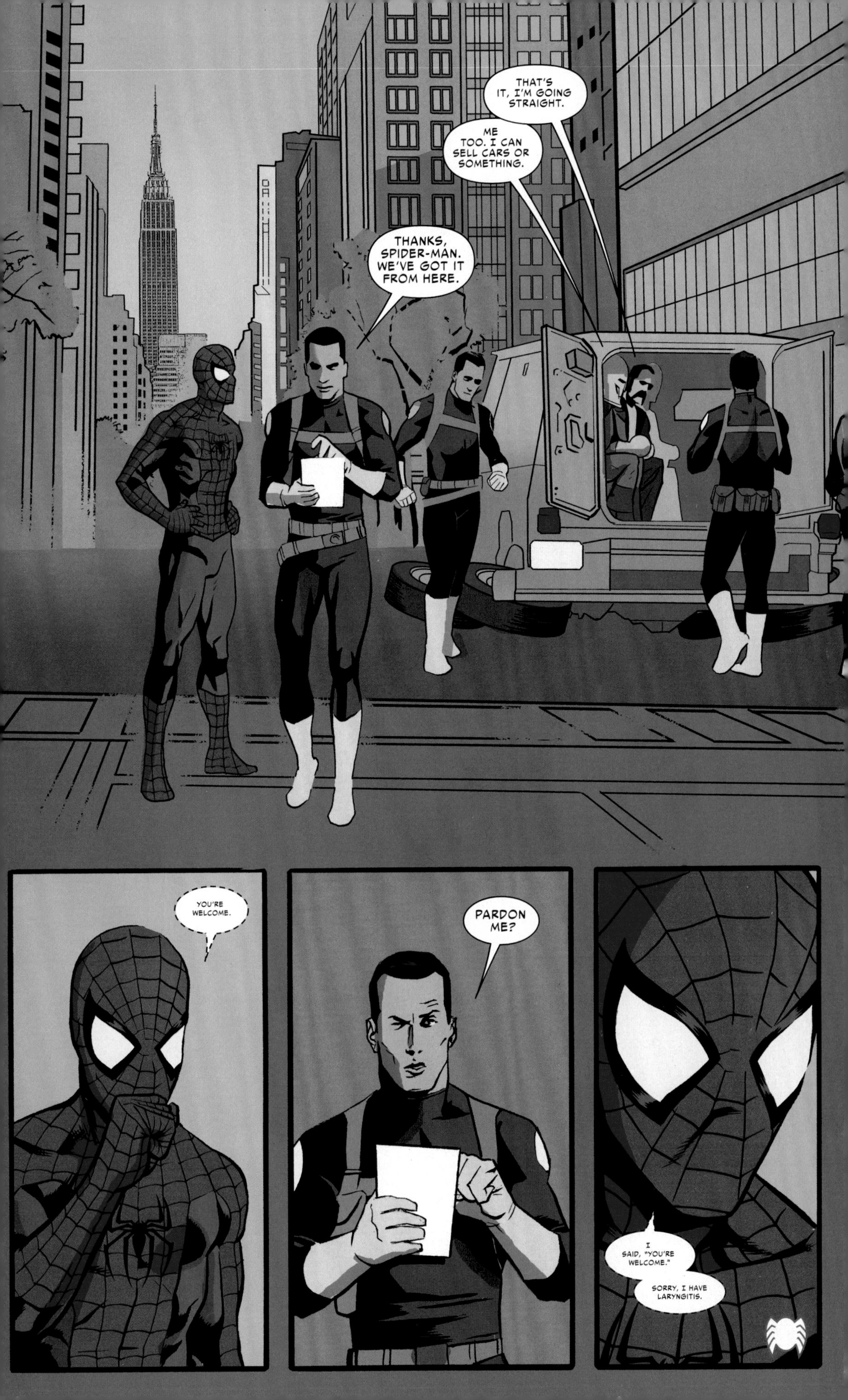
THAT'S IT, I'M GOING STRAIGHT.
ME TOO. I CAN SELL CARS OR SOMETHING.
THANKS, SPIDER-MAN. WE'VE GOT IT FROM HERE.
YOU'RE WELCOME.
PARDON ME?
I SAID, "YOU'RE WELCOME."
SORRY, I HAVE LARYNGITIS.

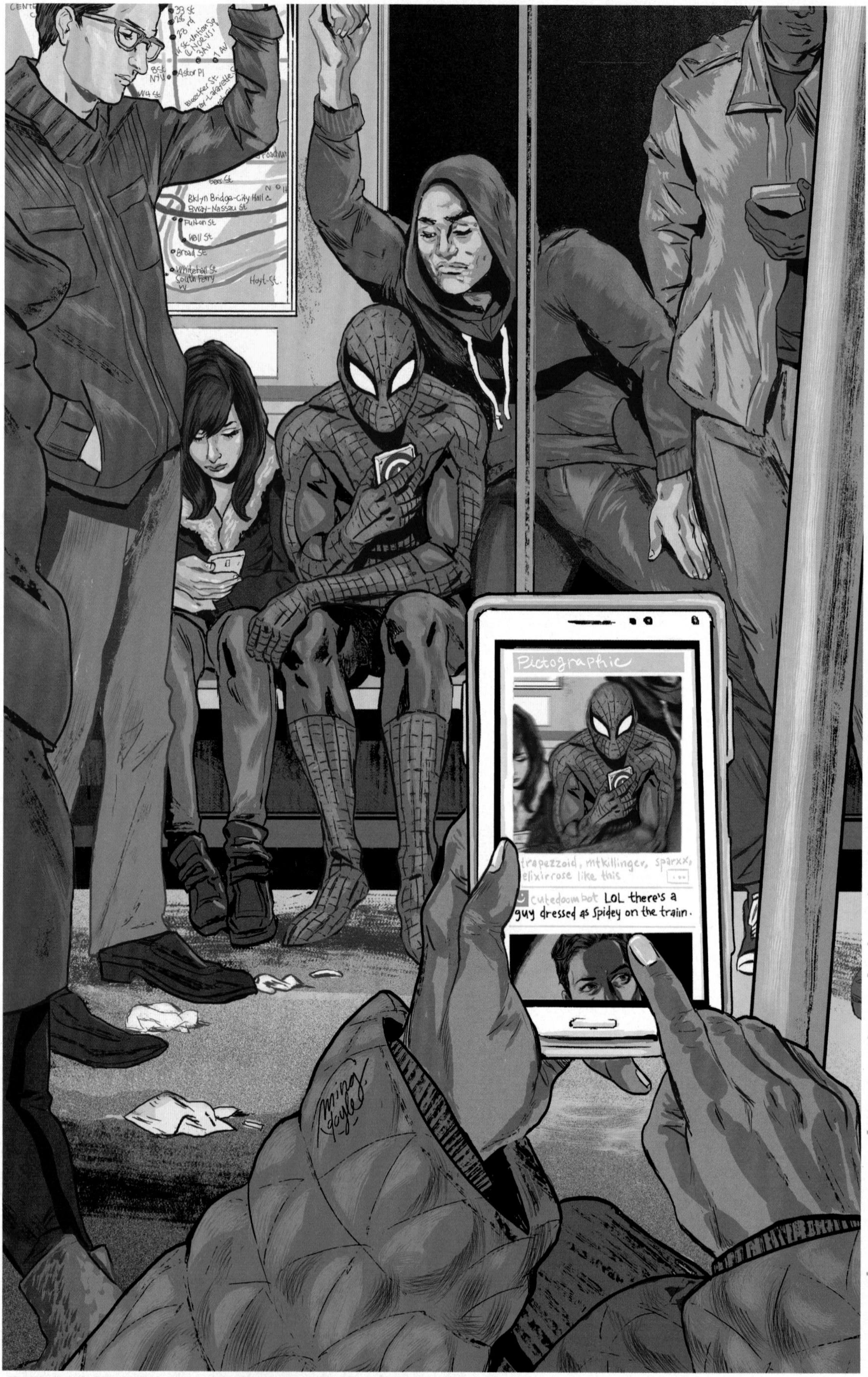
Astor Pl
Bklyn Bridge-City Hall
Bway-Nassau
Fulton St
Wall St
Broad St
Whitehall St
South Ferry
Hoyt-St.
Pictographic
trapezzoid, mtkillinger, sparxx, elixirrose like this
cutedoombot LOL there's a guy dressed as Spidey on the train.

AMAZING SPIDER-MAN 17
WOMEN OF MARVEL VARIANT COVER BY MING DOYLE

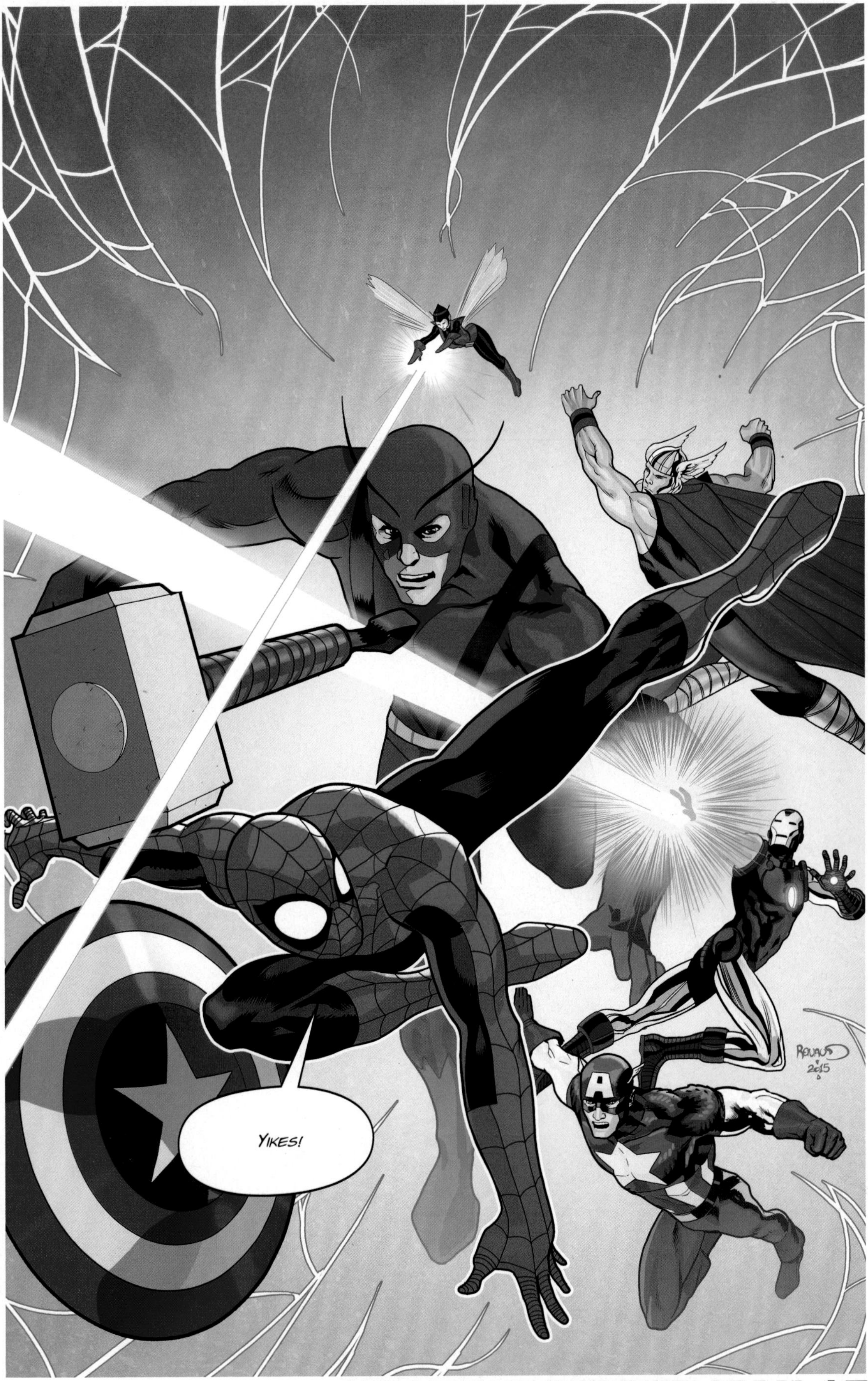
YIKES!
RENAUD 2015

AMAZING SPIDER-MAN 17
VARIANT COVER BY PAUL RENAUD

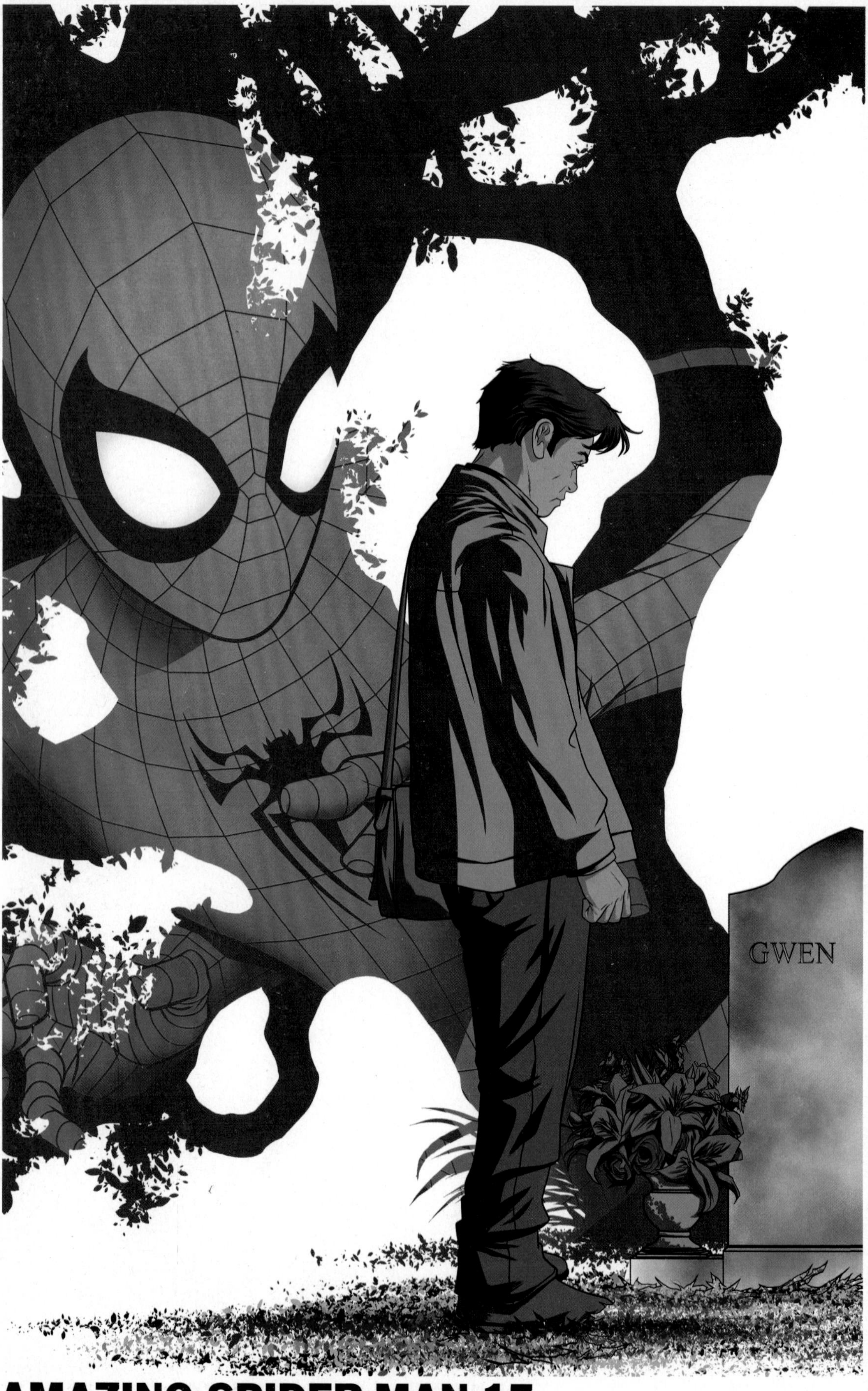
GWEN

AMAZING SPIDER-MAN 17

VARIANT COVER BY MIKE McKONE